The
Japanese-Speaking
Curtain Maker

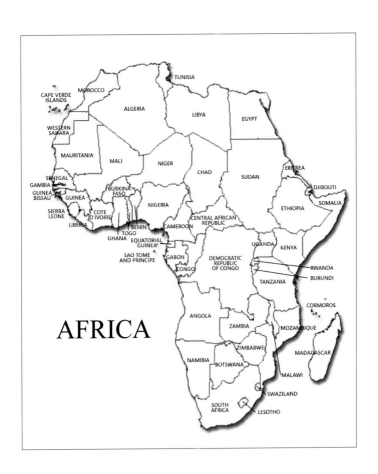

The
Japanese-Speaking
Curtain Maker

SPENCER JAMES CONWAY

Spencer Conway's solo circumnavigation of Africa by motorbike raised well in excess of £30,000 for Save the Children.

ISBN 978-0-9956290-3-5

Set in Times New Roman 11pt

Inside back cover photo, Spencer Conway and Cathy Nel, by RADKO

Editor
Michael Conway

Cover graphics
delipps

Typesetting
YouByYou Books
www.youbyyou.co.uk

Printing
Scan-Tech, Hastings

Contents

Dedicated to my parents Wendy and Michael to whom
I owe everything

Prologue

Ashraf apologised: "Sorry Mr Spencer, they do not see white people as they are very young and have only left the village once."

"I understand Ashraf, I must look pretty ugly to them," I quipped.

He laughed spontaneously, then thought he shouldn't have and spluttered, "No, no, not that, not true." Then, as if in apology, he busied himself with preparing a hookah pipe. He spent ten minutes diligently washing out all the component parts.

The pipe was a work of art in itself, a single glass instrument with brass edging and a brightly coloured tube leading through a water basin. Once it was cleaned out he packed it with flavoured tobacco, dropped a pre-prepared hot coal on the bed of tobacco and proceeded to inhale furiously until his cheeks puffed out like balloons. As soon as it was burning smoothly he handed me the wooden nozzle. I inhaled deeply and then spluttered and coughed my way around the entire compound. I apologised and decided to stick with the slightly less harsh Cleopatra cigarettes. I suspect Ashraf enjoyed the whole spectacle, judging from the tears of laughter running down his face. I think he came off better as tears were also flowing down my cheeks.

Chapter One
A Motley Crew

This book is not about motorbikes. I just happen to be sitting on one throughout it. If you were hoping to read about sprocket size, knobbly depth, torque and chain lube, then you will be disappointed. Anyway, here goes.

It's not every day that one hundred hairy, tattooed, leather-clad bikers meet up with the Bishop of Dover and twelve angelic choirboys. But this was the scene unfolding in the tiny village of Biddenden, South East England (pop: more than five) early on a blustery November morning, 2010. Why, you might ask. Why were most of the village lining the street (at least six of them)? Why were the BBC, Diesel Films and various newspaper reporters setting themselves up in various strategic locations in the quaint Tudor High Street? Why was there a massive banner looming over the scene with my ugly and bewildered mug plastered across it? Why were my family gathered in the village car park, my two daughters in tears? But, more to the point, why were all these people braving the driving rain, drenched to the bone, shivering uncontrollably as they were buffeted by cyclone-strength winds. The stiff upper lip of the English. Superb. This whole, over-the-top scene of stoicism, in the face of the elements, was entirely my fault.

I had decided to undertake a journey. Don't ask me why, but I woke up one morning and foolishly thought that I would try and become the first person in the world to circumnavigate

Africa on a motorbike, solo and unsupported. Not the smallest of journeys. It was a ridiculous idea really when you consider that if I was to be successful I would have to travel through thirty five different countries. I would have to cover one fifth of the world's surface area and travel a distance of over 50,000 kilometres, the equivalent of one and a half times around the equator. Through some of the most dangerous and unstable countries in the world, I might add. (Cue drum roll.) My initial intention was to leave quietly, kiss my family goodbye, wave cheerio to my loyal Border Collie, Millie, and return a year older, but having 'conquered' Africa. Simple.

It didn't turn out like that. For some odd reason my trip caught people's imagination and my departure turned out to be anything but incognito. By some strange osmotic process, by the time I was prepared to head off to insanity, I had partial sponsorship for the bike, sponsorship for my gear, a book, DVD and TV programmes in the pipeline and Save the Children announcing me as an extra-ordinary fundraiser. My website and blog had 700,000 visitors and my bike hadn't even left my front door. (When I did eventually leave, I crashed before I even got out of the garage. The foot peg caught on a piece of carpet and deposited me unceremoniously on the concrete floor; the motorbike completed the sandwiching.) Right, I hope you can appreciate that the pressure had surreptitiously sneaked up on me. Try and imagine yourself in my position. I had been swept up in a tide of enthusiasm and now had too many people relying on my hair-brained scheme succeeding. No turning back then. Except in Cape Town of course. Right, let's get the introduction over and maybe it will give you more of an insight into how ludicrously unsuited I was for this challenge.

My name is Spencer Conway and I am six foot four inches tall and weigh 95 kilogrammes. I am 42 but look 25. I have the body of Hugh Jackman and the combined looks of Brad Pitt and Johnny Depp. I have the tenacity, courage and will of all the great explorers, from Livingstone to Thor Heyerdal to Sir

Ranulph Fiennes. I have climbed the highest mountains and swam the deepest oceans. Ok, let's get back to reality. The first sentence is the only one that's true. More accurately, I may look superficially fit, due to sporadic attempts at weight training, which never evolved into a strict routine, despite my intentions. My exterior is therefore passable but I suspect my interior would not pass quality control, due to a couple of suspect habits; avoidance of fruit and vegetables and a weakness for Golden Virginia. I have been told on occasions that I am reasonably good-looking; on a good day, from a distance, in the shadows. A case of good from afar but far from good.

As far as my adventurer/explorer credentials are concerned, I fall well below par. Although I have managed to stumble around various countries in awe, I happen to be extremely accident-prone. I have broken most of the bones God provided me with. To add insult to injury, my sense of direction is exceedingly poor. I get lost in my own house. But I could not let these small details deflect me from my present task. I was about to head off around Africa. I still had to make the 1,500 miles through France before my circumnavigation commenced. Incidentally, I hadn't ridden for ten years and didn't even have a licence. Small technicality. I passed the bike test a week before I left.

After a year of planning and fundraising, fast forward to the day. I felt like a fraud. All these people had turned up to see me off. I was to be scrutinised by thousands, followed on the web and expected to film my experience when not being filmed by a crew. I had been asked to do two adverts for a laser surgery company to be shot in Egypt and Kenya. ('Shot' actually being prophetic.) I had never even been on TV. (This is glaringly obvious if you google 'Spencer Conway, laser eye surgery' - the corniest, cheesiest advert ever made, with cringeworthy lines like, "Just go for it. Don't let poor vision hold you back".) Forgive me if I jump subjects randomly, but this was what the week before I left panned out to be. Chaos. I had to do radio interviews, learn how to use an HD helmet camera, become familiar with sound bites, voice-overs, pieces to camera, diary cams, GVs and a multitude of other terminological inexactitudes. I had meetings with Save the Children about fundraising and projects to visit on route.

I had several rendezvous with famous adventure bikers, survival experts and an African Land Snail expert. (He didn't turn up, or maybe was just extremely late.) On top of this I had to decide what was vital equipment for my travels and minimise the load as best possible. I failed dismally in this department and my bike ended up so absurdly overloaded that it looked like a yak about to attempt Everest Base Camp. As someone else put it, it looked like I had thrown the entire contents of my house from a second floor window and it had all stuck to my bike. You live and learn.

My state of extreme confidence, sorry, I mean trepidation, was tempered slightly by the offer from The Bishop of Dover to bless me before my trip. I am not overly religious but I must say I was pleased with the gesture and would have welcomed a blessing. I suspected however, that it was going to take a greater power than the Bishop of Dover (no disrespect) to deliver me safely around the African continent. But if He wasn't available then the Bishop of Dover was worth a try. It wasn't to be though, as weather intervened. Maybe I should have taken the intervention of rain and life-threatening lightning as a sign that I wasn't meant to be blessed. Or didn't deserve it.

I took the 'blessing/no blessing' decision into my own hands and when it chimed 10am on the village clock on the scheduled day of departure I decided I couldn't wait and I would have to leave without it. More to the point, the elderly villagers were getting blown around the High Street and I was worried about serious injuries and, at the very least, the loss of a wig in the hurricane conditions. I had never seen weather like it and I had been in this part of England for fifteen years. Trees were bending, people were bending and it was generally unpleasant.

I was thinking to myself, 'I have ridden a motorbike *once* in the rain and never ever in winds like this. I am doomed.' My preferred course of action (run away and hide) was highly restricted as immediately I announced my departure a hundred macho bikers started up their monster machines. Talk about peer pressure. These bloody supportive bikers. Why did they have to turn up? It had to be action stations. I was beginning to well up and gave all of my family cursory hugs, which was very tough. The look in my daughters' eyes cracked me up. I wanted to get my helmet on and get out of there before I descended into blubbering uselessness.

And so it came to pass, as some pretty well known verse said, that I was on my way down the romantic M20 motorway, heading to the south coast of England. The spitting, angry weather swirled about me and it was all I could do to keep the bike upright. I glanced behind me and peered over the sofa I was carrying on the back, to see how the other hundred bikers were doing; there were only three. What happened to the promise of 'seeing you off to the coast?' Weaklings. But the more I thought about it the more sensible I realised they were. Who in their right minds would ride in this weather? There was a ninety percent chance of a bitter end. As I pondered this issue the last three bikers hooted, waved and peeled off down a motorway exit. I was alone in a cyclone on an unsteady yak. My mood began to darken. But then an inspirational quote came into my head, one that has been repeated numerous times: 'In a car you are watching a film, on a bike you are in the film.' Douglas Adams was the provider of this quote in *Zen and the Art of Motorcycle Maintenance*. It was repeated by the female adventure motorcyclist Lois Pryce in her excellent book, *Red Tape and White Knuckles*. This philosophy is along the lines of 'on a motorbike you feel the wind, the rain, the sun, the road surface, the bugs, the hazards of life and wildlife. In a car you can close out the world, set your own temperature and listen to music. Biking therefore brings you a raw experience and a closeness to nature and the environment that is unsurpassed.'

As I weaved down the drab M20 motorway, huge droplets of rain stinging my face, struggling to keep my monstrously overloaded bike upright, I thought, 'What a load of rubbish. Give me a car!' In a flash I came up with a cunning plan. I would ride the thirty miles to the coast and set up in some secluded coastal town. I would get a job, rent a cosy bedsit and hide out for a year. I would then roll about in some English mud, head back to Biddenden, suitably dirty and triumphant, and wax lyrical, between heavy sighs, about how difficult the trip was. Dream on. I had to do this. I had started, so I would finish.

After forty minutes of wobbling and weaving, it was with relief that I spotted signs for the Channel Tunnel Rail Link that would take me over to France. I had succeeded, with difficulty, to complete the first fifty kilometres. Only 49,950 to go, approximately. I pulled up to the terminal kiosk and was immediately asked by the smiling Customs lady, "Are you the man who is going around Africa?"

What! They even know about me here. "Yes, that's me; how did you know?" I replied incredulously.

"There is a lady here, Mrs Trudy Beazley, who has brought your wife and children down to say goodbye. A van will take you back out of the terminal area to meet them."

My initial reaction was, 'Oh no. I have to go through saying goodbye again.' The Customs were great and treated me like a VIP, even taking photos with me and wishing me luck. It was actually wonderful to stand there in the pouring rain, hugging my girlfriend Cathy and my daughters Jesamine and Feaya. There was no one to witness my tears and the rain beating down helped to partially camouflage them. I headed onto the train boosted by a proper goodbye. Who knew when I would see my children again, if ever. (Yes, I was swinging from confidence to despair already. I had better pull myself together quickly.) I remained lost in my thoughts and within what seemed like seconds I was in France, the weather conditions still atrocious. (I think God was taking the Mickey Mouse out of me.) Thankfully, I only had to ride for an hour as I had pre-booked into a classy establishment for the night called 'Hotel Mister Bed'. Luckily it was in a small town in northern France called Rang du Fliers and the hotel was easy to find. It was a great relief to strip off my soaking wet clothes. Unfortunately there was no heating, so no chance of drying my sodden clothes by morning. I wrapped myself in a grotty Mexican-print-inspired, moth-eaten blanket and sat in front of the cracked, lopsided mirror. I got one hell of a shock. I had managed to pick up a livid red rash that covered my entire face. I looked like a giant angry strawberry. I didn't know it then but I was to suffer this rash on and off for the next nine months. It would eventually spread to my arms and back. I would become quite used to people looking at me as though I was some kind of loner motorcycling leper. To this day I have not a clue what it was, but the rash was a source of some embarrassment as well as a slight barrier to social interaction. People are not keen on getting to know you if they think you are infectious and if they shake your hand it might fall off. Looking into that mirror set me off into a hysterical fit of laughter. I was alone in France, soaked to the skin, with the complexion of a burns victim and with no real plan for what lay ahead.

I fitted my camera onto the top of my helmet, put it on and looked in the mirror again. I couldn't stop laughing. I wasn't just out of my depth, I was at the bottom of the ocean. I was heading alone through the whole of Africa, and with no satellite navigation system. I only had one large map of Africa which showed the main towns and cities but little else. There was a fine chance that I would get lost in the wilderness of Africa, with no Henry Morton Stanley to come and find me. I had no back-up crew, mechanics, doctors, psychologists, etc. à la Ewan McGregor and 'The Long Way Down'. Not that I had any choice; I am not a Hollywood superstar. I would be living on a budget that would feed a sparrow, at a stretch, and would be camping for the next 270 nights or so, with no means of self-defence except a camera tripod. I removed my helmet, wiped away the tears of laughter and tried to settle down to sleep in preparation for a 5am start. Sleep evaded me as my mind would not shut down. When I eventually nodded off I had a heart-warming dream that my wheels fell off at 120 kilometres an hour (literally and metaphorically). That boosted my confidence and I left the next morning like a shaky drunk.

I immediately drove the wrong way down the road, narrowly avoiding a fatal head-on with the world's largest truck. The French driver screamed something at me which was definitely not "Welcome to France". I had to pull over and calm down my heartbeat or cardiac arrest would ensue. After five minutes and a sneaky cancer stick I rode off again. Over the period of the next hour a strange thing happened to me. My frame of mind changed and I clicked into full-scale biker automaton mode. All my senses were heightened and my focus and concentration took over. I was in the groove and became more and more elated with my progress. I started eating up the miles. In one sense it was wonderful because I knew that most motorcycle problems are caused by the nut that connects the handlebars to the seat. On the other hand I could not tell you a single thing about the landscape of France or Tunisia. I hit what riders call 'white line fever'. I became obsessed with covering the miles, to the detriment of my surroundings. Looking back on it, I suspect it was a necessary action, to boost my confidence, and it was with a sense of disbelief that I covered the trip from England through France and Tunisia and reached the border of Libya in six dreamlike days.

My only break from this focused, blinkered riding was the twenty one hour ferry from Marseilles to Sfax, the northern Tunisian port. It was a trip of a lifetime. Never again! Although the ferry was plush and clean I made the fatal mistake of booking a cabin. I decided to pay the extra $30 to upgrade, as a final treat to myself before I started roughing it for a year. It was not justifiable, I suppose, but I just wanted to experience one last night's sleep before I stayed awake for probably… the next year. I was shown to my cabin by a cheeky little monkey; yes, it was a cheeky little monkey. He had escaped from someone's clutches and careered down the lower corridor with no intention of being caught. I followed and he suddenly stopped right outside the door that I confirmed from my embarkation card was mine. The monkey then screeched, ran up the wall and disappeared round a corner. Intriguing. I opened the cabin door and was immediately surprised to find three Moroccan men already in there, all fast asleep.

I assumed for that price I would have my own room. There was a spare upper bunk bed on my right, wedged almost up to the ceiling of the tiny cabin. After a few problems and some acrobatic moves I managed to squeeze in and lie down. My nose was about four inches from the ceiling but I tried to relax. If I swung around to turn over I would hit my elbow on the roof. I had to swivel round, arms by my sides, a bit like a mummy in a sarcophagus. (Not that they move around.) After fifteen minutes of squirming around in this cabin/cave I eventually found a comfortable position. As I was just drifting off, my roommates simultaneously burst into snoring, all at a different pitch and rhythm. The volume increased as they tried to outdo each other to be the lead snorer, rather than one of the rhythm back-up sections. After fifteen minutes of this crescendo, the snorer directly below me, abruptly stopped snoring and let out a yell. He then rolled around groaning before standing up and stretching noisily. He shuffled over to the tiny cabin toilet that was, oh, at least half a metre from my head. There followed, what I can only describe as the most horrendous, longest and loudest sound I have ever heard emitted from a toilet bowl. If I had diarrhoea of that violent intensity I would be straight off to hospital. The smell started oozing out of the door and filling up the room. The other two kept snoring and it dawned on me that this was unpleasant. The show, however, was not over. Ablution man number one finally finished up and returned to his snoring slumber. No sooner was he asleep than the second snorer opposite me went through exactly the same ritual and headed to the loo. The results, and sound and smell effects, were the same. Suffice to say this routine went on all night and involved all three. I slept for, maybe, five minutes. What shocked me the most was how they were all still alive in the morning. I just expected to see three dehydrated corpses. I have no idea, to this day, what they had all eaten, but the results were spectacularly disgusting. In future, it's the upper deck for me. I apologise profusely to the French and Tunisian Tourist Board for the lack of insight into the beauty of the landscapes and the cultural richness of the people. I can at least report that both countries have high quality roads and I am pleased to announce, 'Excellent road signs'.

My arrival at the Libyan border was superb. In Libya it is the law that all 'tourists' have to have a guide throughout their visit, at a whopping $100 per day. I was dreading being shadowed by a surly, officious tour guide but I needn't have worried. I was approached by a thin but rock-hard, scarred, skinhead Libyan who on first impressions looked like he would stab a school child for their pocket money. But looks can be extremely deceiving and this was definitely the case with 27-year-old Sami Osman. He approached me with a massive, pearly white grin, extended his hand and said warmly, "Welcome to Libya, Spencer." What surprised me the most was not the warmth of his greeting or the vicelike, crushing handshake, it was his exceedingly broad Glaswegian accent. During the five days I spent with Sami I couldn't help laughing as he switched effortlessly between Glaswegian English and Arabic. It was such a strange cultural combination. Sentences like "Allah Akbar, ye didnee did yee, ye havnee have ye," set me off in stitches. Luckily Sami was exceedingly laid back and was not remotely offended.

Sami was the first member of a trio that kept me highly entertained throughout my Libya visit. Scottish Sami's boss was another Sami; Sami El Ghibani, the owner of Al Muheet Tours. Whereas Scottish Sami dressed casually in jeans and a T-shirt and looked like a serial killer, Boss Sami was suavely immaculate and friendly looking. Throughout my hot, sweaty and sandy visit, Boss-Sami remained unfeasibly pristine. His suit was spotlessly clean and expertly ironed no matter the time of day. His gold chains were nearly as shiny as his brown leather shoes. His sunglasses, mobile phone and watch all looked eye-wateringly expensive. His swarthy complexion, slicked back hair and caterpillar moustache reminded me of Omar Sharif, except Omar would look like a scruffy hobo next to Boss Sami. Both Samis were super friendly and I felt totally relaxed in their company. The third member of the group was Ahmed, who was the driver. This was unfortunate, if not downright dangerous as he was a serious whisky guzzler. This is more surprising when you realise that alcohol is illegal in Libya and if caught he could face many years in jail. Ahmed was exceedingly overweight and constantly sweating. His eyes worked independently from each other and it was quite difficult to ascertain who he was talking to. This lack of eye co-ordination was exacerbated by his whisky glugging. By late afternoon one eye would be facing the heavens while the other scanned the ground randomly. It was not the perfect recipe for a safe driver. Scottish Sami seemed totally unfazed by Ahmed's driving, shrugging calmly when he weaved across the road or misjudged a corner and ended up in the desert sand. I was super relieved that I wasn't in the car but I still had to follow them into Tripoli. I decided early on, after seeing Ahmed reach under the seat for liquid refreshment that I would hang back at a safe distance. It turned out that I had no choice as Ahmed was a serious Formula One fan and we averaged one hundred and fifty kilometres an hour all the way to Tripoli. It was a totally nerve-wracking trip and took all my concentration to keep up. I would have lost them for good if it wasn't for Ahmed's penchant for regularly leaving the road. On a number of occasions I came round a corner and saw them digging the back wheels out of the sand. I wouldn't get in a car with Ahmed if I was paid, but the two Samis seemed oblivious to his erratic swerving and tyre screeching.

It seemed that the whole of Libya was a race track so I presume they were immune to the fear of speed. I am, and always have been, more of an escargot driver, and it was an extreme relief when the outskirts of Tripoli came into view. The strangeness of Libyan driving was only matched by the oddness of Libyan parking. The rules are simple; park anywhere you like. This varied from cars three deep on the side of the road, to cars on the pavement, to cars parked in the middle of the road. Like many African countries, hooters were used permanently as some kind of bat sonar. The problem of 'parking people in' was solved by an ingenious method. Everybody left their keys in their cars, so if you were blocked in you simply jumped in someone else's car and moved it. If for some reason the keys were not left in, the handbrake could be released and the car pushed out of the way. If a more complicated manoeuvre was required a team of twenty or so were always on hand to manhandle a car out of the way. In the case of larger cars this consisted of a bouncing technique, whereas the smaller cars could be simply picked up and moved. Cars were never moved too far for the owner to lose them but the constant shuffling and sharing kept the flow of traffic fairly sane. It goes without saying that this method of communal parking duties would be an impossibility in a country where stealing was common. If they tried this in South Africa, for example, everyone's car would be stolen every day and it would end up as some sort of car roulette. Everyone would have a different car every day. In Libya, stealing is punishable by death, or something nearly as extreme, like leg removal. (I had better Google that.)

We pulled up outside a plush-looking hotel and Ahmed demonstrated a different parking method that removed the necessity for anyone to get out. He simply pulled up slowly behind a car that was marginally blocking a parking space, until they were bumper to bumper. He then drove off gently in first gear and simply pushed the car out of the way. I pulled in behind them and jumped off the bike. I noticed that there was a short man who had gone unnoticed in the driver's seat of the car Ahmed had just gently rammed. He seemed totally unnerved and simply waved to me when I caught his eye. Excellent.

Boss Sami led us into a hotel foyer and immediately ordered tea and ushered us to a plush set of sofas. Boss Sami had two permanent habits. One was to constantly check his mobile phone, literally every thirty seconds. It reminded me of the fixation thirteen-year-old English schoolgirls have with their mobiles. Between checking his mobile, Boss Sami had the habit of constantly smoothing down his tie and his hair. His image was of paramount importance to Boss Sami but strangely he seemed in no way arrogant or conceited. It was just the way he was. Although softly spoken, he commanded respect and over the next few days I would often see people leaning in towards him to make sure they caught every word. Whilst we sat there

Sami arranged all my accommodation, food and petrol as well as setting up an interview with Libyan TV. This turned out to be a serious fiasco. The two Samis then left me at the hotel, promising to meet me the next morning at six.

They were true to their word, arriving at one minute to. Scottish Sami looked like he had not slept a wink and had smoked twenty joints, whereas Boss Sami looked even more immaculate than the day before. His moustache even looked ironed and I was convinced his socks and underwear would have been similarly prepared.

Within five minutes the cameraman from Libyan TV turned up. He was a tall, slight, curly-haired, moustachioed man called Abdul. (Picture Borat.) Abdul had two striking characteristics that could not be ignored; his eyes and his unbelievable command of English. Abdul displayed all the symptoms of someone with hyperthyroidism. His large round eyes protruded out of his head like ping pong balls and he blinked infrequently lending his eyes a staring quality. Where normal people have no visible white between the top of the iris (the coloured part) and the upper eyelid, Abdul's irises were islands in a sea of white. It was quite disconcerting at first, as he was also a very intense person who stood extremely close to you during conversation. His English, though magnificent, was peppered with clichés. His sincerity, passion and speed of delivery, combined with his unwavering goggle-eyed stare, were a mildly disturbing sight, but I thought he was great. A typical conversation:

Me: "Hi Abdul, how are you?"

Abdul: "I can't complain, my fine sir. I am on top of the morning indeed, despite the onset of inclement weather. I would surmise that it is going to be a peach of a day: morally, mentally, physically and spiritually, but not climatically as I commented earlier. What are we planning to do on this one and only, individual, special, non-repeatable, non-refundable, non-returnable day? God Almighty has prepared this day in advance for us to cherish, grasp, nurture, enjoy, thrive in and eventually burst forth through. We will then bask in the dusk, slumber in the night, before waking refreshed and recharged with a new conviction, motivation and zest for life which will only culminate in new goals being set for the future of our blessed lives. And so the beloved cycle continues."

Me, laughing: "Calm down Abdul. I only asked how you were. Take a breath."

Abdul: "A breath is only a moment in time... "

This may not be verbatim but you get the gist. I was taken with Abdul's energetic persona. I may be mistaken but I suspect Boss Sami was not so enamoured with Hyper Abdul. He kept tutting and looking at his million dollar watch until Abdul finally took the hint.

"Okey dokey, let us press on with this venture. I suggest we relocate to the Beach road and film an interview with Spencer overlooking the indomitable Mediterranean Sea. Ahmed, do you know the corner of Ramadan Road and Tariq-Al-Shat?" (Not the nicest sounding road.)

"I do," answered Ahmed, sleepily.

"Excellent. We will rendezvous at that location in one hour from the present. Sharp. En route I will direct and film from the back of the truck, with my driver, Arse," (it sounded like that, but I can't be sure), said Abdul, pointing to a chubby, robed man leaning against a white Isuzu truck. "Spencer will follow on the veritable motorcycle and if Mr El Ghibani could take it up the rear." (Not Abdul's finest choice of English words.) And so the team was assembled and ready to go: Scottish Sami and Posh Boss Sami, Whisky Ahmed, Hyperthyroid Abdul and Arse. It was to be the most farcical and chaotic film shoot in which I would ever be involved.

All started smoothly as we pulled into the centre of the city in convoy. Abdul positioned himself in the back of the truck with the double doors open. His handheld camera was the size of a washing machine and he reeled and staggered every time the truck pulled off or braked in traffic. I was sure he was going to fall out and I would then run him over. Within minutes the scene had degenerated into absolute chaos. I am no expert but it seemed poor timing to try and film a road scene during rush hour, in a city with a population of almost two and a half million. Abdul turned into a lunatic. He seemed oblivious to all the traffic mounting up. He screamed at Arse to slow down to a crawl, to enable him to film. He was directing me to move left, move right, accelerate up to within inches of the truck and gestured wildly for me to remove my helmet. I looked in my rear view mirror and could see Ahmed raising his arms in despair, Scottish Sami laughing hysterically and Boss Sami leaning through from the back gesticulating frenziedly at Abdul. Behind them I could see rows and rows of cars hooting and revving their engines, people leaning out and screaming out of every window for us to move on. Abdul just waved them away with the back of his hand and continued filming. He was looking more and more maniacal and unhinged. I was seriously worried that his eyes were going to pop out completely and bounce down the road next to me, followed by his body.

Thankfully the inevitable happened and the Police managed to weave their way through the traffic jam to confront Abdul. He steadfastly ignored the two Police cars, forcing the four officers to get out and confront him. (Strangely enough, Libyan taxis are black with white wings, whereas Police cars are white with black wings. I strongly suspect the government bought a cheap batch of white cars and a batch of black cars of the same model and just swapped the wings. Hey presto; Police cars and Taxis sorted!) I sat there and watched as Abdul berated the Police at the top of his voice in Arabic. His arrest seemed inevitable, but astonishingly the Police turned on their heels and left. Abdul slowly drifted back to reality and ushered us off the road to let the raging commuters pass.

"Can you believe those ignoramus Police sons of dogs? They do not understand the importance of art and creativity. All they care about is upholding the law," he raged.

I almost pointed out that this was exactly what Police were supposed to do, but decided against it, what with his present volatile mood. "What did you say to them, how did you get rid of them," I asked.

"I told them in no uncertain terms that I was the President's cousin. I pointed out that because of their insubordination I would have all of them chopped up into very small morsels of humanity. I would then feed them to my camels, in front of their families. Then I would use the dung from the camels as fire wood." Fair enough.

Common sense prevailed and it was decided that we would head out of the centre, along the Beach road, where we could hopefully record an interview without the intervention of a million commuters. It was certainly quieter along the coast but our interview was hampered by gale force winds. In no way was this going to deter Abdul and he filmed whilst almost standing at 45 degrees. We wrapped up the scene after half an hour. Abdul seemed happy but as far as I was concerned it seemed absurd to assume that we would have any dialogue whatsoever recorded. I presume that this was indeed the case as no footage from our chaotic day has ever surfaced. Maybe, after I left, Abdul had just spontaneously exploded in the street due to excess kinetic energy. I will never know.

After that debacle it was time for me to head towards the Egyptian border. My route was simple and required no map. I would follow the one and only coast road east through Misrata, Sirte, Benghazi, Tubruk and to the El Salloum border with Egypt. It was a mere distance of 1,390 kilometres through the Sahara. Luckily Boss Sami had decided we would split the trip into two sections; the first day we would travel to Benghazi, a mere 1,014 kilometres. You will find this difficult to believe but we nailed this distance in 13 hours 48 minutes. The only stop we made was a brief visit to Leptis Magna. The site was originally founded by Berbers and Phoenicians around 1000 and became the third most important city in Africa. It was developed by the Romans and remains the most spectacular and impressive ruins of the Roman period in the whole of Africa. There were reports that it was used as a cover for tanks and military vehicles by pro-Gaddafi forces during the 2011 civil war. When asked about conducting air strikes on the historic site, NATO refused to rule out the possibility. Luckily this did not happen and without dwelling on it, if you get a chance to visit, it is spectacular in its size, beauty and position, bordering a golden sand beach. The majesty of the place is only enhanced by the lack of tourists and, believe it or not, Scottish Sami and I were the only people there. It was magical. After this brief break it was go, go, go and I was shattered and delirious when we eventually stopped in Benghazi. I slumped over the petrol tank as we pulled up outside a truck stop. Boss Sami headed inside to organise accommodation. He returned shortly, looking exceedingly sheepish for the normally in control Boss Sami.

"Spencer, I am one thousand percent sorry, but they will not let you inside. We have to stop tonight because Ahmed is not so good." I made a quick mental calculation; fourteen hours of driving for Ahmed probably equals two and a half bottles of whisky. It was a logical and necessary time to stop, especially as Ahmed was nodding forward and hitting his head on the steering wheel. I put on a brave face, but inside felt angry and discriminated against. "Don't worry Sami, you guys sleep inside and I will sleep in the truck."

And so it came to be that I was lying in the back of a truck, staring at the distant stars in the blue night sky, feeling like a true outsider. All the 'team' were great, if not a little eccentric and I had no idea why one rebuttal for accommodation could make me feel so down. But it did. On top of that my wrist was beginning to give way from fourteen hours of riding. This was to be an injury that would worsen steadily, until it eventually threatened my journey altogether. At least my ego would heal and I tried to settle down and recharge for the next big push to the Egyptian border.

The next morning I still felt grim, but Boss Sami, Scottish Sami and Ahmed acted as though there was nothing untoward with me being banished to the car in sub-zero night temperatures, so I left it. I had to focus on the trip ahead and stop being so childish about a rebuttal because of what; the colour of my skin, my religion? It happens a lot, all over the world. I knew that there would be other more serious obstacles ahead of me, so put it down to experience. To be honest, I had already faced some prejudice. I will always sing the praises of Sami and Sami but on a number of occasions in Libya already I had been faced with open aggression. People shouted at me, "American, American!" and spat on the ground in contempt. I am not going to argue this point because I am not a fan of the American, bullying 'we are the world's police' attitude. What I do know is that in most African countries (despite what Americans think), once people had ascertained that I was not from the US or from China (the new colonials) they were much more friendly.

Our pace continued and the journey from Benghazi to El Salloum (the Egyptian border), a total of 633 kilometres took us an astonishingly quick nine hours and fifty four minutes. I was eating up Africa. It was not from choice and no matter how much I enjoyed the two Samis I was looking forward to going at my own pace rather than at Jenson Button Ahmed's pace. So it was with mixed emotions that I said goodbye to the 'team' at the Egyptian border. I never managed to say goodbye to Ahmed as he immediately fell unconscious when he reached the border. Scottish Sami gave me a photo of a road bike that had been given to him by Gaddafi's cousin with a comment on the back, 'Best of luck with the rest of the journey. See you again. Sami Osman.' Boss Sami gave me a big hug, which I was quite surprised by as he was too smooth to hug. However, he did revert to his correct persona by smoothing out his suit and tie afterwards. He rapidly put on his sunglasses after the hug. I am not saying that he shed a tear, but I did get the feeling that he liked me and had enjoyed our brief friendship. I tried contacting both Samis as the Libyan civil war unfolded in all its horror. I heard nothing and have not heard from them since. I pray they survived.

Chapter Two
Desert Nomads in the Qattara Depression

'If you reject the food, ignore the customs, fear the religion and avoid the people you might better stay at home.' James A. Michener

'Sunshine all the time makes a desert.' Arab proverb

Although I didn't know it, I was about to have a spiritual eating experience in the sand dunes of the Sahara desert. Within two hours of being in Egypt I decided to do some desert riding instead of following the standard coastal tarred route. The asphalt road snakes along the northern border of Egypt, joining the city of Marsa Matruh to the famous city of Alexandria, the second largest city in Egypt. Although it is a stunning ride with the Mediterranean on the left of the bike, and the vast expansive sand of the Sahara Desert on the right, I was yearning to divert off this main thoroughfare and shoot into the desert and the middle of nowhere. I stopped in Marsa Matruh to prepare properly for what could be a hazardous expedition, especially if ill-equipped.

The Qattara Depression where I was heading was considered, during the war, impassable by tanks and most other military vehicles, although German Afrika Corps patrols and the British Long Range Desert Group did operate in the area. Its presence shaped the Battle of El Alamein. The features that make the Depression so impassable include its salt lakes, high cliffs or escarpments, and Fech Fech (fine powdered sand). I also knew that there was the Mogra Oasis but there was little chance I would find this uninhabited, brackish lake. Without the proper planning and provisions the Qattara Depression could easily become more than depressing. I was determined that this would not happen to me. I had a ten litre bladder bag which I filled with water, a handy bit of equipment, as it contracts as you drink, thereby taking up less space. I also bought two new, yellow, plastic jerry cans from a street vendor who was also selling plastic litre bottles of fuel. I purchased ten and siphoned them into the new containers which I then strapped to the back of my panniers. He was also flogging small plastic dolls (?!) and flip flops but I decided they were a luxury and not at the top of my list of survival equipment in the Sahara. I declined his offer to buy two dolls and get one for free, thanked him, and headed off to a food stall I had spotted earlier on, a hundred metres further back up the street, on the opposite side of the sandy road. A large lady in a bright headscarf was busy selling handmade Egyptian bread, and that's what I had my eye on. The bread, known as Eesh baladi, is whole-wheat, circular and about fifteen centimetres in diameter. It is very filling and more to the point was the perfect shape for slipping into my rucksack.

The proprietor of the stall had her hands full over an open fire. She softened the bread by placing it under running water from a stand pipe sticking out of the sand, next to her stall. She would then pass it over a naked flame and serve it up on battered tin plates, with various sauces, to the waiting customers. I purchased five loaves of bread and a variety of sauces which she poured into the corners of plastic bags and tied off. She then cut off the excess plastic above the knot, letting it drop into the fire, causing an instant cloud of acrid, thick smoke. This seemed to have no effect on her whatsoever, as she stood in the dead centre of it, negotiating with the clientele. At times only her arms were visible sticking out on either side of a column of smoke, happily gesticulating to the patient group. I also bought three cans of chilli sardines, thanked the column of smoke, and headed out of Marsa Matruh towards the Qattara Depression.

As soon as I was in the open desert the atmosphere changed

completely. Anyone who has been in sand dunes will tell you that it is an experience so magical, so personal, yet so otherworldly, that it is never forgotten. The hairdryer heat, the stillness and the beauty of the contrasting horizon; dazzling, clear blue sky turning to pristine yellow/white sand produces a feeling of such vast immenseness that you cannot help but feel humbled. As I was riding I imagined an overhead camera view of me on the bike, the camera slowly pulling further and further back, a snaking tyre trail disturbing the patterns in the sand behind me, until I disappeared like a grain of sand in the ever-changing dune landscape. I defy anyone not to feel small and insignificant in this environment.

Riding in sand is hard work until you get the hang of it. The desert's sole intention is to swallow up the tyres of the bike at every possible opportunity. The first thing to do is let them down to about 5 psi to allow the tread to spread out, create a bigger footprint, and therefore prevent them sinking so easily. It is important to keep the throttle steady and even and to keep pushing forward without hesitation. It goes against normal instincts but it is better to stand up, go as fast as you feel safe, and then a bit. I fell often before I learnt these techniques, but luckily, the landing was fairly forgiving apart from the odd rock jutting out of the sand.

I rode steadily, but stopped often to soak up the experience and to check my compass bearings. I did not see anybody for two days. The only living thing that crossed my path was a small sand fox which appeared briefly, standing on a dune, silhouetted against the immaculately blue sky, momentarily checking me out, before disappearing into the desert. It was liberating to be alone. Everything is so much more personal, vivid and unique. Being unable to share experiences with others verbally adds beauty to life. Loneliness puts a special burn on sunsets and makes night air smell better. Loneliness is really the wrong word. Language has created the word 'loneliness' to express the pain of being alone, and it has created the word 'solitude' to express the glory of being alone. I was feeling the full glory!

On the second night I stopped before sunset to set up camp. I unpacked my tent and rolled it out on the desert floor as a ground sheet, blew up my mattress and lay it on the tent. There was no way I was going to enclose myself in the tent in a place like this - scorpions and snakes or no scorpions and snakes. I took off my boots and socks, laying out the sweat-soaked socks in the last dying rays of the sun to dry out. I stuffed the tent bag full of extra clothes as a pillow and lay it down on my sleeping bag. I flopped down and wiggled my bum around in the sand to make a comfortable indentation. I undid my water bottle and took a generous swig, before retrieving my notebook and pencil from my rucksack. I wanted to write down some thoughts under this beautiful amphitheatre of rapidly appearing stars. I wrote steadily for thirty minutes or so, adjusting my position regularly, as my elbow succumbed to pins and needles, straining my eyes against the glare of the paper, beads of sweat dripping onto the page, despite the fact that it was early evening. I was starting to feel very heavy-lidded, so decided to prepare some food and get an early night, in preparation for a sunrise start tomorrow. I'm not sure if something caught my eye, but for some inexplicable reason I stood up and decided to scan the shimmering horizon. What a stunning sight was unfolding in the far distance. I was transported straight into my own Indiana Jones movie. (What a western comment.) Walking towards me through the haze came four tall, angular Bedouin nomads. They were swathed in black and white cloth, their heads wrapped in burgundy and white and all were carrying rifles. Three of the men had coal black beards whilst the fourth, with a hawk on his shoulder (no, I am not making this up) was obviously older, his beard speckled grey and his gait less steady. As they came closer, two things became obvious; firstly by his demeanour, it was obvious the more elderly man was the leader, and secondly, to my delight they all had beaming smiles

32

and looked genuinely pleased, if not a bit surprised, to see me. They had cloth sacks on their backs which they gently offloaded onto the sand as they approached me. The leader stepped forward and offered me his hand. Although I did not speak a single word of Bedawi Arabic and they had no words of English, we somehow muddled through. Once all the introductions and etiquette were observed I couldn't believe how quickly and how elegantly they set into action, organising a camp for the night.

They worked in silence, each having a specific job to perform, so I just busied myself with setting up my part of the camp. The nomad who I judged to be the youngest, disappeared silently into the desert and returned forty minutes later with a bundle of wood. I must have missed the 'Nomad Supplies Shop' on the way here, because I had not seen a single tree or branch on route. He proceeded to offload the wood and slowly but steadily dug a circle out of the sand, broke up the tinder-dry wood with a large dagger, and made a small pyramid of kindling in the centre of the circle. He then unwrapped a piece of cloth containing dried camel faeces, broke it up and placed it under the twigs. He lit the fire, gently blowing it until it sparked into life. He sat back on his haunches to survey his work. The nomads were so incredibly graceful and peaceful, and the desert was so still, I was having a real experience here! Everything about their mannerisms and movements seemed in tune with the atmosphere of the desert: they oozed poise and serenity. This is the sense of the desert hills, that there is room enough and time enough. What a contrast to the frenetic, everyone-for-themselves, impersonal mayhem of many urban centres. People's characters and behaviour do reflect their environment. I sincerely believe it is rarer to find happiness in a man surrounded by the miracles of technology than among people living in the desert or jungle who, by our society's standards, would be considered destitute and out of touch. I was so happy. It's the simplest things in life that are the most extraordinary.

Within minutes they had tea brewing on an open fire and made an incredible meal. We had aubergines with onion, a salad with diced carrots, tomatoes and whole chillies and *fuul* (Java beans cooked with oil and lemon and unleavened bread) and minced, seasoned meat and *'ta amiyya'* (falafel). It was a meal fit for the finest restaurant. During the dinner all we really managed to ascertain from each other was that my name was Spencer and that their names were Ali, Ali, Ali and Ali (in that order from youngest to oldest) and that they were from the Bedawi Arabic tribal group of Eastern Egypt. Somehow it did not matter in the slightest that we had communication problems, we managed with sign language and a lot of smiling and gesturing. I was in a strange way pleased, as it minimised the conversation and added to the magically silent atmosphere of this insanely different picnic. (Well, it was certainly different for me!!) As darkness began to fall we settled down to sleep, but not before 'Main Man Ali' offered me his own blanket. I refused politely and we all set about wrapping up in preparation for the cold desert night ahead. I slept outside my tent, my head sticking out of my tightly drawn sleeping bag and stared up at the stars. Poets say that science takes away from the beauty of stars; that they are mere globs of gas atoms. I, too, could see the stars as I lay there on this desert night. But did I see less or more? I felt like the luckiest person alive and the awakening in the morning only confirmed this.

As the sun rose, I felt its first rays warming my face and slowly opened my eyes. My four friends were gone and the camp was completely spotless, no litter, no sign of the fire and no sign of them. It was as though they had swept the desert clean. But right in front of me, on a small piece of cardboard stuck in the sand were the words, "Thank you". *They* were saying thanks! It's me that should be saying thank you, thank you, thank you, thank you, the four Ali's, and long may you roam the desert in your serene way. I am forever jealous. I thought it ironic that the term Bedouin, which predominantly refs to camel-raising tribes, is sadly often now used among various Arab groups as a derogatory term for another, implying a lack of culture and refinement. How far from the truth is that!

Lying there in the silence looking out at the sand stretching endlessly before me it was difficult to believe that Egypt has a population of 80 million. But having said that it does have an area of 997,739 square kilometres and I was sure I would get the shock of a lifetime when I saw how many people were squeezed into the capital, Cairo. There is a saying that 'the desert has its holiness of silence, the crowd has its holiness of conversation'. I know where my holiness vote goes.

Having said all that, although the desert is unbelievably beautiful there is still no denying the fact that the Sahel, the area bordering the Sahara, is shrinking at an alarming rate as animals graze on its fragile land, and trees and bushes are cut for fuel. Without the vegetation to hold it in place, the thin topsoil of the Sahel blows away, leaving stony land where neither grass nor crops can grow. I realised that I was looking at it through the wondrous eyes of a visitor but to the people of the Sahara region it is a constant battle against the elements and the encroaching desert. Sadly it is much easier to create a desert than a forest.

As I packed up my things to head to Cairo I pondered on the amazing four Bedouins who arrived and disappeared, as though it was a dream, back in to the desert that they had conquered and made their home. They had adapted perfectly to their environment and I felt privileged to have spent a short time with them. I love it when life resembles a novel more often than novels resemble life. That is the wonder of travel, it's an unpredictable pursuit. As I bungeed up my possessions to the bike, eager and ready for the next experience, the sun exploded into the sky and showered me with warmth. Within five minutes I began to feel hot, hot, hot. It was time to start the bike, get the breeze through my body and find the sealed road.

Nothing could go drastically wrong as far as directions were concerned, because if I just continued north and rode into the Mediterranean Sea then I would know that I had gone a little bit too far and should have turned right earlier. My orientation skills are top class, bar none, don't you think? I rode steadily all day, not taking any risks. I was well aware that if I fell and broke a bone I would be in deep trouble as I had not seen a single track or person in the last seven hours. Furthermore, I had broken the golden rule of survival training; tell somebody where you are going and when you are going to be back. Compounding the risk was the fact was that I had no mobile signal whatsoever, so had no contact with the outside world. I began to have a slight feeling of rising panic thinking that I should have reached the main asphalt coastal road when over the rise came a man on a red Chinese motorbike. On the back was a little boy, his son, I presume, who was dwarfed by the biggest bundle of firewood I have ever seen in my life, tied up with cloth and balanced precariously on the back of the bike. The little boy was sandwiched between his father and the wood but managed to extract his arm and give me an enthusiastic wave as they rode past me. The father also tried to wave, but as soon as he took his hand off the handlebar he went into an out-of-control wobble and had to rapidly grab the handlebars to prevent being dumped, load and all, into the sand. He smiled, shouted something excitedly, and they were gone. It was silent again, except for the thump of my bike's engine and I cracked on, hoping that having seen someone else was a sign that the main road was nearby.

After ten minutes or so I heard a noise behind me, glanced back and there he was again, minus son and wood. I stopped and he introduced himself as Khalid, saying that he would show me to the road. I thanked him and we headed off with him in the lead, weaving and sliding in the sand, but somehow staying upright. As we rode his head wrap started unravelling and by the time we got to the highway it was blowing two metres behind him, in a crimson trail. The road was absolutely perfect and I felt confident that if I pushed on I could make it to Cairo. I gave Khalid some water and a loaf of bread and said farewell. What a contrast Cairo was going to be compared to the mainly solitary last two days.

I arrived in the outskirts of Cairo at about six o clock in the evening and what a spectacularly insane driving experience it was. I thought that maybe it was rush hour, but quickly came to realise that Cairo *is* rush hour, full stop. It was mad, exhilarating, thrilling, and more. The cars were bumper to bumper, all hooting constantly while mopeds wove ludicrously fast through any tiny gap they could find. All the cars were dented. The smoke from the traffic was making my eyes stream, and the pulsing heat emanating from all the car engines, added to the heat of the late afternoon sun beating down, made the cauldron-like temperatures stifling. There are no traffic laws except to keep moving whenever you get the chance, or else your eardrums will be hooted to death.

I was singing Bob Marley again, thrilled with the challenge of trying to get through this mayhem with all my limbs intact. The bike was not so happy however and was beginning to overheat. I pulled over onto the pavement which was no safe haven, believe me, because mopeds used it for short cuts and children used it to surround you with tacky tourist souvenirs. I then made the error of a simpleton. I opened my oil reservoir to check the oil level and a jet of boiling oil spewed a foot into the air and all over the engine, where it immediately turned into a cloud of thick black smoke. An excellent way to stay anonymous; arrive on a massive blue motorbike and then set fire to it in the centre of Cairo! My next problem was to get some oil in this heaving metropolis without leaving my bike and my entire luggage. My saviour arrived in the form of a raven-haired boy with dark rings under his eyes, who stood in front of me, arms crossed in front of him; chest puffed out and said confidently, "I can help you". I was indeed impressed by his confidence and command of English, especially as he was the same size as one of my motorbike boots, and couldn't have been a day over nine years old. I was not about to get into a discussion about the morals of child labour and sent him off to find me some oil. His confident air was justified and ten minutes later he struggled back with a litre bottle of oil. I thanked him and offered him some sweets, but he was having none of those kiddy diversionary tactics, he wanted hard currency, which was fair enough, I thought. I handed him a few notes, as he had kept up his part of the bargain, and I headed down the main drag to a place called Tahrir Square. I had been told it was possible to find a cheap room, along the smaller roads running off the square. Tahrir Square is actually a circle but God forbid I would criticise Egyptian geometry, given their long cultural and architectural history; pyramid schemes and all that. I made my way off Tahrir 'Squircle', passing by the world famous Egyptian Museum and into a dingy side road which was blocked by a lorry offloading electrical goods into an even dimmer alleyway.

I stopped the bike and asked one of the men if there were any cheap hotels nearby. He gestured to a derelict four-storey building at the end of the alleyway that they were offloading the boxes into. I squeezed through the gap between the boxes, which they had thoughtfully left clear for visiting motorcyclists and made my way to the entrance, leaving the bike in the street. At the entrance was a small neon sign with the welcoming words, 'Downtown Palace-4th floor', the w's in Downtown flickering on and off. I made my way through the entrance (there was no door) into the interior. In the dim light I could see a double, sweeping staircase with an incredibly intricate wrought iron banister running its length. Directly in front of me between the two staircases was a similarly intricate lift, set inside a wrought iron flower exterior. The walls of the building were covered in an array of jumbled wires leading to hundreds of LG air conditioners which looked like they had stopped working around the time dinosaurs were beginning to struggle.

The electrical set-up was such that the interior walls looked as though a giant had angrily thrown his bowl of spaghetti at them. It must have been a magnificent hotel at some point and was obviously a remnant of the old British colonial era. I decided to risk the similarly dilapidated lift. It jolted to a start and made its way reluctantly to the fourth floor. Through the open grill I could see that the first three floors were also derelict. The fourth floor was exactly the same except for one particular door which was painted baby blue and had a light emanating from it. Pinned on the door was a squint piece of paper with the words 'Welcome to Downtown Palace' scrawled on it. And another notice not to have 'guests'.

Just inside the entrance was a small wooden reception desk with a young Egyptian guy in thin glasses standing behind it, in an immaculately ironed pink and white shirt, busy on his mobile phone. Ahmed's English was excellent but unfortunately he sounded exactly like Scooby Doo and was as thin as a cotton bud, so it was quite difficult to keep a straight face. He showed me to a vacant room which was reasonably clean. It consisted of a bowed double bed with a wooden headboard with the name Downtown Palace carved into it. Also in the room was… nothing else, but at least I had a small balcony to watch the comings and goings on a Cairo street. It turned out to be $8 a night, which if you had seen it, I am sure you would have agreed, was massively overpriced. I settled in for one minute (I have been called hyperactive in the past) and then decided to head into the street for a snack before I tried to catch up on much-needed sleep. I have always had a fear, verging on phobia, for lifts and my ultimate nightmare happened. I got caught and stuck in the lift halfway between two floors. I eventually got the attention of Scooby Doo and he prised the doors open and I had to squeeze out of a gap.

For some odd reason which I can't remember, after my escape we started a highbrow discussion about music and Scooby proudly informed me that, "the foreign music that is much popular with Egyptian people is the Kenny Rogers, the Rolling Stones and the Samantha Fox."

For those of you not lucky enough to be familiar with her considerable talents, Samantha was a Page Three English glamour model in *The Sun* from the eighties, a favourite pin-up amongst hormonally over-run teenage boys, who later became a singer/songwriter. How hilarious was that.

I think Scooby noticed my quizzical look as he stressed, "You know this lady, Samantha Fox, from England, she is very beautiful lady." I assured him that I was well aware of her star qualities and headed down to the street, leaving Ahmed AL Scooby to his fantasies.

After some forgettable food I headed back to my palace and eventually managed to get a good night's sleep. When I left the Palace the next morning to head to the Pyramids of Giza, the lift had disappeared. Apparently it had fallen four floors and, true as God, when I made my way down the winding Colonial staircase to the ground floor, there it was, a crumpled wreck. Excellent, my dislike of lifts is now officially a phobia.

I will be one hundred percent honest: I am not Michael Palin who keeps his cool under any pressure (respect to him) and I very nearly lost mine during a very disappointing visit to the Pyramids. I would not be so foolish as to deny that they are iconic and defy description. They have been visited and studied for 4000 years, for Pharaoh's sake! Islamic caliphs understood their spiritual power and tried to tear them down. Napoleon understood their political power and used them for target practice. The theories about why and what for, the speculations of divine intervention and apocalyptic foreboding ensure that the Pyramids fulfil their function of keeping alive the names of a father (Khufu), his son (Kahfre) and grandson (Menkaure). This really is the wonder of these pyramids and it seems certain that they will continue to succeed in their function for many years to come.

Every generation of schoolchildren in countries around the world studies Egyptian culture and at the very least knows the names Cleopatra, Tutankhamun and The Pyramids. I was enthralled to learn about the culture, the art, the building, etc. I was so disappointed in the experience that I find it difficult to put into words. But I will try. I will explain exactly how it happened. Maybe I was in the wrong mood, I accept that.

I took a taxi at around 10am in the morning to get to the Pyramids. I had done the route the day before on my bike and knew that it was a straight road from my room to the Pyramids of about 6km. The taxi driver took me all over the place despite the fact I had told him clearly that I wanted to go straight there. We ended up arguing and when we stopped he charged me a ridiculous price and tried to charge me extra for having a conversation during the trip and for a cigarette he had offered me on the journey.

Good start! I told him where to go. I told him he was a dodgy Giza and if he Sphinx he can rip me off, he better think again. Sorry couldn't resist the weak puns. The immediate impact of the Pyramids was lost on me mainly because of the sixty buses and thousands of tourists with rucksacks. I joined the queue of baseball cap-wearing, camera-wielding, guide book-reading, binocular-twiddling, sun block-applying, tourists (yes, I knew I was one of them), and after a good forty minutes I eventually got my clutches on a ticket for the Great Pyramid. It was E£100 for the ticket – can you believe it, but they weren't finished there. I went through the turnstile and was asked by the spectacularly grumpy ticket collector for my other ticket, 'For the Area.' The area of what, a triangle, polygon? Apparently I needed a ticket of E£30 to visit the area that I had a ticket for. The E£100 was only for entry to the Great Pyramid but to actually get there you have to go through 'the area'. What was I supposed to do, float over 'the area' to get to the Pyramid? That would have made the news. I told Grumpy, in no uncertain terms, to give me a refund for the Pyramid ticket and to just give me a ticket for 'the area', and I would roam far and wide like the desert breeze. He sighed and tutted, and generally overacted before eventually throwing my money at me.

As soon as I got through this first hiccup and made it to the promised 'area' I was accosted by a young man of about sixteen who, according to him, was definitely *not* a guide and didn't want my money at all. Never, never, over his mother's dead body (or more accurately over his mother's dead Mummy) would he ask me for money. He then spoke non-stop for about half an hour, seemingly without drawing a single breath. He stuck to me like a limpet that had fallen in superglue, which wasn't too pleasant as he smelled like he had eaten a dead rat for breakfast and his teeth were stained black from copious amounts of tea which only added to his alluring appeal.

The last straw (or papyrus reed) for me was when he grabbed me by the arm, pulled me forcefully on to a mound of stones and pointed at the Pyramids stating, "This is the best place to take a photo, you take photo now, you take photo here, good photo here, as memory present for me. You take photo of me, my friend, and good photo. Take photo, take photo!"

The last thing I wanted was any memories of him. I resented his constant invasion of my personal space and his general attitude. It was as though he owned the rock, the view, the photo, the camera – and me! I can hear the politically correct brigade saying, "He's only trying to make a living, he probably doesn't have much, give him some slack." That may be true but it doesn't mean I have to pretend to enjoy him telling me where to walk, where to take a photo and generally ruining an experience that I had looked forward to since I was a small boy. I finally got rid of him with a few mumbled words about training the Egyptian Army, bipolar disorder, violent blackouts, trained killer, exSAS etc., and he sloped off to find a new person to bore to tears.

As soon as I got rid of him and brought out my camera another Woody Allen look-alike, Egyptian official came walking towards me at a rapid rate, waving his finger manically saying, "Not all your fingers are the same." I had not an inkling of what he was talking about or whether he was threatening to cut mine off but the long and the short of it (the story, not the fingers) was that he wanted dollars for me filming in a prohibited zone. I just laughed in despair at this point and said, "I am not giving you money now, or in the near future, or in my or your lifetime, even if you pull my body apart with two horses." His facial expression, gun and moustache visibly drooped at such a direct refusal and he headed off without a fight, completely deflated. I was surprised, maybe he'd had a bad day too and an argument with his wife before work. Who knows? I headed down to the base of Cheop's Pyramid to see the entrance, which I wasn't going to enter because I was too moody to pay the entrance fee. The entrance wasn't visible anyway as there was a very large lady in a red T-shirt wheezing and coughing and blocking the whole entrance with her abnormal posterior. I took a photo of tourists, taking photos of tourists, while their guide waved a yellow and red table tennis bat to herd them to the next attraction while sporting a fixed grin, which was beginning to look remarkably like a side-effect of constipation. I know this is one of the most famous sites – and sights – in the world, but couldn't they just close it for one day so that I could enjoy it in the peace and serenity that such a place deserves. I guess everybody would like that but it's too late. When you go to a football game or live concert you want it to be heaving with people to create the atmosphere but you want the absolute opposite when you visit something as magisterial as the Great Pyramid, the Sphinx, the Grand Canyon and even Victoria Falls. I suppose the beauty and wonder of these places is their own worst enemy. The absurd thing is I was probably being filmed by a tourist filming the tourists, filming the Pyramids. I do realise I am part of the chain, but what a disappointing day.

The most striking thing to me about the whole day was the location of the Pyramids. I had some impression that I would be riding across sand dunes on a camel (à la Lawrence of Arabia) for a couple of hours and would come across the Pyramids standing majestically on their own in the middle of the desert. Instead, they are right on top of the city with a winding tar road leading up to them with a McDonald's within view. That's a small thing, I suppose.

But forgetting about political correctness, the aggressive selling attitude has ruined the 'Pyramid Experience'. After all my moaning, I absolutely love the vitality of Egypt and would recommend it to anyone with a bit of gumption. What a vibrant, twenty-four hour, full throttle life!

On the trip back from the Pyramids the taxi driver told me he was going via the ring road otherwise it would take three hours for six kilometres – God! The traffic is bad in Cairo. During the journey he parked in the middle of the road and jumped out to rearrange the shape and style of a man's shirt, the owner of which had dared to hail his taxi, when it was obvious that there was already a tourist ripe to be fleeced within his very car. Whilst the driver was venting his road rage I peered out the window and realised that there was nowhere in the world where I had seen so many cats and dogs. They look exactly like they do in hieroglyphics and unlike any species I have seen anywhere in the world. The dogs look like the cats which look Siamese, and they are everywhere. Brilliant! We made it another two miles, until the driver drove straight into another car's driver door and that was that. He took off his sunglasses, looked at me, raised his eyebrows, shrugged his shoulders and said, "Sorry." I thought that was quite cool and asked, "How much, I will walk from here." He insisted on the full amount so I gave him E£10 less and walked off with his Arabic swear words ringing in my ears. So glad I wasn't on the bike!!

Another thing that became crystal clear during my Cairo visit was that all the Egyptians who prey on tourists must have been to the same School of Tourism. Here are the basic conversations you will have to repeat many times over:

HIM: Hello – where are you from?

YOU: England.

HIM: London? Manchester?

YOU: London (even if you are not from there).

HIM: I like London, I like English, I have friend in Yorkshire (why Yorkshire, I don't know, but it seems every single Yorkshire man in the world has an Egyptian friend he is unaware of).

YOU: Mumble, mumble.

HIM: All of the following –
"Tally ho"
"Lovely jubbly"
"In a while crocodile"
"See you later alligator."

YOU: Ha! Ha! (or suchlike).

HIM: I like English. Because you English, I give you good deal on camel ride, horse ride, taxi ride, boat ride, food, drink, alcohol, hashish, hotels, souvenirs, my grandmother, etc. Actually all except the last: have some respect!

If you want to vary the conversation slightly and have a bit of fun you can vary your country of origin:

HIM: Where you from – (what's your nationality)?

YOU: Mars.

HIM: I like this place. I give you good deal on… etc.

Despite all my complaints, I was actually loving Egypt, and still had the pleasure of travelling down the Nile to Luxor and Aswan ahead of me. I couldn't wait.

Chapter Three
Ashraf and the Scarabs

'Travel is fatal to prejudice, bigotry and narrow mindedness.'
Mark Twain

'Human beings who are almost unique in having the ability to learn from the experience of others, are also remarkable for their apparent disinclination to do so.' Douglas Adams

Wadi Halfa! The name itself had become a mystical landmark for me in much the same way as the exotic sounding Timbuktu or Ouagadougou. I was on my way there but first I had a torturous twenty-four-hour ferry journey to deal with. I was leaving Egypt for the border port of Wadi Halfa, in Sudan, which was only accessible by ferry as the road that did exist was limited to organised tour buses and the military.

I had been warned that the ferry was a steel hulk with human cargo crammed on it to the absolute maximum – so much so that if you were a little slow getting on and up to the top deck, you could end up standing for twenty four hours which, I frankly, was quite keen to avoid. Armed with this knowledge, I was like Usain Bolt at the starting blocks when the gangway was finally opened. Unfortunately, there were at least a hundred Egyptian Usain Bolts in front of me and the whole embarkation process turned into a semi riot of pushing, shoving and general mayhem as women in traditional yeleks (kaftans) and men in gallibayas (robes) fought their way up the steel stairway to the top deck. I eventually managed to scramble my way up. The general principle seemed to be that you threw yourself down like a lunatic in the first available space, of which there were very few already. I stepped over people who were lying prostrate and spotted a free sliver of space at the stern of the ferry, on the very edge, underneath a massive steel pipe. I wouldn't be able to stand up, but that was my space! I squeezed under the pipe and sat down. Quickly I pulled out my sleeping bag, unfurled it and hopefully had 'booked' my sleeping berth for the next twenty four hours. On the one side I was jammed against two small metal railings which would be my only safety guard against falling into Lake Nasser if I fell asleep.

Ferry Fear

On the other side sandwiched between me and a steel panel was a Turkish guy and his two young children, their knees folded up against their bodies so they could squeeze into the available space. I had met them in Aswan when I went to the Nile River Transport Corporation Office to obtain my ticket for this ferry. The remarkable thing about these three was that the father, Davut, was blind, and his daughter, Abutab, who must have been about nine, was running the whole show; sorting out paperwork, organising tickets, negotiating with officials and the myriad of other tasks and responsibilities that are all part of travelling. It was very moving to see, as Abutab hung on every word her father spoke and obviously worshipped the ground he walked on. Through a brief conversation with them I ascertained that they had been travelling for three months. Davut wanted them to see the world that he never could.

We settled down as best we could to watch the scene in front of us. More and more people were still pouring onto the deck, until there was not a single available space. Most people were laden down with goods. There were all manner of boxes, held together with plastic strapping, bulging sacks, colossal piles of woven mats, engine blocks, electrical appliances, suitcases, and even a man carrying a full size fridge on his shoulder. People were busying themselves with various activities; arranging their goods into piles, brewing tea on tiny stoves, playing cards and wrapping themselves up against the early morning cold. At the front of the ferry a group of four or five families were busy barricading themselves into a circular configuration using their luggage as a barrier against the jostling masses. Once they had achieved their Stonehenge-like effect, a couple of the younger men proceeded to tie together ten or fifteen large pieces of cloth which they tied to various parts of the ferry above them, thereby creating a makeshift tent. I only came to realise, later in the day, when it got hotter and hotter, and the steel hull became boiling to touch, that they had made a prudent move. After rolling out carpets on the deck, their makeshift home for the next twenty four hours was complete. They then proceeded to have a very loud and volatile discussion in Arabic which, to my astonishment, continued unabated for the entire journey. Talk about verbal energy.

I cast my eyes around the deck and further down, on the same side of the ferry as me, were four Westerners. Three of them were destined to play a significant part in my journey, but more of that later – a lot more. Having set myself up, donned another sweater and a balaclava against the early morning cold, I ventured down to the lower deck, stepping over, and often vaulting, three or four bodies. I made my way down the slippery metal step, pushing my way through groups of people who refused to move an inch. A low door led into the dark interior and I stooped down and went in. It took a few seconds for my eyes to adjust to the light, but when they did my immediate impression was that it was like a slave ship. People were lined up top to toe over the entire room. It was like a human carpet. In the tiny spaces left between the people that were lying down, other people were standing, trying to keep their balance so as not to topple on those lying around them. The smell of urine and faeces from the overflowing public toilet on my left was overpowering and was collecting in a pool by my feet. I could see that it was fruitless to negotiate this lower deck and my eyes were stinging. I was beginning to gag from the stench emanating from the toilet, it was time to head back to the not so bad upper deck.

As I returned to my sliver of a space the ferry finally pulled out of Aswan and we were off. I was pleased about that, as to tell you the truth I was not overly impressed with the section of the Nile around Aswan. Apart from the cramped space and constant worry in case I fell into the Nile all proceeded well and we finally reached our destination. It is an extremely touristy area. The river is littered with feluccas (traditional boats with a tall triangular sail) ferrying tourists around. They are a beautiful sight but the tranquillity is constantly broken by the huge ferries, barges and cruise ships ploughing their way through the water. Tourists can be spotted in their hundreds, sunning themselves on the lido deck whilst sipping expensive, fluorescent cocktails. Added to this, in the area around Aswan, the Nile is a muddy brown colour and the banks are littered with plastic bags, broken bottles, wood, toilet paper (used and otherwise), nails, glass, tins, bits of clothing, etc. I tried to find a peaceful spot during my week in Aswan but came to realise that this was just not the nature of the place. It was a tourist magnet. (Yes, I know, I was one of them.) As a foreigner, life on the streets was marked by constant approaches from the locals to sell you something; anything from "the cheapest, best deal in Aswan felluca trip," to horse-drawn carriage rides (I had a particular dislike for these as the donkeys and horses in Egypt were in appalling condition and were worked mercilessly in the baking sun), to fake papyrus manuscripts and scrolls, 'original' statues and artefacts as well as the purely tacky, gold-sprayed pyramid souvenirs and statuettes of famous Egyptian Kings and Queens. It was a relentless barrage of sales pitches, but I completely understood, so made a concerted effort to turn people down politely.

On the fourth day when I was stuck in Aswan waiting for my Sudanese visa, I headed out of town a few kilometres to try and get the head space that I craved and, more importantly, to try and catch a famous Nile Perch which I knew could grow up to one hundred and seventy pounds! When I finally thought I had found a secluded spot, within minutes crowds of children came running down the banks of the Nile, elbowing each other and pushing to get a prime position in front of me. They proceeded to carefully lay out pieces of cloth on the sand which they covered with an array of necklaces and cheap trinkets, all set out meticulously in neat rows in order of size and length. I was quite impressed with the military precision with which they erected their instant shops. They had obviously done this before. I steadfastly ignored them, fiddling with my fishing line or staring contentedly over the river, briefly giving them a smile, trying to make it clear with my body language that I was just not interested. It did not work. I then had to make it even clearer that not only was I the poorest man ever to visit Egypt, but on top of that I had a serious medical allergic reaction to cheap fake artefacts and on top of that I had a hatred for anyone under the age of fifteen. They eventually took the hint, when I pulled out a knife (no I didn't), and just as deftly and expertly as they had set up shop, they merrily packed up their displays and chased each other up the river bank and into a field of papyrus reeds. Like all children the world over, they were showing off for my benefit, pushing and poking and tripping each other, doing handstands and cartwheels, surreptitiously stealing a glance in my direction to see if I was highly impressed. When this didn't work they proceeded to throw stones at an unfortunate, tan-coloured ox with unfeasibly large horns, standing forlornly on the river bank. When they tired of taunting the oxen and had given up on entertaining a gloomy tourist they disappeared through the grass in fits of giggles.

I then had a window of fifteen minutes of calm and quiet where the beauty of the Nile washed over me (not literally of course, but metaphorically). As I sat there burying my toes in the warm sand and removing my shirt, on cue a Nile Perch swam right in front of me, lazily gliding through the shallows. The sun broke from behind a cloud and illuminated the water. The river bottom was beautiful, visible through suddenly crystal clear water. The river bed was covered in grass as vivid as a well-watered and tended football field. Small, brightly coloured fish darted over its surface and around the Perch as he scooped up plankton with his wide open mouth. All I had as fishing equipment was a small piece of blue nylon rope, which I had unwound to get a thinner strand from to serve as the line, a piece of wire I had fashioned into a hook, and a stale falafel to act as bait. My chances of a catch were slim, to say the least.

I could see my prey, for God's sake: how difficult could it be to snag a delicious meal. I literally lowered the hook in front of the Perch and waited. Not only did he not take the bait, but he turned to me, nodding his head in disgust, or maybe pity, and took a wide berth around the hook, disappearing slowly into the murkier depths, not before looking back at me with disdain (are fish physiologically capable of looking back?) and a theatrical flick of his tail. OK, I imagined a lot of the body language, but the point is he got away, after a gruelling fight. How big did I say he was?

No sooner had he vanished into the depths when a number of

motorised boats shattered the vibe. I am sure the fish also get annoyed with the constant humming, buzzing and whirring of boats. The ceaseless activity on this stretch of river, the pure human element of it, was to me an eye opener. If it was not a wedding or party, or a religious festival, or weekend goings-on, there would always be someone with a mobile phone playing tinny, distorted music, or groups of boat boys chattering loudly as they washed their cars or motorbikes or boats on the riverside. It also takes some time to adapt to the passion and volume of the conversations that go on in Egypt.

On my arrival at the Libya-Egypt border, I heard two men in an animated discussion. Because I couldn't understand a word, I assumed, from the intensity of the verbal sparring, that families had been cursed and daughter's virtues had been brought into question. But I am sure, in retrospect, that it was more likely that they were weighing up the virtues of different eggplants that were on display at last week's market. In fact, come to think of it, the frenetic pace in Aswan is mirrored perfectly by the volume of noise that emanates from its inhabitants, whether it is a conversation on the street or an Iman over a microphone. The volume of noise permitted in public buildings is unbelievable.

I stayed in a seedy little dive called the Horus Hotel where it felt like the foundations were about to collapse from the vibrations of belly dancing music. It was day and night, believe me! As if that was not enough to deprive a weary traveller of sleep, to add to the din, directly adjacent to the Hotel, was a school where three hundred girls were marching and drumming in the concrete playground, so vigorously it was as though they were worried that they would be sold to the nearest man as a bride if they didn't drum more loudly and enthusiastically than their nearest chum. Competing with this din were the three Imans chanting from the mosques that had surrounded the Hotel in a pincer movement. All were trying to outdo each other, firstly through speed of delivery, secondly through emotion and most importantly through volume. They all had massive PA and megaphone systems perched on the apex of each Mosque. Add to this the thousands of shouting tradesmen in the streets below, and the hundreds of hooting cars, trucks and motorbikes making their way through the traffic-jammed, litter-strewn streets. Bellowing, whistling policeman with white gloves and white outfits desperately tried to control the chaotic traffic at junctions. Consider that this is all played out in a maze of hot and dusty streets and you are getting some inkling of life in Egyptian towns and cities. Actually it is fantastic, marvellous and stimulating, but after a week of sensory overload I was now glad that I was heading into the middle of Lake Nasser and ultimately into the almost tourist-free Sudan.

As the ferry ploughed through the water, leaving Aswan behind in its wake, the whole atmosphere changed and bit by bit, kilometre by kilometre, I began to soak in the magical history that surrounded this unique country. Water is the geographical marvel that shaped this nation and I was beginning to appreciate the enormity of its importance. The effect that the Nile has had on Egypt's history cannot be underestimated. At 6,650 kilometres the Nile is the longest river in the world. It runs through the countries of Sudan (where I was heading), South Sudan, Burundi, Rwanda, Tanzania, Kenya, Ethiopia, Uganda and Egypt. The river has two major tributaries, the White and Blue Niles. The White Nile is longer and runs into the Great Lakes region of Central Africa. Despite the almost superhuman efforts of iconic explorers such as Burton, Speke, Livingstone and Stanley, to this day the distant source is still undetermined, but believed to be in either Rwanda or Burundi. The Blue Nile is the source of the most water and fertile soil. It begins in Lake Tana in Ethiopia (where I was going too), and flows into Sudan. The two rivers meet near the Sudanese capital of Khartoum (where I... OK, you get the point). The northern section of the river flows almost entirely through desert from Sudan into Egypt. Most of the population and cities of Egypt live along those parts of the Nile Valley north of Aswan and nearly all the cultural and historical sites of Ancient Egypt are found along the river banks.

The importance of the Nile is that Egyptian civilisation would not exist without it – it is as simple as that. Silt deposits from the Nile make the surrounding land fertile because the river overflows its banks annually. The Ancient Egyptians cultivated and traded wheat, flax, papyrus and other crops. Wheat was a crucial crop in the famine-plagued Middle East. This trading system secured Egypt's diplomatic relations with other countries and contributed to economic stability. The Nile is also considered to be a causeway from life to death and the afterlife. The east was thought of as a place of birth and growth and the west considered the place of death, as Ra, the sun God, underwent birth, death and resurrection each day as he crossed the sky. Thus, all tombs were west of the Nile, because the Egyptians believed that in order to enter the afterlife, they had to be buried on the side that symbolised death. As the Nile was such an important factor in Egyptian life, the ancient calendar was even based on the three cycles of the river.

As I sat gazing back at the riverbanks we were leaving behind, the transforming effect of the river was stunningly obvious to the naked eye. On either side, a strip of land approximately a hundred metres wide was lush green and neatly cultivated. Beyond those fringes there was a visual, almost linear, demarcation point where the land immediately returned to desert dunes, stretching as far as the eye could see. The desert was stunningly beautiful in its own right, but obviously not conducive to large scale human occupation. The more we ventured south, the more beautiful the river became and closer to my preconceived idea of what it would look like. The towns turned into villages and quickly became more and more sparse until all you could see were small settlements dotted along the bank in the shade of massive palm groves. The sun was beginning to bathe the deck of the ferry and warm up my shivering bones. There was not a cloud in the sky and the contrast of the pristine yellow sand dunes against this faultless blue sky made for an awe-inspiring horizon. As the human settlements disappeared, so the wildlife appeared. Grey and Green Herons could be seen wading in the shallows busying themselves with breakfast. As we passed a small island dotted with Ibis, Egrets, Sanderlings and skinks, much more imposing figures were sunning themselves on the rocks – Nile crocodiles. The noise of the ferry interrupted their morning snooze and they reluctantly rose and made their way to the water's edge before silently sliding into the depths. Nile crocodiles are the largest in Africa, growing to twenty feet and weighing up to fifteen hundred pounds. As well as their legendary status underwater they are also able to 'gallop' at thirty miles an hour on land. Best not to meet up with them at close quarters in either environment then! Not to mention the hippos and venomous snakes that I knew lurked beneath the surface, ready to attack any 'sleepy, fallen-over-the-side tourist'. I jest: I'm sure they are more than busy with the Nile Perch, soft-shelled Turtles, Tigerfish, Lumpfish and Catfish that the river is teeming with.

I felt elated and my mood lifted even more when I glanced down the deck and spotted a striking figure coming towards me, who I had met briefly, but memorably in the Horus Hotel, in Aswan. Little did I know it then but this man was going to play a significant part in my story. It was Carl, a twenty-seven-year-old French Canadian. A tall, muscular man, with the world's largest beard, he was negotiating his way carefully, barefoot, over the still prone bodies of sleeping Egyptians and Sudanese, giving me the thumbs up with both hands as he approached. He wore his sun-streaked hair long, tied loosely with a red elastic band into a ponytail and was sporting a pair of dirty blue jeans and a grey T-shirt. His T-shirt looked so old and worn through, that it more closely resembled a fine tissue in texture. He was darkly tanned, except for his hooked, distinguished-looking nose, which was bright red and had obviously taken the full brunt of the sun's rays. His lips were dry and cracked and his forehead and cheeks had peeled, giving him an uneven, blotchy, two-tone tan. He had a dirty, army-green rucksack slung over one shoulder, a Nikon camera round his neck, with a telephoto lens whose length rivalled his beard, and under his right underarm he carried a black metal camera tripod. To all intents and purposes he looked like a rugged, old-fashioned adventurer under the employ of The National Geographical Society, or some institution like that.

"Hi Carl, good to see you," I said, as I gripped the handrail, pulled myself up and offered a strong handshake.

"You too, man, can I join you? This is the sunniest part of the ferry and I'm bloody cold," he replied.

"No worries, grab a place," I gestured next to me. He sat down and we got talking about our time in Egypt and inevitably got round to reminiscing about the two, frankly hilarious occasions we had met previously.

On the second occasion we came across each other, and the first time we really spoke, it was in an elevator in Aswan's cheapest, but the world's noisiest hotel, Hotel Horus (The God of the Sky). I glanced over to Carl and he was stifling a yawn.

"You're the guy I met on the donkey aren't you?" I asked.

"That's me," he answered, still trying not to yawn.

"The music kept you up all night, hey?" I queried.

He laughed and replied, "Yes man, can you believe this place. I stayed up until four in the morning with the bed and walls vibrating. I got so sick of it, that I went up to see what was going on. It was a belly dancing club, very x-rated, but they chased me away. I'm having breakfast and moving out. What about you?"

"I think I'll do the same. I'm having breakfast now, do you want to come? Sorry, it's Spencer by the way," I said, extending my hand.

"Hi, I'm Carl, yeah, let's go and eat," he replied, shaking my hand, as the elevator doors clattered open.

We made our way out into a dark, shabby, mud brown-coloured corridor, with a single naked bulb wall light, illuminating a rusty metal sign on the wall, which stated 'Horus Restaurant – the best in every way'. That sounded promising; my stomach was rumbling in anticipation. The corridors opened out into a large empty room, except for two plastic tables, with filthy, 'once were white' plastic tablecloths. There were five of the ubiquitous plastic chairs which had seen better days and looked like they had been carefully arranged by throwing them into the room from the entrance. The walls were probably originally magnolia, but were now stained a tobacco-smoke brown. The row of windows down one side of the room were so filthy that it was impossible to see outside. There was only one surviving net curtain which hung limply and torn from its railings, the material peppered with squashed and trapped flies embedded in the fabric. I picked up a chair from the floor and the metal leg clattered to the ground, snapped from its plastic mounting. "That will be your one then," laughed Carl as he pulled up another chair and sat down. I retrieved a slightly happier chair and sat down cautiously. We looked at each other, looked around and laughed. There was nothing else in this room; no décor, no pictures, no other furniture, no carpet and definitely no sign of any breakfast related activity in the last ten years. Carl gestured behind me, saying "We're OK then, should be a good breakfast." I peered behind me; there was another sign on the wall that had lost a screw and had consequently slid sideways down the wall. I craned my neck and read 'Welcome to Horus Restaurant – the best in the worl'. (Yes, the 'd' was missing.) So, although it was the world's noisiest hotel, at least it had the world's best restaurant.

I turned to Carl to register my delight, when a waiter appeared from a hole in the far end of the room and shuffled his way towards us. He was extremely small and looked like a miniature, swarthy Charlie Chaplin. He was between the age of six and forty, it was difficult to tell, maybe the moustache was a fake. Although he had the classic waiter outfit, with black trousers and a white button-up tunic, the image was slightly spoiled by the fact that he looked like he had been rolling around in a muddy puddle. I've never seen anybody that dirty in my life – well, maybe the odd coalminer. As he approached us and enquired, "Breakfast, two?" he broke into a wide grin revealing tea-stained brown, broken teeth. As I replied, "Yes please, two breakfasts, Chokran," he scrunched up his redder than red eyes, nodded manically, wiped his hands on the front of his trousers and headed back to his hole in the wall, where I presumed his 5-star kitchens were situated. "Food Poisoning City!" Carl exclaimed as the waiter disappeared.

While waiting for our sumptuous feast I ascertained from Carl that he was travelling from Cairo to Cape Town, by any means possible; walking, public transport, hitching, etc. His intention was to pick up a Rhodesian Ridgeback in South Africa and fly it back to Canada. Carl was soft-spoken and gentle and I warmed to him immediately, although his eyes somehow gave me the impression that he could look after himself and was undoubtedly as hard as nails. After a good half hour there was no sign of our hygienically challenged waiter.

"I'll go and see what's going on. Maybe he only uses the freshest ingredients possible and that's why he's taking so long," I joked, as I made my way to his hole in the wall. It wasn't strictly a hole, but the doorframe had long since disappeared and the bricks were beginning to crumble onto the bare floor. I stepped over the rubble and into the interior of the darkened room. When my eyes adjusted to the light I made out a small fridge and a slim wooden table with a knife and a half-cut tomato poised on it. But there was no sign of 'Soap Dodger of the Year'. To the rear of the room there was a faint light emanating from a flight of irregular concrete stairs. I followed them and they led me out onto the roof of the hotel. The roof top was littered with broken glass, broken chairs, rubbish and a number of satellite dishes in various stages of decay. Sitting on the edge of the building, on a wall overlooking El Corniche and the Nile was our missing waiter, smoking an enormous hash joint that would have made Bob Marley proud. He made no attempt to conceal his carrot-shaped cigarette, on the contrary, he started inhaling deeply and rapidly as I approached him. I asked him incredulously, "What about breakfast?" tapping on my watch to indicate how long we had been waiting. Between bouts of coughing, he managed to muster up, "I come," whilst slapping himself on the forehead with the palm of his hand, as if to indicate that he had forgotten we were there. I shook my head and went to report to Carl, who just laughed and raised his arms to the heavens stating simply, "Africa!"

Within ten minutes, the spliff-smoking puddle roller had returned with our breakfast, his joint having now been replaced by a Cleopatra cigarette which dangled out his mouth, liberally sprinkling ash on our feast. As he presented the plates with a small flourish, I burst out laughing. No word of a lie; each breakfast consisted of one boiled egg, one thin slice of tomato and one thin sliver of cucumber. As we prepared to grapple this mountain of food, two women came into the room and sat on the remaining table. They were obviously belly dancers but not of the exotic, mystical, sensual type. Both were smeared with copious amounts of badly applied make-up which had run in rivulets down their sweating faces. Their glistening foreheads and sweat-stained underarms hinted at some very recent vigorous physical activity of some sort or another. Both were wearing lurid boob tubes and tightly banded trousers which only served to concertina their generous rolls of midriff fat. The one facing me had a livid bruise on the side of her stomach. They couldn't have been a day over ninety.

"Might put me off my superb breakfast," said Carl, gesturing towards them with his eyebrows. It didn't put us off however, and we ate and ate and ate until we were satiated (no, not really!). After breakfast (which turned out to be complimentary, which was more than I could say about the service), we packed up our stuff, left the illustrious Horus Hotel and headed off into

El Corniche chuckling about what should really have been called 'Whorehouse Hotel – the worst in the world.' We exchanged some manly pleasantries about meeting up some time later on, wished each other well and went our separate ways. I sensed that both of us wanted to make a more firm commitment to meet up later, but I was fully aware that my whole approach was to travel solo and I am sure Carl had his own agenda. So nothing was said.

The first time Carl and I met was exceedingly brief but no less surreal. I was winding my way through Central Egypt, following the east bank of the Nile. I had just negotiated the town of Asyut and I was relaxing into my ride when I came across a scene straight out of the Bible. On my right-hand side, the Nile was visible through the palm trees with the sunlight gleaming off the rippling surface. A single, white-sailed felucca glided gracefully by on the light wind. On my left-hand side were beautifully cultivated fields, dotted with date palms and wild flowers. The small dusty road was fringed by a boulevard of palms. As I turned a sweeping bend, in the road ahead of me, in the shadows of the trees, Jesus was sitting on a donkey. He was being led down the track by a young Egyptian boy in white robes and tatty brown leather sandals.

Of course, it was Carl on the donkey. He had removed his shirt and had tied it around his head with a thin leather belt. With his long brown hair, streaked blonde by the sun, cascading down his shoulders, his bushy beard and piercing eyes he could have easily fulfilled the title role of Jesus in any Hollywood production. As I drew closer I pulled in the clutch, to quieten the bike, so as not to spook the donkey. It would be bad Karma to unseat Jesus. I came to a stop next to him and removed my helmet. Realising he was a foreigner I said, "Hi, for a minute there I thought I was hallucinating, you look just like Jesus."

I realised that I was using the stereotype Western view of the image of Jesus, but just as I thought that, he replied in a strong French Canadian accent, "Don't worry, everybody here calls me

Jesus, with or without the donkey. They even shout it out from the other side of the road."

I replied, "Well, he's a good role model if you were to pick one." He laughed and dismounted the donkey. We introduced ourselves and I offered to share some fried fish and rice I had purchased in Asyut. As we sat down to talk Carl explained that he had walked about thirty kilometres but was so blistered up from his hiking boots that he was in agony and had been forced to offer a few dollars to the young boy. He had been on the donkey for more than two hours and quipped: "Now I have got sore feet *and* a sore arse." I offered to give him a lift on the bike to the nearest town of Sohag, but, he politely refused saying, "Actually I am enjoying myself and feel safer on the donkey than on the bike." I couldn't persuade him so I took off, shouting through my helmet and over the noise of the bike, "Maybe see you in Aswan, Mr. Christ." He gave me the thumbs up and I was gone. I kept that vision of Jesus on a donkey in my mind and it kept a smile on my face. What a character.

So, it was a great pleasure to be chatting to Carl for a third time and the depth of our conversations wiled away the long hours on Lake Nasser. Carl quizzed me about Ridgebacks and it was obvious that he was serious about his plan.

I remarked, "So you are travelling the length of Africa to get a dog. That's one hell of a journey, and one hell of an effort. I suppose at least you could say to your girlfriend that you were 'going to see a man about a dog', and you would be telling the truth. Did you not consider checking the Internet for a dog?"

He laughed, "No, of course I could find a Ridgeback in Canada, but I have always wanted to see Africa and this just gave me an extra end goal." (Little did he know that it would eventually transpire to be far from his end goal.) Carl explained that during the winter months in Canada he worked slavishly for sixteen hours a day, clearing roads with a snowplough for his father's company. This provided him with enough money to travel for a number of months a year. He had already trekked extensively through South America, but stated that he was enjoying this trip to a much greater degree. This led us onto the subject of Egypt. We both agreed that Egypt was breathtaking but the intense level of tourism in Aswan overpowered the special atmosphere evident in more remote villages.

"What did you do for the week in Aswan, because personally I found it frustrating and claustrophobic?" Carl asked.

"Ah Carl, I was lucky enough to meet the Jewel of the Nile, a guy called Ashraf." I then proceeded to regale him with the full story of the exceptional Ashraf.

Ashraf was the proud owner of a traditional Egyptian wooden sailing boat (a felluca) that happened to be moored directly opposite the hovel of a room I had rented during the ten days I was stuck in Aswan. The felluca owners used to congregate on the main thoroughfare, El Corniche, overlooking the Nile to tout for business. I fell into a routine of going for an early morning coffee at a small café overlooking the river. On route I had to run the gauntlet of a barricade of sales pitches from groups of highly enthusiastic 'won't take no for an answer' salesmen. They could highly recommend, at the best price in Egypt, of course, horse-drawn carriage rides (which, more often than not, were powered by tragically overworked, forlorn looking donkeys that looked like they were on the verge of permanent collapse with every step. What do donkeys get for lunch in Aswan? Answer: ten minutes). If it wasn't a horse-drawn carriage that tickled your fancy they could provide taxis, buses, bicycles. No? What about a top meal, a statue of Nefertiti, one of Tutankhamun's bracelets (with a one hundred percent genuine letter to prove it is a one hundred percent genuine ancient artefact)? No? What about a trip to the Pyramids, a sail in a felluca, a woman, some hashish? No? Well then I will just walk with you then. That was the basic daily routine.

What set Ashraf apart from this group of hagglers was that

he was completely devoid of this aggressive selling attitude that had taken grip of the rest of the galabeyan-clad (traditional Egyptian robe) salesmen, who were on you like a rash as soon as you were spotted. In complete contrast to this, Ashraf would just lean against a wall, chewing a small twig and brushing his teeth with its tip. (He was in fact following an ancient tradition as 'chew sticks', twigs with frayed ends resembling toothbrushes, were found in tombs from 3000 BC.) As I strode past he would remove the twig from his mouth and softly say "Good morning". It was not only his relaxed demeanour that prompted me to start a conversation (I am so glad I did) but also his appearance. He had a striking aquiline face, a thin, well-defined nose and strong high cheekbones. He was, however, extremely slight, almost bird-like, his thin, almost emaciated arms and legs visible under his pristine, white galabeya. He had a severe droop to his left eye, but it did nothing to detract from his striking good looks and in some ways made him more approachable and endearing. I immediately ascertained that he had a wicked sense of humour, was laid back to the point of horizontal; if I get clients I get them, was the aura he exuded. "Inshallah" – If Allah wills it – was his favourite statement.

We immediately fell into a ritual where we would meet at 7am each morning and stroll the streets of Aswan. Ashraf showed me the back street markets, his favourite coffee shop, the cheapest places to buy food and provisions for my trip, all the while filling me in on the traditions and history of Egypt. He told me about his family, how his mother had died when he was six, about his wife and two children in a nearby village and about his beloved 'Bob Marley Family' Felluca. The great thing about Ashraf was that his conversations constantly twisted and turned and changed subject, his speech peppered with memorable quotes and insights – pearls of wisdom that could easily be missed, without due concentration, as he delivered them in a soft, sometimes barely audible, lilting tone.

On one particular morning he started, "Mr Spencer, you

know how I buy my felluca boat and how I build my village bayt (house) for my wife and babies?"

"It must be difficult to save money with a young family to support; tell me, how you managed it," I responded.

Ashraf continued, "It was about ten years ago, yes ten. I was twenty one, when a friend of mine, Mohammed, who had been away for five years returned to our village. He was a rich man now and told me if I come to Luxor next month I can get a job as a sand shifter."

"What is a sand shifter?" I asked.

He continued. "A new archaeology dig made by the Israelis was starting, at a possible buried tomb, just outside of Luxor. A sand shifter uses spade and passes sand through a sieve to find antiquities. It is hard work, Mr Spencer, ten hours a day, seven days a week in hot, hot sun," he stated solemnly, furrowing his brow. "But very good money for Egyptian man," he added, putting emphasis on 'very', widening his eyes and looking to the heavens.

He went on. "I ask Head of the village to lend me the money for bus and I would repay when I got back to village. He gave it to me because he trust me and he is my father." (Ashraf always expressed himself like this, slipping snippets of information into the conversation, casually, like his father was the Head of the village, but with no sense of arrogance or self-importance ever in his tone.) "I made it to Luxor and found Mohammed. I start work same day, after bus journey of all night. It is hard, but good work. I work every day for six weeks and then everything change." He paused.

"Oh! Yeah! What happened?" I encouraged him on.

"It was early morning and I was walking from my tent in the desert when a white 4x4 Land Rover carrying an Israeli woman digger, has problem and gets stuck in the sand. We were one kilometre about from tomb site so we help to dig and push Land Rover out of sand. When Land Rover moves we see four gold Scarab beetles (Egyptian sacred symbol) in sand. It was a good day, Mr Spencer, a good day," Ashraf exclaimed, raising both hands above his head and shaking them back and forth, towards his God.

"I start digging with Mohammed but many people come quickly. We find eighteen more Scarab, some green stone and some gold, but Israelis and Egyptian government quickly close area and start new dig in new position."

I was fascinated and pushed him further, "Did you get any of the beetles?"

Ashraf answered that he had managed to conceal two in his galabeya and Mohammed took four. He went on, "We decide to go to Cairo where my uncle was selling Egyptian jewellery in the market. When we arrive there he was very happy and introduced us to an American dealer. We received E£10,000. That is how I buy my Bob Marley Family Felluca and the material for my house."

He paused but I got the impression there was a bit more to the story, so I remained quiet. After a brief lull in the conversation, where Ashraf stared downwards and pushed his toes into the sand, he went on. "I make big mistake. The American man wanted more Scarab but I did not have more. I buy some that were not gold and were modern-day. I take them to him and he call the Police."

"Why did they not arrest the American for trying to take antiquities out of the country?" I asked, shocked.

"He pays the Police, it happens every day in Egypt."

"What, even now?" I asked disbelievingly and obviously naively.

"Every day, Mr Spencer. Tomb robbing happens every day. You must not be surprised as the Nile runs the length of Egypt and there are tombs all the way. I know two brothers in a Nubian village near Aswan, who are tomb raiders every day and are millionaires, from American, Russian and Chinese."

In an obvious, but insightful comment Ashraf said, "If the foreign people do not want to buy then the Egyptians would not sell." He looked at me awkwardly and then changed the subject and the melancholy route our conversation was going.

"You come to my village tomorrow to visit my family. You buy beers and food and we go on free trip in Bob Marley Family Felluca."

I laughed at his directness and replied, "Of course I will come Ashraf, and it would be my pleasure."

"That is decided, Inshallah, I go now to tell my family and tomorrow I meet you at 6am at Bob Marley Family Felluca." With that he shook my hand and left.

Unsurprisingly, Ashraf was waiting for me at the designated time, as promised and we made a whirlwind visit around the local market. I could tell that Ashraf was highly respected in this community for two reasons. Firstly, everybody was overly attentive to all his needs, and secondly, no one asked him for any money. He had this alarming manner of leaning his head over slightly and staring directly in people's eyes, giving them the impression that what they were saying was of great importance and highly knowledgeable. To put it in a nutshell, he put everybody at ease. His thousand-watt smile didn't hurt either. As we went rushing around ordering things, I realised that we were not taking any of the produce with us.

"What about the things we have bought?" I quizzed.

"Don't worry, they will bring everything to the boat before an hour is gone." Lo and behold, when we returned to the Felluca everything had been delivered and Ashraf's sidekick, Spider, was busy packing away the provisions and setting the sail. Spider was a mahogany-dark Egyptian with a shock of black curly hair. He was a man of few words, more accurately he was a man of no words. I only received the odd grunt from him throughout the trip but observed that Ashraf received the same verbal treatment, so it wasn't the language barrier.

"Why is he called Spider?" I asked Ashraf, when he had headed off to a neighbouring boat to procure some spare rope and cooking gas.

"The reason for this is that when he was a small boy on his father's Felluca a spider crawled on his arm. He jumped into the Nile, all time shouting, 'spider! spider!' From that day, he has been called Spider."

Spider returned shortly and we set sail for Ashraf's village. Aswan is blessed with a wind that runs against the flow of the Nile so it is possible to sail upstream powered by the massive triangular sail and return via the power of the flow of the river. Within an hour we were the only boat in sight and I lay back on the deck, gazing up at the sail, taut in the wind, framed by the spotlessly aqua blue skyline. In the centre of the white sail, stitched into the fabric, was a three metre by two metre, cloth image of Bob Marley, backed by the famous Rastafarian colours of red, gold and green. Ashraf clocked me looking at the image and said, "An English man called Steve send me this picture from his brother in London." He told me Steve's story and he spoke so lovingly of this man, it was clear that this was an important experience and relationship he had had. (No, he is not gay.)

Steve had been living in Cairo and various places in Egypt for fifteen years and had fallen in love with it and vowed never to return to the UK. Tragically, he was involved in a minibus accident, which overturned when it was hit by a bus. All of the occupants had been killed, except for Steve. He did not escape unhurt and after months of hospital treatment, he survived but lost his left leg and was left with problems controlling his bodily functions. After gruelling rehabilitation he decided to escape Cairo for a while and travel the Nile by Felluca. For two weeks Ashraf looked after Steve, 24-7, sailed the Felluca, cooked all the food, helped him around the boat and to the toilet, as well as bouncing him around little villages in his wheelchair. He is still in contact with Ashraf and it was obvious from our exchanges that on this occasion the fee for the trip was of secondary importance: it was the relationship between these two men that counted. Ashraf pulled out his wallet and showed me a photo of Steve. He looked like Tom Hanks and was pointing at the camera, winking. Next to Steve's photo was another one of a strikingly blonde Danish family. Apparently the parents were making a documentary about a certain green bird found only along the Nile (I don't know the name unfortunately), and had spent a month on the Bob Marley Family Felluca. How excellent to see these two photos in Ashraf's wallet rather than ones of tourist girls he had managed to lure into his bed. In my experience, that would have been the norm, amongst the often arrogant, dreadlocked boat boys that scour the coastal areas of Africa in search of naïve young tourists to seduce and fleece of their money.

We cruised peacefully down the river and as the sun started dipping below the horizon we made for shore. As soon as we were grounded Spider leapt off the front of the boat, landing nimbly on his bare feet in the soft sand and with military precision started gathering wood, rapidly getting a fire going before the last rays of Ra disappeared, and cloaked us in darkness. He rolled out two wicker sleeping mats (Spider apparently slept sitting up on the sand, his knees tucked up to his chest) and then proceeded to prepare dinner.

Sleeping Spider

We feasted on a cucumber, tomato and chilli salad, boiled eggs, pitta bread and *fuul* washed down with a bottle of Sakara, the more-than-acceptable Egyptian beer. We slept early. I felt supremely happy.

When I awoke, Spider was fast asleep in the exact position Ashraf had predicted, except his head had slumped forward between his knees, in silhouette his posture giving the impression of a statue with the woes of the world on his shoulders. Once we had all stirred and were ready to move, to my surprise we did not re-board the boat but made our way up the dunes and into a stunningly beautiful palm grove. We followed the route of a thin irrigation channel that snaked through the grove, before it eventually widened out into a channel six foot wide. Naked children were swimming in the channel, whooping and splashing each other by slapping the palm of their hands across the surface of the water or filling their mouths to the limit, firing jets of water at each other's faces. Twenty metres further on, the palms gave way to a clearing where a large ox with a wooden pole strapped to its back was walking in circles pulling water up from a traditional well. We shouted a greeting to the young boy attending the beast and he called back in delight when he saw Ashraf, before running off through the trees, presumably to relay the information to the village that Ashraf and Spider were on their way with a pale face beanstalk.

It was a serene walk and, as usual, Ashraf entertained me with various tales of past and present. He told me about the Old Cataract – the famous Hotel on the Nile where they filmed the highly successful Agatha Christie film, 'Death on the Nile', in 1978, with Peter Ustinov playing the famous detective Hercules Poirot. He told me about the Mausoleum of the Aga Khan of Pakistan, the leader of a Shiite sect based principally in India but with followers around the world. The Aga Khan loved Egypt and would spend two months a year at The Old Cataract Hotel enjoying serenades along the banks of the Nile. He used to say that Egypt was the flag of Islam. Apparently the revered leader had serious problems with his joints and was advised by an Egyptian holy man to bury himself up to his neck in sand for a whole day. The remedy worked and from that day he decreed that when he died he be buried in a spectacular pink granite mausoleum. The decision on the location was decided whilst the Aga Khan was on a felluca trip. His wife, tiring of his fixation on finding a burial site, spotted a closed and neglected house high up on the river bank. "Why not find somewhere to live in Egypt, not somewhere to die?" she suggested, pointing out the neglected but still stunning house in the distance.

The Aga Khan replied, "We will buy that house if I can build a Mausoleum on the hill behind it." So it was agreed. Now, high up on the west bank in Aswan stands the spectacular tomb of Muhammad Shah Aga Khan III, the 48th Imam of the Ismailis, who died in 1957 and of his French-born wife, the Begum, who died in the year 2000.

The words flowed smoothly from Ashraf's mouth and I was fully involved, but as we reached the outskirts of the village, I began to notice that this beautiful landscape which hadn't changed for thousands of years, to my annoyance, was succumbing to the scourge that is litter. It is the blight of most African countries; plastic bag trees, hedges strewn with bottles, cardboard and sweet wrappers, rivers and drainage channels awash with debris. It is something I find difficult to fathom. As we headed down the narrow sandy streets, squeezed between white and dun-coloured mud buildings, Ashraf paused with his stories and started to apologise to me in advance of our arrival. "I have a good wife and a son of six and a daughter of four, but my house is very small. I have TV, music and hot water but I am sorry, Mr Spencer – no air con." I laughed out loud and said, "Don't worry; I don't care about things like that."

Ashraf's house turned out to be an immaculately neat, mud-brick house with a small kitchen and two bedrooms. The compound was surrounded by a six-foot mud wall which enclosed a pretty courtyard. Strewn around the sand of the courtyard, in a rough semi-circle were a number of colourful carpets in the centre of which was an impressive, unbelievably vivid green tree, about eight feet tall which provided the only shade from the unforgiving Sun God, Ra. It was obviously Ashraf's pride and joy as he wasted no time in watering it – his first chore upon arriving at his beloved home. A small wooden door on failing rusty hinges at the front of the house opened creakily and Ashraf's wife timidly peeked out. He beckoned to her and she came out of the dark interior, making a concerted effort to avoid my gaze, by staring at the ground. What struck me first about Habibah was how incredibly young she looked, no more than seventeen, it seemed, with unblemished, creamy, coffee-coloured skin and perfect bone structure. She was tiny-framed, much like Ashraf, and her large hazel eyes, which I glimpsed fleetingly as she stole a glance upwards, were accentuated by heavy black make-up, not dissimilar to that associated with the classic image of Cleopatra. Habibah was beautiful. The two children were behind her, gripping tightly on to her legs, peering out and giggling.

After a brief introduction where she shook my hand, while steadfastly holding her downward gaze, I didn't see her again until she returned with a feast fit for King Rameses II. She carefully laid out all the dishes on one of the carpets. The pungent aroma of garlic and onion wafted through the air and I realised why Ashraf had pre-warned his wife of my arrival. It must have taken a great deal of preparation to come up with such an array of dishes so lovingly presented. First she laid down a tin plate laden with stacks of Aish Merahrah, a traditional flat bread made with fenugreek seeds and maize. Bread forms the backbone of Egyptian meals, not only because all the ingredients are readily available, but because bread is also used as an edible utensil. Knives and forks are rarely used outside tourist areas. As I watched Habibah setting down a bowl of steaming mashed fava beans (Ful Medames), rice-stuffed pigeon (Koshari), and eggplant with chick peas and lemon (Baba Ghannoug), something struck me. She had an aura similar to Ashraf. The only way to describe it was elegance. They both had poise and grace of movement that someone of my height, size and clumsiness could only admire. I sometimes feel that people in the West have lost many elements of social grace and we must often seem brash and boorish to other cultures. Every movement and gesture Habibah made flowed into the next seamlessly, and seemed controlled and choreographed, yet self-conscious and vulnerable. It was a pleasure to watch. This elegance did not stop her from being a mother and she scolded the children for running up, touching me and then rushing off screaming, before herding them back into the house and disappearing. After a few minutes the children built up the courage to come out and watch us eat from a safe distance. They stood in the shade of the wall of the house, stealing surreptitious glances at me. Ashraf beckoned them to approach, saying something in Arabic, but they refused, shaking their heads vigorously.

Once again we slept early in preparation for leaving at sunrise to get back to Aswan. I was surprised that we were leaving so quickly but I realised that Ashraf had to catch stolen moments with his family, because in reality he had to get back amongst the throng of tourists to have any chance of making any money. It was with admiration and respect that I bade farewell to Habibah, and after a failed attempt to catch the screaming children for a hug we headed back to the Felluca. The trip back was again a pleasure and it was with some regret that we docked in Aswan once more. I was preparing to head back to the Horus Hovel to spend an evening being vibrated to with an inch of my life by the belly dancing music, but luckily Ashraf had more plans up his sleeve. "I take you to Egyptian nightclub tonight, because I know you are leaving for Wadi Halfa ferry in two days. Meet me here at Bob Marley Felluca at eight." Can't argue with that.

The Egyptian nightclub was a once-in-a-lifetime experience that I would not like to repeat (get it). The approach was down a flight of stairs, squeezed between two derelict-looking buildings. The Club was at basement level and when we opened the double doors a wall of smoke and music poured out. We ventured in and squinted into the cloud. The whole place was decorated to resemble a cave but was so badly done that I assessed the interior décor bill to be around the $30 mark. The walls consisted of scrunched up clumps of papier mâché, stuck at random on the walls, and spray painted in green and brown streaks. There were strips of coloured paper hanging from the ceiling, interspersed with wires, some with coloured bulbs hanging off them at a precarious angle, many just bare wires. I was not surprised that the electricity was intermittent and on some occasions during the evening we sat in absolute pitch darkness for up to fifteen minutes, chatting as though it were perfectly normal. Ashraf told me that the owners' last venture was a restaurant, but it had burned down. (Anyone smell smoke, or an insurance scam?) Judging by the chaotic wiring in this establishment he obviously had the same plan in mind for this venture.

The fact that the lights were dim and intermittent was probably a blessing as it was obviously a brothel and not of the best class. An unfeasibly ugly woman of extremely advancing years took a shine to me and kept bringing us complementary samoosas, until there were enough to feed a small Egyptian army piled on our table, making it difficult to see Ashraf on the other side. The table legs were threatening to collapse even before she came and leant on it, thrust her face into mine and screamed like an army sergeant, "You want something," and wiggled her fat provocatively. I was scared stiff and nearly flipped over the back of my chair, but had to laugh when Ashraf shouted above the music, "She likes you, Mr Spencer." Well fair enough, she might do, but if we can go beyond the fact that she is older than my grandmother, looks like a troll of some sort

– short, squat, with a strawberry for a nose. That's not to mention that she had (an optimistic estimate), approximately five teeth, the colour of used teabags, then maybe there might be a chance. I felt like I was in *The Lord of the Rings*. The whole atmosphere was made more dingy, dank and airless by the fact that the clientele, exclusively men, seemed to be involved in some sort of smoking competition. If it wasn't cigarettes, it was traditional Shisha pipes. The combination of coloured paper hanging in your eyes, no lighting, chairs positioned at random, not to mention the voluminous smoke with scantily-clad women darting back and forth through it, made it a dangerous mission to navigate your way to the toilet. I was quite surprised I didn't break a leg.

It became evident that Ashraf was quite anxious that I was feeling comfortable. He was getting to know me, showing me different sides to Egyptian life and seeing how I reacted. After all, we did not know each other that well, and I was genuinely pleased that he had no hesitation, and wanted to introduce me to different experiences away from the tourist trail. I would never be so callous as to tell him that this particular scenario was a nightmare; I liked and respected him too much. When he constantly asked me if I was having a good time, I told him what he wanted to hear, and what I wanted to say. "Of course I am," I replied coughing and eyes streaming. "Who said that by the way? Are you still there Ashraf? Good, just checking." I could have been sitting with the 'Troll of the Night' for all I knew.

When Ashraf suggested at one in the morning that it was time to leave I was extremely disappointed, but managed to blurt out, "Really, oh what a pity, let's go then!" As we made it out into the cool fresh breeze of early morning Ashraf sprung it on me that one of his friends would like a lift on the motorbike. I was about to protest but realised that it was the norm to have three on a motorbike. I had even seen five on a 125cc motorbike – mother and father, two children and a baby strung to the back of the daughter, perched precariously on the rear luggage rack. I firmly believe, no one would bat an eyelid if a donkey with goggles on, drove past on a motorbike. Although I was sorely over the limit I couldn't find a way to say no. So it was with this decision that I ended up weaving my way back to the Bob Marley boat with two drunken Egyptian men on board. I think I even had to close one eye at certain points to stop the white line dividing into two. The situation was complicated by the fact that Ashraf and his connections made no compensation for the fact that they were on a motorbike, squirming and changing position constantly, chattering away in Arabic while I negotiated the traffic. Car drivers in Egypt have a misguided conception that if they refrain from using their lights it saves the battery. They compensate for this by flashing you a warning as they approach, which served, on this occasion, only to blind me in my one remaining, functioning eye. It was a wonder to me that we made it, but my passengers seemed oblivious to my weaving riding style and merrily jumped off when we arrived. I was truly shattered from my day in the blistering sun and my evening in the brothel (no, not like that) so I hugged Ashraf, shook his friend's hand and bade them good night. I parked up the bike sloppily and staggered across the road and up to my hovel. I sprawled out on the sagging, pungent mattress fully clothed, closed my working eye and was immediately asleep.

My deep sleep was shattered by a manic, loud rapping on the flimsy door. I looked at my mobile, it was five twenty. I had managed three and a half hours' sleep, oblivious to the 3000 decibel belly dancing music. But it was not enough. This was not acceptable.

"Who is it?" I managed to mumble groggily.

"It is me, Spider, Mr Spencer; please come quick, Ashraf is very bad." I jumped out of bed, well creaked out, pulling on one leg of my jeans as I hopped towards the door. I opened it to find a much stressed-looking Spider, with a furrowed brow, and deeply worried expression on his darkly sun-tanned face.

"What's happened, what is it?" I asked frantically.

"No, no come quick. Ashraf," was all he could utter.

I was getting worried by this point so negotiated the stairs, two at a time, out onto the already busy road, barefoot. I ignored the Policeman waving us back, weaved through the traffic, down to the jetty, negotiated some sharp rocks and then jumped from boat to boat, desperately trying to keep my balance as they bobbed up and down in the water under my weight. I leapt up on to the side of the Bob Marley boat and stopped dead in my tracks. Ashraf was lying on the deck. I knew it was him, but the appalling thing was that he looked nothing like Ashraf.

His head was twice the size it should have been. He looked as if he had been stung by a swarm of bees and had suffered an allergic reaction. His eyes were almost completely shut and weeping a thick yellow fluid. To add to the horror was a livid cut, which was so deep it split his hairline apart. His lip was swollen tight and split directly down the centre. I stepped gingerly down next to him and the expression he gave me was heart-breaking. He looked so small and vulnerable, like a broken child. I put my hand on his right shoulder gently, and said quietly, "What the hell happened to you?" He looked up at me, trying to mouth some words through his swollen lips and bloodied teeth, but grimaced in pain as he looked down to his left. I followed his gaze and saw his left arm. The other injuries paled into insignificance. His arm was twisted at a horrific angle and was obviously seriously broken. All down the left side of his body, his galabeya was shredded and the exposed skin was raw and bubbling yellow goo.

My head cleared slightly and I turned to Spider, who was standing behind me, leaning over in horror and pleaded with him to run up to the Corniche and hail a taxi. He bolted off and I turned my attention to getting Ashraf off the boat and up to the road. It was a painstakingly slow, and for him, an agonising thirty metres, but the only sign he showed of what must have been intense pain, was the odd grunt and groan. I supported his right-hand side as best I could and after what seemed like an eternity we made it up to the main road where Spider was waiting with a taxi. Ashraf was sweating profusely and his usually dark and tanned face was looking drawn and pale. He looked on the verge of passing out so I quickly helped him into the back seat and followed him in, motioning Spider into the front. On route to the Aswan Hospital I had to frequently remind the driver to keep his eye on the road as he was constantly looking back at Ashraf in horror. It would not be a great help to the situation if we were now involved in an accident. We did make it.

To my absolute relief the Hospital staff could not have been more impressive. (I broke my golden rule of travelling and handed over $50 to the necessary people. Yes, I know, it's a bribe, but so what, in a situation like this.) Over a period of three hours they cleaned Ashraf's wounds, stitched up his head and lip and disinfected his raw abrasions, and finally straightened and set his left arm. It was with great relief that when I walked in he was conscious and attempting a weak lopsided smile. I thought it miraculous that he was alive, let alone awake and talking. Slowly and painfully he filled me in on what had occurred.

It transpired that after our over-indulgence at Top Notch Nightclub, or whatever it was called, Ashraf and his friend had come to the ludicrous conclusion that they had not tested the quality of Sakara beer to the necessary extent so popped into an all-night bar for further imbibing. They proceeded to get carried away and attempted to drink enough beer to sink the Titanic and every felluca known to man. Having come to the conclusion that he had behaved immaturely, and suffering from serious dizzy spells, Ashraf made the wise but crucially delayed decision to catch a taxi back to his village and the comfort of his wife and home. Inshallah! Unfortunately, on this occasion God was not willing. Although successful in procuring a taxi, for some reason Ashraf had no intention of reaching his final destination. While the taxi motored north out of the city, on the main sealed highway, at fifty miles an hour, Ashraf nodded off. Whether it was through tiredness or heavy intoxication, probably a combination of both, when he woke, Ashraf decided that he had definitely arrived at his village. He opened the taxi door and got out at fifty miles an hour. Although he could remember little of the incident after that, when I returned to El Corniche after the hospital visit, the familiar face of a taxi driver, who touted in the same area as Ashraf, filled me in on a few details. "Your friend Ashraf Mohammed is very sick, he fall out of taxi, and he is in Felluca Bob Marley."

I assured him that I had seen him and that he was in hospital already and was okay, if a little battered, stitched up and bruised in places. The driver explained, in broken English, that he had heard the car door open, had instantly looked out of the rear view mirror, only to see Ashraf rolling down the road in the headlights of a following car. Luckily the car managed to swerve sharply to avoid him. The taxi driver rapidly pulled a U-turn, to miraculously find that Ashraf was not only standing, but was insisting on returning to the Felluca. Reluctantly the driver agreed, although he could see clearly in the moonlight that Ashraf had a nasty gash. Ashraf must have staggered back to the boat and fallen asleep, drunk.

As he lay there in the hospital bed, the alcohol and medicine were keeping him fairly comfortable, but I was sure that when he awoke he would realise that he had ended up with more than just a Frankfurter lip and a bass drum headache after his marathon drinking session and stunt car work. It could have been much worse though. I leant over his bed and whispered, (like they do in cheap soap operas), "I will come and see you early tomorrow before my ferry. Get some sleep." This would not be the greatest way to say goodbye to someone who I had got so close to, in the amazingly short period of what turned out to be ten days. He lifted his right hand from the bed (again, like in a cheap hospital drama) and croaked, "Thank you."

The following morning I rose early, packed up my sleeping bag, inflatable pillow, and donned my bike gear, quickly and efficiently, and headed down to the bustling street to my bike. As I approached a white stone column, where my bike was chained, I saw that a figure was leaning against the seat. I was astounded. It was only Ashraf-bloody-Mohammed, trussed up in bandages, like an Egyptian Mummy! (Why was the Egyptian boy confused? Because his Daddy was a Mummy.)

"What are you doing here at six in the morning you lunatic?" I asked, jokingly but incredulously.

"I wanted to say goodbye," was his simple answer. I actually felt tears well up in my eyes (no I didn't, I'm a tough, unemotional, adventure motorcyclist), but managed to brace myself and suppress them. We hugged gingerly and walked – well I did, he hobbled – to an early morning coffee house, across the street where the proprietor had just opened and was setting out tables and wiping them down. We ordered two strong coffees, and had a two-hour chat, during which Ashraf confided in me that he was worried about the way his cast was set. He felt that they had botched the job and feared for his future mobility on the Felluca. He also came up with some theory that a jealous member of his village had put a curse on him and that's why he fell out of the taxi. I put it to him that it might be the case, but more likely it was the curse of Sakara. I tried to do all the talking to save Ashraf the trouble through his severely swollen lips until the time came for me to mount my steed and head to Lake Nasser. As I jumped on the bike, ready to speed off, Ashraf left me with a classic 'Ashrafism'. "It was very good to meet you, Mr Spencer. You are welcome in Egypt. All fingers are fingers, all are useful, but none look the same." Excellent, he didn't let me down. I left with a tear in my eye, but a grin on my face. Oh, and with an address, scribbled on the torn-off side of a Cleopatra packet which said, 'Ashraf Mohammed, Bob Marley Family Felluca, Aswan.' Superb.

The wonderful Ashraf and his friend Ahmed

"That is my story of Ashraf, Carl," I concluded, as he sat there silently, nodding his head. After a minute, he commented, "What a guy, hey Spence. I know it's a cliché, but it's the people who make a place, not the surroundings." I didn't really subscribe to this cliché but on this occasion I did. We both sat back in comfortable silence until the sun set over the horizon. The temperature dropped dramatically and I donned my green Army surplus balaclava and squirmed into my sleeping bag. I had come to the end of a small, but significant chapter in my trip and was eagerly anticipating the next stage. But why was it significant, what had Ashraf taught me?

Although I have lived in Africa for more than twenty three years, I had been away for ten, and on the first stages of this journey, I have to confess I had a negative, untrusting and pessimistic attitude towards the people I met. I had adopted this attitude without really realising it. Living in a small, safe, picturesque, predictable village in the south of England, with no challenges, no hurdles, no shocks to overcome had taken its toll on my character. Although I have nothing against anybody in my village, it became very difficult for me to become enthusiastic about the next village fête, or the new swings in the park, or the serious dog excrement problem threatening the lives of the children of the village. I had almost become a recluse and it was only when I started planning this project that I actually spoke to anyone in the village. I mean 'spoke' – not merely passed the time of day with a comment about the weather. Part of why I had to undertake this challenge was not only to test myself and achieve what no one had done before, and thereby, hopefully raise some money for Save the Children, but from a purely selfish point of view to save my whole character from imploding.

I knew Africa was out there, and that I was existing, not living, while I was away from it. But something had changed in me since I had been away. My confidence was in tatters and I think, consequently, that my social skills had suffered similarly. I had become socially aggressive and suspicious of people. There is no getting away from the fact that as a Westerner in Africa, you are inundated, no assaulted, with requests for pencils, cigarettes, food and by far the most common request – "Give me money." It is constant and understandable. There is no need to debate about the gulf in wealth between myself and the people that were asking me for money. That is obvious, from the moment a £7000 motorbike turns up on the scene. But that does not mean that it is not frustrating and that once in a blue moon it would be nice if someone wanted to talk just for the pleasure of it. But that hope is naïve and unrealistic.

My transformation from this negative stance was largely due to Ashraf. I am ashamed to admit it, but I was expecting him to ask for money right up to the minute I left. The fact that he did not, and struggled all the way from the hospital to say goodbye to me, is testament to a man with character traits I can only admire. It was, of course, stupid to get as drunk as he did, but I am fully aware that he was only getting carried away with the moment. He had spent time with his wife and children, and brought provisions and love for them, was having a ball with me (I hope!), and I learnt from Spider, that he had recently secured a three-week charter from a couple of photographers. So let's give him a break. (A bad choice of words there!) What's more important were the positive character traits that he displayed in abundance; intelligence, patience, generosity, humility affection and kindness. All these provided him with a grace I have rarely encountered. (Except when he's rolling down a road of course.)

I was also grateful that he had provided me with access to another side of Egypt – the Egypt of now. I was well aware that millions of tourists were rushing around experiencing the marvels of Ancient Egypt, but to me, the opportunity to spend time with Ashraf and visit his village was precious. Africa is so hectic, frenetic, chaotic and beautiful; it can only give your senses a massive jolt. I realised, more importantly, that beneath the chaos and filth people were getting on with their lives; they had their family, their street, their friends and were all having the same day-to-day worries as everybody else in the world. I realised that there were genuinely altruistic people, who were not just interested in a 'fast buck', but wanted to help and wanted to have a shared experience. Ashraf was one of these people. In the journey to come, that was destined to swing from episodes of excessive violence to scenes of great tenderness, it was these people that would keep me going.

I promised myself that if I ever got this story published I would give Ashraf a plug, so here it is. If you ever find yourself in Aswan, go to the Nile River Road, El Corniche and ask for Ashraf Mohammed, the captain of the Bob Marley Family Felluca. Not only will you learn a great deal and be entertained by a first class man but you will be guaranteed some beautifully peaceful experiences in an area of the country where tranquillity is difficult to come by.

I fell asleep, the ferry powering noisily through the waters of Lake Nasser, with the words of another unfathomable 'Ashrafism' in my head. "If a fly lands in your drink, you must push it all the way under, then remove it, because one wing can make you ill, but the other holds the cure."

"Right that's clear then – do I still have to drink it?"

I woke up in the morning with no feeling in my legs and a bruised hip bone from the unforgiving metal deck. I was quite glad I had not rolled into Lake Nasser during the night. I attempted to straighten and stretch my legs but there was a head in the way, cocooned in a blanket. I tried to turn to one side, but was sandwiched between Carl and a Sudanese guy, who must have rolled down the deck in the night and landed between us all, an extra sausage added to the pack. I slowly wiggled out of my sleeping bag and managed to sit up. I looked over the lake to the shore. The green banks of yesterday were replaced by rocky, barren outcrops, interspersed with layers of sand dunes, cascading down to the edge of the lake. It couldn't be too far to the port of Wadi Halfa and a new country – Sudan! I felt like I was in a different country already. I was excited and wanted to share it with someone. I prodded Carl gently (not too gently) in the side through his sleeping bag and said, "Wake up, we are in Egypt."

A muffled, groggy, hoarse voice replied, "I know we are in Egypt, we were in Egypt yesterday, what's new. Are we by any chance on a ferry on The Nile?"

"Oh come on, show some enthusiasm," I suggested. Slowly Carl poked his head out from his hiding place, his hair dishevelled and his beard doing some weird pointing trick to the right. He grinned as he looked out. "The river has got wider," he observed.

"This is Lake Nasser you idiot," I said, tutting and shaking my head. To his credit, Carl can wake up and be alert in a fraction of a second, and he reached for his tatty green rucksack and pulled out (I am embarrassed to admit) *The Lonely Planet Guide*. He proceeded to read from it aloud in, what I can only assume, was supposed to be an academic, upper-class English accent. He scrunched up his nose, as though he had pince-nez on, as he read, and got a few odd sideways glances from the locals. To me, he just sounded like Inspector Clouseau with a hangover.

'Lake Nasser is one of the largest man-made lakes in the world. Strictly, Lake Nasser refers only to the much larger portion of the lake that is in Egyptian territory (83%), with the Sudanese preferring to call their similar body Lake Nubia. The lake is five hundred and fifty kilometres long and 35 wide. The lake was created as a result of the construction of the Aswan High Dam across the waters of the Nile between 1958 and 1971. The dam project was not without opposition as many thousands of people had to be relocated and a number of historical sites were undoubtedly drowned.'

"What about that, hey Spence," Carl exclaimed.

I replied, "Well it's impressive and it's vast, but… "

I stopped in mid-sentence. On the starboard shore were two magnificent, colossal figures carved out of the solid rock mountainside as though guarding the lake. Directly below the statues we could make out some tiny colourful shapes; people milling around. They looked like ants contemplating Everest. "What is this place?" spluttered Carl. I recognised the figures from the internet. "It is the temple of Abu Simbel!" I answered.

"Right, let's look it up!" was Carl's enthusiastic reply. He started reading from the book, this time, I presume, in the style of the Richard Attenborough whispered delivery, in his famous mountain gorilla scene, copied ad infinitum by other television presenters since. Once again Carl succeeded in sounding like Inspector Clouseau with a cold. How fantastic not to be on an organised tourist boat, or bus, with a guide suffering from verbal diarrhoea, proudly announcing, "In fifteen minutes we will be passing, on our right hand side (cue hand gesture to the right), the iconic temple of Abu Simbel… " and thereby ruining the awe of surprise. Much better to play 'historical catch up' after the event and hear it from a Canadian, snow-clearing, Jesus look-alike, albeit with a squiff beard.

'The Abu Simbel temples are two awe-inspiring temples in

Nubia, southern Egypt, about 230 kilometres southwest of Aswan. The twin temples were originally carved out of the mountainside during the reign of Pharaoh Rameses II in the 13th century as a lasting monument to himself and his Queen, Nefertiti, to commemorate his alleged victory at the Battle of Kadesh and to intimidate his Nubian neighbours. The complex was relocated in its entirety in 1968 on to an artificial hill. The relocation was necessary to avoid them being submerged during the creation of Lake Nasser'. Carl paused.

"That is incredible," I enthused. Not only is the original a feat of engineering that created a great art work, but modern engineering was utilised to preserve the ancient. How history can twist and turn on the whim of individuals. Although Abu Simbel was saved during the flooding of the Lake, what historical sites were submerged, maybe to be discovered by future generations of archaeologists. I was once again feeling very, very privileged to be on this epic journey. Too soon, this magnificent vision was gone as we powered past towards the Sudanese shoreline. Over the next twenty minutes the ferry slowly came to life as people woke, yawned, stretched, rubbed their eyes and hair and generally kick-started their minds and bodies into gear (sorry, motorbike analogies slipping in – won't happen again). There was a significant gathering of people at the front of the ferry and it seemed our arrival was imminent. There would, however, be one more twist in my ferry trip story before docking. I would meet a couple who were going to put me through a serious moral dilemma over the next week of my life. I headed up to the railings at the bow of the ferry, to see if I could glimpse any sign of land and found myself standing next to someone I recognised from a brief encounter in Aswan.

Chapter Four
African Castles, Austrian Parcels

'Calling upon my years of experience I froze at the controls.'
Stirling Moss

'Everyone crashes. Some get back on. Some don't. Some can't.'
Anonymous

I had not seen a foreign biker in Aswan, so when I spotted a guy wearing a Honda jacket sitting outside a McDonald's on a terrace overlooking the Nile, I headed over. (Yes, a McDonald's, can you believe it, in such a culturally historic area. It goes without saying that I wouldn't have set foot in there if I had not spotted old Honda jacket. I wouldn't let poisonous McDonald's food enter my finely tuned body... Two Big Macs and a packet of fries please!)

As I approached Honda jacket, he clocked me, and immediately stood up and introduced himself. "Hello, my name is Ernst and I am from Austria," he said, extending his hand and giving me a wide, thousands of dollars of dental straightening and bleaching, smile.

He seemed very friendly, but I wasn't about to say, "Hello, my name is Spencer and I am from Swaziland," because it would sound weird, so instead I answered, "Pleased to meet you, I'm Spencer, do you mind if I join you, I noticed you are also wearing a bike jacket."

He gestured towards a chair and replied, "Yes, I'm travelling to South Africa with my wife on Honda Transalps." He certainly cut an odd figure and I was trying to picture him on a Transalp. It didn't escape my attention, that when he stood up to greet me, he was fairly vertically challenged. Now, I am loath to use the word midget, what with political correctness and all that, but let's put it this way; if he stood on a cardboard box, wearing the kind of high heel shoes you associate with 'Clockwork Orange', then he would possibly reach my chin. So imagining Ernst on such a large bike was intriguing.

He was sporting a tiny, well-manicured triangle of hair, hanging on to his lower lip, like many a biker is known to sprout. I was pretty sure it was dyed blonde, as he was over fifty, in my estimation. His hair was blonde, cropped very short, and was receding radically in two semi circles (almost to behind his ears), leaving an extended widow's peak in the centre of his head, which looked like an arrow pointing to his face. Completing Ernst's image were a pair of white-framed sunglasses, straight out of the Elvis catalogue. Excellent: different characters make the world a richer place.

"Are you taking the Wadi Halfa ferry?" I asked.

"It's possible but we might stay one more week," he replied. I suddenly realised what was so disarming about Ernst; he sounded exactly like Arnold Schwarzenegger, the same accent and the same deep pitch. It was a bit of a surprise coming from such a diminutive figure. We chatted amicably for ten minutes or so, but I couldn't help but notice that he was stealing furtive glances at his burger, in case it escaped into the Nile, so I decided to leave him to his food poisoning – sorry, meal. "I'll leave you to eat, as I have loads to arrange, and maybe I'll see you on the ferry," I said, pushing back my chair and standing up, so that he wouldn't feel obliged to ask me to stay.

"Yes, I hope so," he replied, his left hand already reaching for his burger as he spoke.

So, when I found Ernst standing next to me on the ferry, I turned to greet him, but he beat me to it, "Hello again Spencer, I was just talking about you to Lena."

"All good I hope," I joked.

"I will go and get her, she is just behind that wall, a bit sick from the ferry, but ok now." Ernst turned to fight his way through the throng of people packing up their belongings. He turned and no word of a lie, said, "I'll be back." I nearly cracked up laughing and said, "Yes Arnie," but restrained myself, as it is a bit racially stereotypical, I suggest. I was intrigued to meet Ernst's wife and couldn't help wondering whether she would be more vertically challenged than Ernst, which usually holds true for couples. It is very rare for wives to be taller.

My hunch was proved correct, as Ernst made his way back down the deck with a lady of about fifty with jet black, dyed, long, straight hair, a deeply tanned and attractive face. She could, at a stretch have fitted in his helmet, she was so small. They were wearing 'his-and-hers' – dressed identically in black Fox boots, black trousers, red and black Honda jackets and even the same Airoh helmets and Fox gloves. She was, thankfully, not wearing the Elvis sunglasses, as I would have had difficulty keeping a straight face.

"Spencer, this is my wife Lena," he said, gesturing with his hand.

She looked up at me, nodded and gave a wide smile. "Hello, I don't speak so good English, sorry."

"That's no problem, I… " but before I could finish my sentence, the ferry's foghorn let out a loud and extended blast which made conversation impossible. I looked over their shoulders and shouted, "Look, land!" They both turned to look – it was Wadi Halfa, a new country, new people, another culture to soak up. New everything! It always gave me butterflies.

Although I was glad to meet a few foreigners, in some selfish way I yearned to be the only one. But I also realised that this was inevitable on this stage of the journey, as this area was a bottleneck. Anybody who wished to travel south of Egypt had no choice but to be on this ferry. Although there was a road that stretched as far as Abu Simbel, this was restricted to organised tour buses and the military. Consequently, I was quite surprised that there were so few foreigners on the ferry. I was quite pleased, something to do with the 'intrepid traveller syndrome'

I was suffering from. Actually as it turned out, Lena and Ernst were going to be two of only six foreign bikers that I would encounter on a journey through thirty four countries. That turned out to be more to do with the insanely difficult secondary roads that I would take, which led me away from the established tourist route. But don't listen to anyone who says that the east coast of Africa is a well-established bike route, because it is just not true. I imagined a constant stream of bikers, but once again it was the armchair bikers that fed me this information. Land Rovers with hairy hippies, yes, but bikers, no chance. But more of that later.

As we approached the dilapidated-looking ferry terminal, my first impressions were of a lunar vista, so alien to me until this trip. I felt a shiver of anticipation down my heavily sweating spine. The landscape was flat and barren and extremely desolate and forbidding-looking. I had never seen topography quite like it. The flat terrain was broken up by bizarre mounds, even mountains, which looked like huge scoops of coffee ice cream dropped on a pancake. Rising up in the distance, barely visible, were the dunes of Nubia. The second thing that struck me was that the jetty and small outcrop of buildings looked shoddy, downtrodden, and extremely small, dwarfed by the mountain scoops they lay at the base of. I assumed that the port would be larger and more organised, as it was the only gateway to Northern Sudan. I also wrongly assumed that the buildings would be new, as this was the 'new' Wadi Halfa. The original Wadi Halfa was also the victim of the Aswan High Dam, flooded with the creation of Lake Nasser. Sudan's military dictatorship forcibly removed 50,000 inhabitants of the area from their lands and relocated them to the desert, where many died of malaria and other gruesome diseases. The amazing thing is that shockingly it hasn't ended there. A word of advice; if you want to visit the ancient archaeological sites of Nubia, be swift, before they too are submerged. A series of dams are under construction which threaten Nubia's remaining pyramids, which actually pre-date those of Egypt. Catastrophic really, how we can create beauty and just as simply destroy it.

OK, enough of the heavy stuff. I was about to set foot in the largest country in Africa with a population of 41 million spread over a massive 1,861,484 square kilometres. I was overexcited. After rushing through Tunisia and being rushed through Libya I was well aware that Egypt had been a turning point. Meeting the desert nomads had sowed the seeds for my love of the desert, which up to that point had been a mystery. The nomads rode tall, fast camels, their lean, powerful bodies protected from the sun by swathes of flowing blue or white robes, fastened at the waist by silver inlaid belts. They moved silently, like shadows in the desert sand. Black ganduras sheltered them from the wind, and turbans protected their heavily lined, slit eyes from the fine penetrating sand. I began to 'feel' the desert and appreciate the beauty of the nothingness they survived in. I had seen the occasional jackal, desert fox, a few scurrying scorpions and herds of camel dotted on the horizon during my North Africa trip so far, but my overriding impression was of barren, yet beautiful dunes, unending like the sea. I could understand how one could be seduced and put under the spell of the Sahara. It is mystical, otherworldly, but I was also aware, deep down, that it was not my Africa, the Africa I knew and love so completely. I had lived in Kenya until I was six and in Swaziland after that. I get a knot in my stomach just saying the names, or if I even glimpse a Swazi flag. But before I reached the subtropical Africa of my youth, I had the expanse and mystery of Sudan to negotiate. I was spurred on by a passage I had read recently in *Lonely Planet*, especially after my disappointing experience at the pyramids of Egypt:

'The pyramids and other ancient sites littering the northern deserts of Sudan may pale compared to the best Egypt has to offer, but you can experience these without another soul in sight. This sense of discovery often repeats itself in the towns too, since Sudan's tourist trail is no more than a trickle. While solitude is a top draw, visitors invariably agree that the Sudanese are among the friendliest and most hospitable people on earth with a natural generosity that belies their poverty.'

I snapped back to reality as everyone was frantically packing their belongings into unfeasibly large bundles that the men loaded onto their backs. They started staggering towards the rickety-looking gang plank that was being dragged into position by two mahogany dark, glistening, shirtless Sudanese. "Let's go get our bikes," I said as I squeezed my way through the crowds of locals, with Lena, Ernst and Carl following in my wake.

A cargo barge was moored and chained to the ferry and was slapping back and forth against the tyres that lined the jetty wall. A sweating line of Sudanese workers had formed a human chain from the cargo barge to the dockside. They were already busy, heaving varying sizes of coloured bundles, wrapped up in string, tape and wire onto the quay. I spotted the handle bars of the bikes, sandwiched, at the rear of the cargo barge, between two huge bales of produce. It was evident that we had a long wait. It was clear that the cargo barge was dangerously overloaded (a common feature with all methods of transport throughout Africa), as it was sitting extremely low in the water and the deck was a good two metres below the level of the jetty. It would be an impossibility to ride the bikes off until the ferry had been relieved of most of its load, and had risen in the water, so I suggested to the others that we wander into the port area to find food and kill some time. We headed through a prefab warehouse, explaining to the Police Officer that we would return in a half hour to retrieve our bikes. He waved us through and we were in Sudan, as simple as that. A dusty track led down to an open square on the right of which was a wooden shack, with tables and chairs laid out in the sand. On the left was an old lady with milky cataract eyes, preparing stringy goat stew laced with copious amounts of pepper. She had a rickety homemade wooden cart where she was serving strong coffee and sweet mint tea in glasses not much bigger than thimbles. The cart was positioned in front of a small, rocky outcrop where she sat and stirred the stew. I noticed the surface of the rock was worn smooth and shiny, presumably through years of her sitting on it, welcoming new arrivals to Sudan.

We walked over to the wooden and corrugated iron shack. A local man was sitting outside on one of the red plastic chairs, preparing himself a hookah pipe and two young Nubian girls were frying fish over a cut-in-half drum, fashioned into a barbecue. Strangely enough, next to the 'café' was a barber's shop, which consisted of a minute lean-to, with two chairs facing a broken mirror. On a whim I decided to get my hair cut very short, as the temperature was already beginning to soar and rivulets of sweat were running down my face, matting my hair to my forehead. I could see that Sudan was going to be an unforgiving terrain as there were no trees and therefore no respite from the blazing sun. I told the others I would see them at the fish-frying shack and approached the hut. The owner spotted me, and quickly lifted up a young boy with coal black eyes by his underarms and deftly swung him into the chair. He had just enough time to fling a small towel over the boy's shoulders and grab a small brush. As I knocked on the side of the hut he made a great show of brushing the loose hair from the boy's neck (there wasn't any of course), as though he was just finishing with a customer. The game was given away, just slightly, as the 'customer' looked like a miniature version of the barber. He shooed the boy from the chair and smiling, beckoned for me to take a seat. It was great theatre. He proceeded to cut my hair very deftly and professionally, but being a novice at this hair dressing lark (I have probably been to a barber's twice in my life), I was totally unprepared for his grand finale. He proceeded to remove every strand of hair from my face, my nose, my forehead, my ears, the back of my neck and parts of my eyebrows. The fascinating thing was that he achieved this all with a piece of string. He held one piece in his mouth and with his fingers fashioned the string into a T-shape, which he spun against my face, briskly, and I must say rather camply, expertly removing all the offending hair. He had also perfected the clicking of the scissors as he tidied up the tiny remnants of hair I had left. For every real cut he made, he executed another ten flourishes in the thin air around my head and ears. It was exciting and entertaining, but the flourishes were a bit too quick, and the scissors a bit too sharp, for my ears to completely relax. I survived unscathed and was more than happy to give him the two dollars requested, as in another life he would have received $150,000 dollars as the Best Supporting Barber in a Robert de Niro film.

I left his establishment, I must admit, hairless and extremely itchy. I felt a bit like the last turkey in the supermarket, bald and a little bit off colour. This image was confirmed when I returned to the café where Carl, Lena and Ernst were engrossed in removing bones from their Nile Perch. Ernst was demonstrating to Lena how to remove the head and backbone in one piece, leaving only the meat. I must say, he was failing dismally, when he looked up and said, laughing, "Jesus, Spencer, where is your hair and why are you so red. Did you have a sauna?" (He pronounced it sow-na.)

"Thanks Ernst, no, I had a haircut, but I seem to be suffering from an allergic reaction to his flamboyant hairdressing methods," I replied.

"Your eyebrows have also had an allergic reaction, they have changed shape," Carl said, stifling fits of laughter. Indeed he was right. When I finally peered in my bike mirror, Mr Spock was staring back, albeit a little more tanned. I filled them in on my theatrical haircutting experience, after which the discussion turned to our plans for the day. Ernst and Lena were heading through the Nubian desert towards Dongola and then on to Khartoum. Carl was going to try and procure a lift to

Khartoum by any means. I deliberately stalled and informed them that I was going to have some food and park up for the night, so as to leave in the cool of the early morning. The others were keen to get going and I did not dissuade them. I am normally a very sociable person and I enjoyed their company, but I was on a different wavelength. I had realised that to absorb the full splendour I had to travel alone. Deserts lend themselves to a solitary experience and I was not the type of person that needed someone around to validate my experience.

Lost in Myself in the Desert

The Qattari Depression and the Libyan Desert had confirmed my conviction that areas so desolate, yet serene, were best experienced within one's head and alone. I knew full well that it was extremely unlikely that I would venture to these parts again. I already knew that my heart, my soul and my future lay in Southern Africa. I was determined not to repeat the mistake of Tunisia where I rocketed along, with white line fever, my whirring mind in overtime, trying to make progress, attempting to eat up the map, wondering why I had left my children and pondering on when and if I would see them again. On numerous occasions during the early part of the journey I had a premonition that something catastrophic was going to happen, although I had no reason to believe this. It was not fear; it was just a fleeting feeling of impending doom, a lump in my throat, a flutter of my heart, which I found unsettling, because it was an alien emotion to me. I always had a positive outlook on life. My biggest conviction, however, was that whatever I had to face, what wonders, what trials, what dangers, over the next year I wanted to face them alone.

So it was with some guilt, but also relief, that I said, "Well guys, good luck and maybe we will meet in Khartoum." I didn't believe for a minute that we would but it felt impolite to be so final. My comment seemed to spark an argument between Ernst and Lena in German. I did not speak a word of German but the vociferousness and hostility in Ernst's voice made me very uncomfortable. As quickly as it flared up, it dissipated and they made their awkward farewells. As they left, Lena seemed to be imploring Ernst with her eyes to say something but the moment passed. Lena was flushed in the face and looked close to tears. Something was not quite right.

Carl went for the macho handshake and laidback farewell, as he grunted, "Good to meet you, good luck, maybe see you again." No more than I expected, excellent guy.

When they had left, I still felt very uncomfortable. Lena seemed like a rabbit in the headlights, too tense, too ill at ease for the trip of a lifetime. I tried to brush it off as not my *indaba* and wandered over to the waitress who was flipping the sizzling crispy fish. I ordered one and a warm Coca Cola. I lingered over my food long enough to be sure that Ernst and Lena had retrieved their bikes and then returned to the dockside.

The glistening, muscle-and-sinew dock workers had made a Herculean effort and had transferred tonnes of cargo through their human chain to the port side. Ernst and Lena's bikes were gone. The barge was sitting much more proudly in the water and it was a formality to ride over a thin plank and onto dry land. The Tenere had reached Sudan! It would soon be time to tackle the vast cauldron that is the Nubian Desert, but not before one last bit of classic Sudanese theatre.

An old man was sitting on an upturned crate, clean, smart but fighting against the elements, his eyes scrunched tight against the sand whipping around his head, the sun beating down on his head gear. Despite the conditions he was engrossed in the task of repairing one of his leather sandals. I was surprised when I pulled off my helmet to be greeted by a "Welcome, friend." He was one of the only people I would meet in Sudan who spoke English.

"I'm looking for the Immigration Office," I told him.

"Go to the end of the road and it's on the right," was his response. I thanked him and true to his word, it was at the end of the road. Literally. The asphalt road stopped abruptly in a perfectly straight line and gave way to the desert sands. On the right was a long building which resembled an aeroplane hangar. Two customs officers were standing at the entrance, their shirts already stained with sweat, their caps lopsided and dripping like taps. My first thought was that they had not physically adapted to their environment very well. Both had extremely hairy arms and Sean Connery chest carpets. They waved me through, with bored and thirsty-looking expressions. I leant the bike against the side of the building in a sliver of welcome shade. I had become extremely 'shade aware', having already returned to the bike a few times and been unable to sit on the boiling seat without cooling it down with bottled water. I had also been told that sitting for too long causes piles, and it was made worse by hot surfaces. That was something I didn't want to risk, whether true or not. Nine months on a motorbike with piles.

I swung open the glass door which creaked on its hinges, and then dropped slightly, so I had to force it across the floor to get in. The room was a long open hall with rows of (yes, you guessed) ten plastic chairs welded together. At the far end of the building was a long wooden desk stretching the width of the room. On the far left-hand side were two partitioned offices. There were immigration forms strewn all over the floor which fluttered around my feet in the sand, as I walked in. There was not a sign of anyone so I headed down to the first office and peeked in through the glass. A customs official was sitting at a desk, fixing a snapped biro pen with a plaster, so I stood back and knocked, not wanting to look like I was peering. I heard a reply in Arabic which I assumed was, "Come in, oh honourable and respected tourist." so I pushed open the door and walked in. The customs officer continued his repairs and after a few minutes, he placed the repaired pen on his desk, wiped his hands down the sides of his blue shirt, looked up at me and said, "Passport." I pulled off my rucksack and rummaged around, retrieving my passport and placed the document on his desk. He picked it up, looked at the photo, looked at me, looked at the photo, looked at me and then with an unnecessarily firm flourish, so loved by African officials, stamped my passport. The flimsy desk wobbled, creaked sideways, and threatened to collapse under the force of his passport stamping. He glared at me, "You speak English?"

"I do indeed, my kind, welcoming and efficient Customs Officer," or something like that.

"You wait outside for to sign Carnet," he said, pointing out into the main waiting area and then returned to the task of testing out his newly repaired pen.

I sat down on one of the blue plastic chairs. It was extremely hot by now, and sweat was running down my forehead, the side of my cheeks, the centre of my back and the back of my legs. Everywhere actually. My heavy bike gear was clinging to my body and I was coated in a layer of sand. After twenty minutes I was getting quite itchy and frustrated, to say the least, as I had turned into little more than a soggy piece of sandpaper.

After an interminable age, finally, another customs officer

came out of the second office and made his way behind the desk in front of me. He was short and was sporting the same blue shirt and moustache as his compatriot. Moustaches seem to be part of the unofficial dress code for customs officers. His official image was finished off with an impressive-looking blue felt beret, with a motif of a Secretary bird bearing a shield, emblazoned on the front. He had a pair of thick black glasses with bottle top lenses, pushed so tightly on to his face that they creased his cheeks. The lenses made his eyes look three times the size they should have been and it was quite disconcerting when he looked directly at me. He looked like a drawing a child might do of a face.

After fiddling around and shuffling some random papers he took a pen from his breast pocket, which had also been repaired with a sticky plaster (must be the plastic-melting heat), tapped it on the desk and gestured for me to come over.

It must be a family affair, this border control lark, I thought, because he looked very similar to the gentleman in Office 1. As he looked through my Carnet de Passage and ticked the relevant boxes, my curiosity took the better of me. I surreptitiously took a step back and glanced to my left to see if his colleague was still at his desk. The office was empty. I was right. This was one and the same man, except he had donned glasses, a beret, and had filled his pockets with a row of different coloured pens. Now I have no idea whether this was a deliberate disguise to pass off as a completely different person, but it mattered little, because I had already become infected with a serious bout of the giggles.

I knew this would not go down well with Mr Serious but I had an overwhelming urge to say, "I know it's you!"

If he had managed to read my documents before without the glasses, then why did he now suddenly require lenses from an Observatory telescope to make out my documents? This, added to the fact that he asked to see my passport again, perusing it as though it were the first time, persuaded me that, indeed, he was in a cunning disguise. I had grave difficulty in keeping a straight face, and stood there with a red face and puffed out cheeks, trying desperately to stifle a laugh. When it became impossible, I feigned a cough to disguise it and turned away to wipe away my tears. I evidently failed as he scowled and glared at me, as I stood there, beetroot-coloured, with watery eyes and a quivering lip. He eventually handed back my documents.

I managed to splutter "Chokran," turned and made my way quickly out of the building. As soon as I was out the door I burst out laughing. I looked up and the other two customs officers were eyeing me quizzically, probably thinking, "Oh no! Ahmed is doing his dressing up ploy again." I wiped away a tear from my cheek, nodded to them, and headed off to my bike with a manly strut.

Great! Into the Nubian desert, with a smile on my face and a full tank of petrol. I knew that it was 1,026 kilometres to the capital Khartoum, through desolate terrain. I knew I would have to split the journey into two stages and decided to make the town of Dongola the aim for the first night. This was a much more manageable 444 kilometres.

Within minutes of leaving the port I was in a spectacular and desolate environment. Craggy rocks burst out of the desert floor, interspersed with massive rugged peaks which cast long shadows over the perfect asphalt road winding below them. I snaked my way through this environment, pleased that the road conditions were so perfect. After a couple of hours the surrounding terrain levelled out and consisted of thousands of small rocks on a sandy base. I felt relieved that the road was so good. I wouldn't like to negotiate those slippery conditions for a thousand kilometres. I settled back against my army rucksack, built up some speed and soaked up the atmosphere – literally. My mind wandered back to the customs officer. How fantastic, how varied and how entertaining are human beings. In a bizarre way, the episode with the border guard revealed that he had some sort of pride in his job. To go through that charade, he must have some sense of importance. After all, he is the gateway into Sudan for every foreigner, and if he says no, then you are not getting in. Or maybe he's just really bored. Or maybe he is schizophrenic. Or more likely, he's taking the Mickey Mouse. No matter which, give me that sort of theatre any day, rather than the village where I live, where you are served by a surly, spotty teenager, manically texting on their mobile phone whilst, just as manically, chewing gum with an open mouth. They manage to give you the impression that they would rather be tortured than serve you. Ah well, it takes all types to...

Thoughts aside, the riding was mesmerising, with beautiful long sweeping bends, rounding the now infrequent hills, followed by arrow-straight sections which stretched ahead to infinity, shimmering in the midday heat. There was no sign of life, apart from the odd camel sauntering along through the haze. It was undemanding riding and I hit 130 kilometres per hour, enjoying the breeze rushing through my open helmet. Although my Fox goggles protected my eyes, my cheeks began to sting from the sand blasting and I was forced to slow down.

After another two hours of constant riding, I also began to suffer from biker's bum. This starts with cramp, but eventually, your body from the waist down becomes so completely numb that if you did a number two, you would not even know. This would not be desirable, and on top of that I was dehydrating. Although the thermometer must have been hitting the high thirties, I kept my full riding gear on. To crash and become badly injured in this place would not only be a catastrophe, it could prove fatal. Consequently, I was soaked to the skin, and was losing water by the bucketload. I decided to stop, rehydrate and stretch my legs. The chance of shade was minimal as I had not seen a tree for an hour, and the craggy outcrops had all but disappeared. In the distance however, I could make out a dim outline of what looked like a mountainside, so I headed on towards it. As I approached I could just make out a dark patch in the centre of the mountain. It was a long and slender cave, resembling a human eye, set back in the rock. My luck was in and I savoured the chance of a brief respite from the brutal sun.

I pulled off the road, kicked the side stand down and placed a rock under it to prevent it sinking in the sand. I slipped and staggered up the steep, boulder-strewn cliff side until I reached the entrance of the cave. As my eyes adjusted to the dim light, after the intensity of the desert sun, I made out a hollow cave about fifty metres wide, two metres high and five metres deep. It was soothingly cool in the interior and I stripped off my jacket, boots and socks. After the intense heat of the sun on my boots, the sand under my feet and between my toes felt almost artificially refrigerated. I lay down on the cool sand, the grains sticking to the sweat on my back. I turned my head to look around the cave from ground level and noticed that the whole floor was covered in animal footprints. I also noticed a small mound of ash at the rear of the cave. Evidently someone had sheltered here fairly recently, and had built a fire to combat the plummeting temperatures of the cold, clear desert night.

I sat up and set about preparing an egg sandwich with red chillies and Maggi sauce (the most famous sauce in Africa – the number of Maggi advertising hoardings rival those of Coca Cola throughout the continent). As I peeled my boiled egg, it slipped out of my hand, rolled along the sand, and came to rest in the indentation of a footprint. My snack was now coated in sand and looked like a Scotch Egg. I wondered what animal made the prints and decided on a desert fox. I scanned the horizon to look for signs of life. The sky was spotlessly blue, the desert clean and serene and the shiny new asphalt road shimmered off into the distance. The haze played tricks with my eyes but I was sure that three of the rocks in the distance were moving towards me. I screwed my eyes up against the glare and tried to focus on the shapes. I was right. The shapes were moving towards me. These were obviously the owners of the cave I was in, but they looked too big to be foxes. As they approached, it became evident that they were the well-known Scrawny-Mangy-Shade-Seeking-Desert-Dog breed.

Although they looked tatty and hungry, I was incredulous that they could survive at all out here. There was no obvious source of water, no obvious source of food (except me) and no obvious source of shade. Oh, except for this cave!

When they were less than fifty metres away, the largest of the dogs, the obvious Alpha male, a tan-coloured, evil-looking creature, held his head back and stuck his nose into the wind. He had smelled me already. As they moved towards me the two smaller dogs moved in to flank the Alpha male, in a classic pincer movement. They all started barking, the leader of the pack snarling and baring his teeth, a bit how I end up looking when I visit the dentist. I was getting worried as they were advancing quickly. I wanted to surrender their piece of shade with the minimum of bloodshed. My blood of course.

I quickly gathered my things together and negotiated the steep scree slope, but not before arming myself with a few medium-sized stones. Don't get me wrong, I am a 100% dog lover, but if it is the choice between having my calf muscle ripped off my leg, or a well-placed stone between the eyes of a Rabid-Alpha-Male-Scrawny-Shade-Seeking-Devil-Dog, then I would go for the second option. Luckily, it didn't come to that as I decided to call their bluff before they were too close. I jumped down the slippery slope in bounding steps, emitting a blood-curdling scream, whilst feigning stone-throwing movements. I looked very elegant, I am sure. They were highly unimpressed, but it did stop them in their tracks long enough for me to mount the bike and roar off, screaming like a sectioned motorcyclist as I went. I looked them bravely in the eyes and shouted "Ha! Ha!" as I rode past.

Onwards and forwards. The Nubian Desert only spans 400,000 kilometres square, so no need to feel small and insignificant then! I drove for forty minutes, all the while expecting to come across a small settlement that the three dogs must have strayed from. But there was nothing; they really did live out there, somehow. I had not seen a single vehicle since I left Wadi Halfa and couldn't help but wonder what would happen if I got stuck out here. As I was contemplating the worst; thirst, starvation, death, etc., the bike started to slide out from under me and I knew immediately that I had a rear tyre puncture. Now, without going into the boring details, over the next three hours I had the nightmare of repairing three more punctures. To this day I have no idea what caused them, but believe me, it is a tough task breaking the bead of the rear tire in 38 degrees, time and time again. Luckily before the fourth puncture I started to notice small settlements not far off the road and realised that I was coming into the outskirts of Dongola.

The empty desert soon gave way to dusty streets, with small white washed shops, the windows closed off by light green, corrugated iron shuttering. Men in flowing white robes and blue headdresses sat drinking tea on the roadside, their necks turning to follow my path, their eyes screwed up against the sun. The shops were all adorned with crude, hand-painted pictures of fish or cans of paint or whatever the shop was selling. The dusty, sandy roads were swept clean but weirdly the flat roofs of the shops were used as a rubbish dump and were strewn with broken plastic chairs, broken satellite dishes, plastic bags and broken bottles. Many people waved from their chairs, and children ran precariously close to the bike so that I was forced to slow right down for fear of pancaking a Sudanese child. It was a great welcome but I was preoccupied with the fact that my tyre was getting softer and softer. I would have to stop and fix it properly before I damaged it irreparably. After passing an impressive-looking mud Mosque, painted lime green and white, like a giant children's birthday cake, I spotted a guy on the opposite side of the road surrounded by a mountain of tyres and a compressor. I pulled up alongside and dismounted the bike, removing my helmet as I walked towards him. He rose from his crouching position and unfolded into an absolute monster of a man. He was two metres tall, and the rest, and although stick thin, his hands were the size of shovels and his feet went on and on across the sand. He extended a bony wrist in greeting but did not smile. (Sudanese like many Africans bend their hand away from you, and offer their wrists if they feel their hands are not clean.) I explained as best I could that I had a rear tyre puncture. He nodded grimly and pointed to where I should park the bike. I wanted to show willing so started to remove the rear tyre. He stood there, crossed his enormously long arms, and watched me, not moving a muscle. I must confess I whipped off the tyre, broke the bead and removed the punctured tube as quick as a flash. A donkey ambled past, looked at me and sauntered on unimpressed. Luckily, the Sudanese Giant puncture-repair man was impressed and broke out into a toothy grin, nodding his head up and down slowly in approval. "Not all Westerners are useless, then," he said. No he didn't, but he thought it. This immediately broke the ice and we shared a brief episode of camaraderie, which often happens when there is a common goal or task to be undertaken. Well, not really a common goal. I wanted my tyre fixed and he wanted the money for fixing it.

I handed him the inner tube and saw that it was badly damaged with a six-inch tear. Giant man sprang into action and I was highly impressed. He proceeded to stitch the whole tear, delicately and neatly, with a large needle made from a nail, and some string. He then cut a thin slither of rubber, covered it with adhesive and spread it over the stitches. He then waited five minutes, before sanding down the surrounding area with a Wilkinson's razor blade and then with the edge of a hacksaw. Lastly he placed a larger patch over the whole area and tapped it down with a hammer. The whole process took five minutes and looked highly airtight. Inevitably, by that stage we were surrounded by a group of smiling men, nodding approvingly and throwing in the odd comment in Arabic. Many things struck me about the Sudanese. They were stunning-looking people with coal black eyes, aquiline noses, high chiselled cheek bones and beautiful white teeth. Their bodies were taut and wiry but the thing that struck me the most was how incredibly tall they were. At 1 metre 93 centimetres I felt like a midget in this group. I couldn't help but wonder how vertically challenged Ernst and Lena must feel in this country.

I thanked Giant man and nodded goodbye to his giant friends, but not before asking how much I owed. He point blank refused to accept any payment and instead organised a cup of tea for me, and a cheap room for the night, which turned out to be just around the corner from the repair shop. The room was spartan but I went to bed feeling elated. Fixing the tyre was about humanity, not money. I slept like a happy log. The next morning I headed out of town and was hit by the fact that the main forms of transport were carts pulled by donkeys, or tuk tuks (three-wheeled motorcycles) in bright colours. I weaved my way through the sparse early morning traffic and within fifteen minutes I was in the open desert once again. In the open desert for the next 631 kilometre, to be exact, until I arrived in Khartoum.

I was once again swallowed up by the vastness of the terrain and after three hours of steady riding I reached that sublime state of suspended animation where, once again, it felt like I was watching myself from above. It is a wonderful feeling that somehow relaxes the physical limitations of sight, allowing me to view myself, alone, tiny, but soldiering on. I could clearly see myself from above, on the bike, powering through this infinite landscape, a plume of dust behind me marking my progress. In a mental state like this, all other humanity becomes marginalised; all my past, my experiences up to that point, pushed aside, to allow full immersion in the present. It is a pure experience, where your mind is full, yet empty, happiness for a brief period is complete. If you have experienced this feeling, the ability to jettison all your past emotional baggage, remove the layers of worries that cloak your personality, even if for a brief period, you will relate to what I now call 'the ecstasy of solitude'. These moments of solitude were enhanced by the massive contrast between the hectic towns that were dotted along my route and the swathes of desert that separated them. In the towns, I was rapidly surrounded by crowds of people, ten deep, who jostled for position, poked me, poked the bike, and if they were not poking, they were definitely pulling. But as soon as I entered the desert the peace washed over me. It was not simply the physical and emotional space only possible in areas such as this, devoid of human beings. It was not just the lack of litter, the lack of noise, the lack of pollution, it was much more. It was a serenity that even extended to every sense. There is no smell in the desert!

I cracked on for an hour and the landscape slowly changed, with massive wind-and-sand-battered rock formations towering above me on either side. As I came round a sharp bend, in the shadow of one of these looming mountains, I spotted my first sign of humans on this particular stretch. It was Ernst and Lena, parked up on the side of the road, in the shade. It was evident that Ernst had a puncture as he was kicking the rear tyre in a cartoon-like manner as I pulled up. Lena meanwhile was sitting on a small rock about ten metres from Ernst.

I greeted them and immediately noticed that Ernst was hyperactive and animated whereas Lena looked forlorn and moody. She waved to me weakly and then put her head in her hands, staring down at the desert floor. Was she crying? Ernst went on to explain that he had experienced a dramatic and instantaneous blow-out. "Luckily I am professional rider; I manage to come in control, yes!" Ernst's eyes were extremely red and he seemed to be slurring his words. I immediately assumed he was suffering from the constant blasting of sand into his eyes, as was I, and that the slurring might be the onset of dehydration. Then it dawned on me that he seemed drunk. No, it wasn't possible. Not in a country where alcohol is 100% illegal and where you could get in serious trouble if caught, even so far as to be relieved of one of your limbs. Maybe he was on drugs. There was definitely something not right but I busied myself with helping them out of this predicament. It became immediately evident that Ernst had no idea how to change a tyre, and even if he did know, it would be pointless as he had none of the necessary tools for the job. My overwhelming reaction was one of disbelief but I kept my thoughts to myself as that would be rubbing salt in the wound and would not help with Lena's mood. So I just said, "No worries, I have everything we need, let's get this sorted."

I turned to Lena and gave her a reassuring smile and thumbs up, but she just shook her head, and raised her eyebrows to the heavens in despair. As I proceeded to fix the tyre Ernst decided to launch into a running commentary on how to do it, without so much as lifting one of his little fingers to help. He was also acting quite obnoxiously and I was puzzled. After struggling for fifteen minutes in the rapidly rising heat, with Ernst watching over me, consumed by verbal diarrhoea, I was beginning to get irritated with him, so decided to take a quick break. I returned to my bike and greedily swallowed a litre of water. Ernst wandered over to his bike and opened his massive homemade back box and rummaged around for a few minutes. He returned to the stricken bike and knelt down next to me. I immediately got a strong whiff of alcohol, and I was no longer in any doubt. Ernst was drunk. I surreptitiously turned to Lena and mimed the act of someone having a drink. She just nodded confirmation and pursed her lips. I suspected this might be an ongoing problem. How else do you explain being drunk at eleven in the morning, in control (wrong word) of a motorbike, in a dangerous foreign country, where alcohol is illegal?

I walked over to Lena and gave her a hug. Ernst seemed oblivious to her woe and was in his own world, tracing circles in the sand with his boot. Lena seemed so vulnerable and small sitting in the shadow of a cathedral of desert spires. Her petite frame and quiet character somehow made her seem more fragile and much younger than her fifty seven years. I felt very sorry for her. I began to suspect she had bitten off more than she could chew, in fact they both had. I didn't see this ending happily – I envisioned, at best, a hundred lashes for Ernst or at worst, a serious bike accident befalling one or both of them. After all this was not child's play. Deserts are dangerous places if you do not respect them.

I fixed the puncture and turned my attention to checking the rest of their bikes over. If it wasn't so tragic it would have been funny. As I stated before, both Ernst and Lena were somewhat vertically challenged, to say the least, but it evidently hadn't stopped them buying two of the biggest bikes on the market – Honda Transalps 600cc. The small problem (excuse the pun) was that seated on the bikes, their little legs would be flailing around in mid-air, a metre above the ground. They had countered this problem with a bizarre adaptation. The seats had been cut away in a box like shape and the engine had been lowered – not a good idea in Africa. This gave the impression that they were sitting inside the bikes, directly on the engine. To add to the absurdity of the image, they had enormous 40-litre fuel tanks which their chins basically rested on. Now I am no expert on bike design but it looked unsafe, uncomfortable and uncontrollable. The most staggering adaptation of all was Ernst's homemade steel top box. It was so large that it looked like he was transporting a small warship. When I eventually found out what it contained, the situation became even more surreal. I will come to that.

After a brief check on the road-worthiness of their bikes (they weren't roadworthy) I blurted out, "Listen, do you guys want to ride with me until we get to Khartoum, in case you have any more problems?"

"I don't care either way," answered Ernst, keeping the obnoxious theme going strongly.

"Yes, yes, thank you Spencer," Lena interrupted quickly.

Ernst scowled and started fumbling with his jacket zip and helmet strap and mounted his bike unsteadily. I wasn't happy but there was no way I could leave Lena in this predicament and vowed to get them to Khartoum.

We set off. I was glad to be inside my helmet again, with only my own thoughts to disturb me. I needed to steal a chat with Lena to see what the situation really was. I knew I should not be getting involved but I felt it was the right thing to do. We continued on uneventfully, but I kept an eye on Ernst and it was obvious his dexterity was suffering as he swayed back and forth across the road. Thank Allah there was no one for him to drive into for the next thousand kilometres. After an hour and a half of riding, our steady but winding progress was halted by a spectacular sight. On our left-hand side, set back about two kilometres from the road, there appeared, out of the heat haze, a row of spectacular pyramids set in a sea of spotless sand dunes. In my astonishment I counted twenty pyramids rising out of the sand, silhouetted against the unspoilt blue skyline. I stopped the bike and stared in awe. I am embarrassed to admit my ignorance, but I had no idea that there were pyramids in Sudan. The setting could not have been more spectacular and was made more so by the fact that there was not a soul in sight. It was in complete contrast to my trip to the Cairo pyramids. There were no ticket booths, no coaches, no tarmac, no cameras with Japanese tourists connected to them. There were no overweight, loud Americans and no pushy hawkers jostling to offload tacky trinkets and gaudy statues of Pharaohs onto the teeming masses. There were no teeming masses. It was pure serenity and I wanted to soak it up.

"What do you reckon we head over there and camp up for the night?" I suggested as Lena pulled up beside me and Ernst wobbled up beside her, nearly careering into her back tyre. Ernst and Lena started a frenetic discussion in German, the gist of which was… I didn't know the gist, so just waited until they had stopped. Eventually Ernst turned to me and said, "Lena cannot ride on sand."

"That's not a problem, it's not too far. I can either ride up to the pyramids and come back for your bike or I can show you how to ride in sand," I suggested.

"You can show, I will try," she answered gamely.

I went through the basics with Lena; standing up firmly on the pegs, legs slightly bent, keeping even revs and power to the front wheel, trying not to hesitate and do not brake or turn too sharply. I demonstrated with a couple of ride bys, while Ernst looked on disdainfully from a distance, pretending (well it seemed like that), not to listen or heed any of the advice. Maybe he's a master sandblaster. When Lena seemed confident enough I urged her to give it a go. She started off well enough, slithering slightly but then corrected it with some acceleration. Unfortunately, spotting a rock in her path she panicked slightly and turned too sharply. The front wheel dug into the sand and threw her sideways, over the tank, her thigh hitting the handlebar before she landed with a nasty thud on her back. It wasn't a serious accident but it wasn't pleasant. We both ran over to see if she was OK, but to my surprise instead of comforting her Ernst began to berate her once again in German.

Although I could not understand a word it was obvious from the tone, that he was not offering words of comfort and assurance. After ranting on for a few more seconds, he turned on his heel and said to her in English, "It is easy, I show you." Now I am not one to laugh at other people's misfortunes but on this occasion I couldn't help it. Ernst jumped on his bike and fishtailed across the sand, like a demented Smurf on speed. He was completely out of control and the inevitable happened. He looked back to see if we were taking heed of his lesson, the front wheel stopped dead in the sand and Ernst was catapulted over the handlebars, landing face down in the sand. It was perfect. He wasn't dented, but his pride surely was.

Ernst had to have the last word though, and all he could think of was the absurd comment, "I had to show Lena I can fall also!" Slightly delusional, to put it mildly. After some more faffing around we eventually got the three bikes to the pyramids. I noticed that it wasn't only Ernst's pride that had been dented but also his bike. I decided not to mention it and darken Ernst's mood even more.

On a more positive note, the campsite was an absolute gem. I defy anyone to camp in the middle of a pristine desert, in absolute silence and serenity, wake up with the silhouette of pyramids above you, and not be moved. It was the absolute opposite of the tourist cattle market I encountered at the Pyramids of Giza. Despite the beauty, I still woke up with the 'Ernst-Lena problem'. I was beginning to have the suspicion that Lena was a battered wife, maybe not literally but definitely psychologically. It was obvious that the bike was not suited to her at all, that she didn't have the riding experience necessary and was consequently way out of her comfort zone. I believed Ernst was in a similar position, but whereas Lena was introverted and mentally battered, Ernst remained arrogant, macho and sexist. I hate to bring up clichés but he seemed to be suffering from the classic Napoleon complex. All my judgements were to be proved correct in the near future but as for the present I had a moral dilemma.

From a selfish point of view I wanted to be travelling alone. I was always going to do the trip solo. In difficult situations I prefer to be alone. If I make mistakes in my decisions, they are my decisions and only I suffer. If I am having a tiring day of dangerous riding in a hostile environment, it is my decision to rest or continue on. If I am suffering from the heat, or lack of food or water, or unfriendly people, it is me alone I am dragging through the experience. Going on a two-week holiday with friends can often put a strain on the friendship. So, on a difficult journey of nine and a half months I didn't want to face anyone else's emotional baggage, fears or physical limitations, any more than they would want to put up with mine. Travelling alone simplifies your emotions and allows you to focus more clearly on the task at hand, rather than the roller coaster of emotions that can spring up when you are living in close proximity to another person for nine and a half months. A trip like this could put a strain on the best of friendships or marriages. The most common two questions I was asked by locals throughout my journey were; "Why are you alone?" And, "Are you not scared?" The first one I generally skirted, not wanting to sound aloof, and the second I answered; "No, I am not scared." I was not being arrogant, because it was the absolute truth. I don't have many good traits but I am pleased to be blessed with a complete lack of fear. It could be plain stupidity, I grant you, but I look at it as a blessing because fear can be a burden that will stop you enjoying life. I am well aware that some people are so crippled by fear that they cannot even leave their own homes. It is often irrational but nevertheless very real for the people afflicted. I realised that Lena had neither of my luxuries – she was travelling with a difficult bully and secondly she was scared.

In a normal day-to-day situation, in the street, in a restaurant or bar, in an urban environment, I could quite easily make my polite excuses and leave Ernst and Lena to their own devices. I could shrug it off with the fickle comment, "It is none of my business," but this situation was completely different. I had a moral obligation to see them both to safety. We were in the Nubian Desert for Allah's sake, a dangerous situation, where two people so ill-equipped could get into serious difficulties. As Ernst was drinking heavily, he was in danger, not only of crashing, but also of suffering dehydration. The glaringly clear bottom line was that it was none of my business, so I had already decided I would not say a word. I would get them to Khartoum and then continue my circumnavigation alone.

I was not so naïve to think that people I met would not affect my experiences. After all, certain characters had already had a massive effect on my journey already. The excellent Scottish-Libyan Sami Osman and the wonder of modern Egypt, Ashraf, would never be forgotten by me. All I knew was that I didn't want to get embroiled in Ernst and Lena's personal problems.

Furthermore, to be completely Ernst (excuse pun), the punishment for possessing alcohol in Sudan varied from the death penalty, to limb amputation, to 40 lashes, to a $5 fine (depending on who you spoke to or what website you looked on). I was hoping, for Ernst's sake, it was the last but I didn't want to be around, and therefore involved, when he found out.

As we packed up to move on, the beauty of the surroundings were marred by Ernst's early morning mood, no doubt due to his hangover and Lena's sullen silence, no doubt due to her bruised body and ego. The atmosphere was tense and I was relieved to be on the road again. We continued south through Atbara and the winding roads turned into endless stretches of arrow-straight perfectly smooth asphalt, dividing the desert sands in two as far as the eye could see. A light crosswind deposited a sprinkling of sand on the road, which swirled around our feet when disturbed by the bike tyres. Every now and then a dried and cracked, sun-bleached fallen tree would break up the landscape, a pile of sand collecting on its windward side. The only other sign of life were the herds of camels lumbering across the desert, their classic shadows following them across the desert floor as they made their way to wherever camels go.

Don't ask me why certain thoughts spring to mind in the strangest circumstances, but the implausibly straight roads reminded me of a friend of mine in Swaziland, a rotund German called Clement. If you imagine Fidel Castro in a pair of blue decorator's dungarees, with a pot belly of massive proportions, there we have Clem. Clem was well known for his wild and fanciful stories but they were told in such earnest that his facts were given the benefit of the doubt. Plus, he was hilarious. He had two favourites which I will briefly summarise. The first was an occasion when two guys tried to mug him (silly them) on the streets of Johannesburg.

"Spencer I tell you, I saw them following me, and one had a knife." Without a glimmer of a smile, he continued, "I do very fast, backward Karate kick and I knock out both bastards at same time." Now if you consider Clem isn't a kilogramme less than one hundred and fifty and has the athleticism of a jelly bean, you can appreciate that I had difficulty keeping a straight face. I tried to encourage him to give us an action replay but he declined and instead ordered another Cane and Coke. Oh well, another time then.

His second story was just as believable and in a nutshell went like this. After complaining about the state of the infrastructure in Africa for the fiftieth time, he would sigh and go: "Listen Spencer, believe me, the area I live, in Germany, the Autobahn, the road, ja, is so straight and so good, I put brick on accelerator and sleep. Good, ja?" This road in Sudan almost made his story plausible. No it didn't. But respect to Clem; he gave me a giggle in the Nubian Desert. But back to the present. Ernst continued as he had the previous day, but this time openly. Every time we stopped for a water break he would open his back box and swig from a bottle of something. Once again he became progressively more obstreperous as the day wore on and I began to pray for some sign of Khartoum.

After an interminably long ride through the desert where we passed only fleetingly through the towns of Ad Damar and Shendi, we finally reached the outskirts of the city. It was predictably chaotic – dirty, dusty, noisy and hectic; all the more so because we had the misfortune of timing our arrival during rush hour. The roads were cracked and potholed and, to cap it all, the clouds literally burst, and we were deluged by a torrent of water which instantaneously transformed the roads into gushing rivers. Anything that was not tied down succumbed to the power of the flood. We were riding in a three foot river of garbage. Debris snagged on our wheels and the blasting rain brought visibility down to zero. Overloaded buses slid in and out of our path, spraying us with stinking, muddy slurry. Minivans and motorbikes rudely spluttered noxious gases in our path, reducing visibility and causing our eyes to smart. Wading pedestrians did their utmost to be run over by the only three foreign motorcyclists in the city, while hawkers attempted to knock us off by waving their goods in our faces as we wobbled past. Our clothes and luggage doubled in weight from the downpour and our boots filled with sludge. The hidden potholes were met by a huge jolt that tended to slide you down the seat and into the petrol tank. At the side of the road, groups of pavement slabs were missing, leaving gaping holes easily capable of swallowing up a motorbike and its rider without a trace. It was tough riding and Lena was moving at a snail's pace, frequently stopping dead when she lost confidence, only to be met with a barrage of hooting, shouting and gesticulating. I ignored them all and stayed behind Lena, which turned out to be a good thing as Ernst had completely disappeared, not once looking back to see if we were following or had been squashed by an out-of-control bus. As we turned a corner the road was blocked by a donkey that had slipped and overturned its cart and contents. The contents quickly disappeared with the barrage of water while the driver did his best to coax the struggling donkey back to its feet.

I pulled up alongside Lena, the water rushing round our precariously planted feet. She looked round at me and I could see her body was shaking and her helmet nodding, almost imperceptibly, back and forth. It was only when she raised her visor that it became obvious, despite the beating rain that she was sobbing hysterically. The tears were streaming down her cheeks from red-rimmed eyes. She looked traumatised. It was too dangerous for her to carry on in that state, especially as a wicked wind had now joined the festivities, so I motioned her to the side of the road, under a canopy. A plucky local man was precariously balanced on an island, a lump of concrete actually, selling sweet coffee, with filthy rainwater swirling around his ankles. He continued stoically despite being battered by the violent rains and being in danger of losing his canopy and urn altogether. He not only continued serving but he did it with some panache and style, despite being in the middle of a tropical cyclone. He poured us two sweet coffees, spiced with cinnamon, poured from a special tin jug with a long spout, known as a 'jebena'. That was a feat in itself as he kept the spout a good half metre from the tiny glasses he served them in. I would be lying if I said he didn't spill a drop – most of the scalding liquid blew off down the road, luckily not in our direction. I got the impression he had dealt with these conditions on many occasions and we appreciated his skill in sending the boiling coffee in the opposite direction to his customers. His tenacity in such extreme conditions was admirable and it put a smile on our faces as the coffee warmed our insides. That was not his only offering either. He was also cooking up a soup called Kawari, made of cattle and sheep's hooves. Fortunately it was not quite ready so we made do with the coffee. After fifteen minutes the rain eased slightly. I put my hand on Lena's arm and said, "Don't worry, we will take it easy, really slow. You follow me and just flash your lights if you need a break. It can't be more than five more minutes to the Blue Nile Sailing Club."

Unfortunately, the Sailing Club where we heard we could camp, was another tortuous twenty five minutes of battering riding, but unbelievably we arrived unscathed. Our destination turned out to be more like the 'Blue Nile Past Its Heyday, Not Much Sailing Done Here Club.' Passing through the rusted gates and past the pockmarked wall we pulled into an open sparsely gravelled car park. A small stretch of patchy lawn led up to a tired-looking thatch canopy. At least there was somewhere to camp. Beyond the canopy was the Nile River (which also looked past its best). Moored on the bank was a boat that looked like it had been through both world wars and then some. To the right of the lawn Ernst's bike lay prone, obviously jettisoned in some hurry, as there were scratch marks in the lawn leading up to where the bike now lay, on the gravelled car park.

A Sudanese gardener who was lackadaisically tending some long dead plants looked up and saw me checking out Ernst's bike. "He is washing," the gardener offered, while miming the act of scrubbing. I thanked him and went about picking up Ernst's bike and borrowing a plant pot from the gardener to place under the foot peg so it did not sink in the waterlogged ground. When I had righted the bike Lena came over, stopped me and said, "Look." She pulled a set of keys out of her bike jacket pocket and proceeded to open Ernst's back box. When I list the contents you will understand why my jaw dropped and my eyes widened until I resembled an out of breath owl:

1. Two deck chairs

2. A tent Colonel Gadaffi would have aspired to, it was so large

3. Three homemade, five-litre metal containers; smaller versions of Ernst's battleship back box

4. That's it.

Lena pointed at the metal containers and whispered, "Schnapps. All."

Schnapps is a Low German word meaning 'swallow'. Ernst was certainly following that instruction. More to the point, it is distilled from fermented fruit, mainly apples, plums, pears and cherries and contains about 40% ABV (80 proof). No wonder Ernst was weaving all over the show for most of the day. Fifteen litres of Schnapps; fifteen kilogrammes of alcohol in a country where it is illegal! Lena closed the box and I turned to her saying, "Ernst has a problem, hey?" This was the catalyst comment that opened the floodgates again and, in a torrent of broken English, Lena proceeded to blurt out all the woes I had recently suspected.

"I have bike experience null. I have licence only one year. Ernst choose bike, Ernst choose Africa, and Ernst choose everything. I only ride on Autobahn three weeks," she sobbed.

I started, "You have to tell Ernst you are not happy and that… " but I stopped abruptly as Ernst appeared around the corner of the thatched hut, wrapped in a red towel and looking worse for wear. He walked up and said in German, "Why are you crying?"

Lena replied, "I am tired, it was a long day."

"Well, go to sleep then," he countered and walked off.

That was the end of our conversation for the evening as I felt uncomfortable sneaking behind Ernst's back for a chat, despite the fact that I didn't hold him in high regard, to put it mildly. I said goodnight and headed off down the ragged lawn to try and get some physical and mental space. I lay down on my sleeping bag on the grass, now dried out, not bothering to put my tent up, as it was still hot despite being nine o'clock at night. I could also safely assume that I would not get rained upon as the sky was totally blue and Khartoum was predicted one day of rainfall at some point in the next month. Sleep escaped me, despite being shattered. My mind was in overdrive, with thoughts, worries and ideas rolling over each other like waves in my head. I thought about what I was doing, what I was trying to achieve and whether I was approaching this whole journey in the right frame of mind. I was fully aware that I should be making constant insights into the local culture, the locals I met and the breathtaking scenery. I could hear people saying, "He has a once in a lifetime experience, if I were him I would… " But it doesn't always work out like that. At the present I was too absorbed in the complexities of human relations. How had Lena got herself into this position? Love? Hope? Bullying? Fear? Weakness of character? A combination? Why was I getting involved?

I also realised that I had taken my eye off my own aim, neglecting my own goal. My goal was to become the first person to circumnavigate Africa solo and unsupported and to document it on film and in a book. I was finding it so difficult to balance my desire to 'get round and succeed' with the necessary tasks of filming and writing. I had no idea why I was behaving like this. I should be soaking up the culture and experiences, but instead found myself in a constant state of animation. I could not relax unless I was making geographical progress. If I spent more than one night in a place I felt frustrated and had a powerful desire to keep moving. I think it is an affliction of most human beings; looking for the next thrill, the next experience, and thereby neglecting the wonder of the present. So much of our life is forward planning, looking for a future, looking to improve our lot. People have been falling for the "Grass is always greener", maxim for millennia.

I had to slow down and take stock of my professionalism and approach to this project. Because that's what it really was; a project to try and improve my future. An expensive one, a dangerous one, and a physically draining one, but a project nonetheless. I had already, in motorbike jargon, succumbed to 'white line fever' having rushed through France, Tunisia and Libya with the minimum of documenting and, to be honest, without as much as a cursory glance. I had somehow managed to divorce myself from the reality of what I was doing. I was living in my own head. I was just trying to cover the miles.

Maybe I was daunted by the massive amount of distance I still had to cover over the next eight months. But the speed had to stop. After all I was not the only one to have sacrificed for this journey. I had to make it worthwhile for the people who cared; my parents, my girlfriend and my two girls. I felt I had been incredibly selfish, leaving them for almost a year, justifying my departure with the throwaway line, "I hope they will be proud of me when I return." Of course my daughters had their own frame of reference and their own worries; school, boyfriends, the odd spot on their face, etc. All they saw was that I left them for a year and possibly put my life in jeopardy. That is why it was so important to succeed, and therefore I had to change my attitude. Otherwise I would feel like a fake and that someone else deserved this opportunity. Someone who would savour the moment, memorise the experiences, not block them out and go through the motions.

Camel warden, Egypt

Adjusting
clobber,
Kenya

On the
road,
Tanzania

Police checkpoint, Mauritania

Carl, Namibia

Sleeping
soldier,
Angola

Sand dredgers, Benin

Good Time Bar, Togo

As was obvious by now I didn't know whether to call this undertaking a trip, an adventure, an expedition or a project. It mattered little. If it all came to nothing, if I failed to finish, or if I failed to document it well, then I could not make my family proud and could not provide for their future. I would be devastated.

A lot of people talk about 'the freedom of the open road,' but this is only true on a simple level, living for the moment. Travelling does not free the mind or spirit, rather it has the opposite effect. It sets your mind into a turmoil of thought about what is important in your life. It is naïve to think that you can be free of your responsibilities just because of your geographical location. You cannot just ignore everyone important to you and wipe the slate clean, just because you are not in close proximity to them. Even when you are born, you are born with responsibilities, you are already part of a unit with people relying on your reactions, behaviour and happiness to provide their own happiness and selfworth. That is my experience anyway. Love is guilt.

These are the issues that were swimming around my mind as I lay in a car park in Khartoum, Sudan, unable to sleep. Inevitably, my mind also returned to the Ernst-Lena dilemma. But my brain felt like it was about to explode. I couldn't hold onto any firm thoughts. Maybe this is the true meaning of travel: not that it stretches you physically; forget mosquitos, dust, filth, heat, disease, etc.; maybe it is the mental gymnastics it causes, making you re-evaluate yourself and your own position in the world. Humans are so complex that maybe it is no surprise that the relationship of two people I hardly knew had overridden my experience of riding through Sudan. In fact, the people I had met had had a much stronger effect on my experiences than I initially thought they would. Both negatively and positively, of course. I had made a decision. I would embrace all the new encounters I would undoubtedly have in the next nine months but not to the detriment of my goals. I would extract myself from the Ernst-Lena scenario when I woke up (in the nicest way possible of course). It was time to resume my solo trip.

I stuck with my plan when I woke up, feeling a new lease of life. I would say my goodbyes but not without urging Lena to consider throwing in the towel. I knew that the riding in Sudan was fairly tame and that the road ahead, into Ethiopia and on to the city of Gonder, was winding and treacherous with steep, deadly curves. In the space of a fifty-kilometre stretch there was an altitude rise of 2,350 metres. Addis Ababa was the highest capital in Africa and I feared for Ernst and Lena's welfare. The crucial difference being that Ernst's problems were self-inflicted. I approached Lena, who was brushing her teeth at an outside tap. There was no sign of Ernst but surprisingly his bike was loaded up and ready to go.

"Lena, I've decided to stay here for a day or two and then carry on to Ethiopia. I'll be taking the same route as you, so if you have any problems I'll come across you at some point."

I thought I noticed a hint of panic in her eyes, but she quickly regained her composure, gave me a hug and with a newly revised, resigned expression, said, "Maybe we meet in Gonder." We both knew that this was not going to happen, but we kept up the charade. I turned to go and pack up my things, but couldn't help myself.

"Why don't you just tell Ernst that you're not enjoying yourself, that you're finding the riding too difficult, and that you want to go home," I pleaded.

"He will be very angry," was her short response. I saw Ernst approaching from the main entrance, so I said, rather lamely, "Well, I'm sure you will make the right decision." They were both ready to head off within fifteen minutes of Ernst's return and after another, warmer hug from Lena and a curt handshake from Ernst, they pulled away. As they turned the corner and disappeared I let out a deep sigh of relief. Guiltily, I was pleased that the burden of marital referee had been lifted from my shoulders. However, I couldn't shake off the fact that I should have confronted Ernst. Would that have been the manly response, or was it none of my business, and should I have never stuck my neck in, in the first place? Ah well, it was over. I sincerely hoped they would make it unscathed.

I busied myself for the rest of the day with routine maintenance and a sketchy plan of my route. I had little choice as the only map I had brought on this mammoth trip was a large map of Africa which only showed the main roads (which I was trying to avoid) and the major cities, Cairo-Khartoum-Addis Ababa etc, and a sprinkling of smaller towns in between. No detailed Michelin map for me. I didn't have a Sat-Nav either. You may think this was appalling planning but it was my whole point and was intentional. I wanted to travel on the roads less trod and to experience a 'deeper' Africa, whatever that meant. I had a compass which assured that I was travelling south, at least most of the time. This and directions from locals would suffice. If I asked ten people for the direction, if three gave the same answer, I would go that way. It did not succeed often. I often had the pleasure of two people pointing simultaneously in the opposite direction to each other to indicate the route. I would have one person state, "It is close, maybe 10 kilometres," whereas the next person would let out a high-pitched whistle and say, "It is too far, too, too far, maybe 1,000 or 500 kilometres, or maybe 2,000." I loved it all and was never upset to be lost or going in the wrong direction, because really there was no wrong direction. It did mean that on the trip from Cairo to Cape Town which is about 12 000 kilometres, I was destined to clock up 23,550. Still, that is getting ahead.

I slept early and awoke before sunrise. My aim was to head south out of Khartoum, through the towns of Al Jadida, Ad Douiem and on to Kosti. At this point I would head west and try and get into Darfur. A golden rule of adventure travelling is to let someone know when you are leaving, which route you are taking and your destination (and ETA).

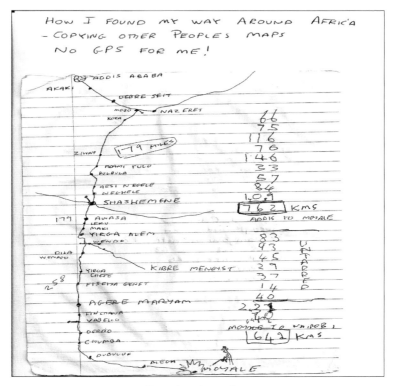

Expert cartography

I was following very few of the golden rules and this was no exception. I felt it unnecessary to burden my family with the worry of knowing I was trying to head into a war zone, that was all but cut off from the world's media. Reports of anarchy, civil war and atrocities were filtering out, but I was keen to see the situation 'on the ground', as news correspondents like to say.

I rolled up my sleeping bag, packed away my few possessions and reluctantly left the palatial surrounds of The Not So Nile Not So Sailing Club, and headed out the shabby gates onto the frantic streets. As I weaved my way around the various obstacles, it was obvious that the city woke even earlier than I did and was already in the full swing of another frenetic day. Street children were sitting in groups, knees tucked under their chins, arms wrapped around their legs, warming up in the weak early morning rays on any patch of grass or verge they could find. Street vendors with gravity-defying loads piled up on their heavy wooden carts were struggling towards their pitch, glistening with sweat. Mobile coffee stalls were making a brisk trade with customers in business suits waiting patiently for the dishevelled vendors to complete their chores.

On the road I battled with the rickshaws, minibuses, buses, cars, battered canary yellow taxis and mopeds. All this was played out in the arena of rotting piles of mud and garbage that were drying out in huge glutinous mounds after the recent flood. I was pleased to eventually get out of the city bustle, but my troubles were about to begin.

As I was hitting the outskirts it was now time to top up my petrol tank, fill up my jerry cans and carry as much bottled water as I could before tackling more endless desert. I pulled into a seriously dilapidated petrol station. The forecourt concrete had literally cracked up in the sun and the pumps were rusted. One of the pillars of the forecourt roof had obviously had a close encounter with a large lorry, as it was twisted and mangled, the metal 'spaghetti' reinforcing poking out angrily from the break. The roof was tilted so wildly, it made the Leaning Tower of Pisa look positively sober. I was frankly loath to ride under it, but needs must. The station was manned by a stick thin, coal black, beanpole of a man, sporting a blue kaftan, a red, grease-streaked Honda baseball cap and white running shoes. He had a slender nose and tight-skinned prominent cheekbones. Perched on an upturned paint tin embedded in the sand, he was busy cleaning a large pile of khat, which was laid out on a scrap of newspaper on the ground in front of him. I had encountered khat throughout my journey. Khat, also known as qat or miraa, is a flowering plant native to the Horn of Africa and the Arabian Peninsula. Among communities from these areas, khat chewing has a long history as a social custom dating back thousands of years. It is an amphetamine-type stimulant which causes excitement, loss of appetite and euphoria. An estimated 10 million people globally use khat on a daily basis. So it was no surprise I had come across it before (but not taken it, obviously). In my experience the outwardly physical symptoms are Chipmunk cheeks, blood red eyes and green stained teeth. If it is a stimulant, Giant Petrol Pump Attendant wasn't showing any signs of it. He looked over and went back to his work. I removed my helmet and waited patiently. The forecourt was littered with bits of machinery, engine parts, glass, nails and numerous oil and petrol slicks. Giant Khat Chewing Petrol Pump Attendant rose slowly from his can and ambled over, brushing debris out of his path as he shuffled across. I jumped off the bike and pointed at the tank, giving a thumbs up and a hopeful raised eyebrow. He turned on his heels without a word and headed to a wooden cupboard behind him. I looked up quickly just to confirm the roof was not about to collapse on me. He extracted a twenty litre, yellow jerry can of fuel and returned to the bike. I looked up quickly again. I stood next to him and at 1metre 93cms I felt like Danny Devito. I couldn't help wondering how Ernst and Lena were feeling in The Land of the Tall. I thanked and paid the attendant and was on my way. I hadn't been squashed by a Sudanese garage roof and I had my fuel. All was good. Or so I thought.

The next 317 kilometres from Khartoum to Kosti were a catalogue of disasters. At the world's dodgiest garage I had managed to pick up three nails in my tyres (two in the rear and one in the front). I had also managed to pick up fuel that had not even smelled a petrol tanker. Most of it was water. Well, I exaggerate but it played havoc with my engine even though I attempted to drain it all. The journey consisted of kangarooing along the road, stopping to repair a puncture in 40 degrees centigrade, kangarooing along the road, repeat… repeat… I was tired, frustrated, sweating like a lunatic and becoming more aware that I was heading into unstable bandit country. With this worry on my mind, after two hours or so I was tiring.

I came to a narrow stretch of road that seemed to lead down to a bridge spanning a dry riverbed. The road had been gouged into two deep furrows from the infrequent lorries that had passed through. The sides of the road dropped sharply away to a steep slope that only levelled out after about twenty five feet. As I negotiated this tricky section I glanced up and saw four men standing there, blocking the bridge I was heading towards. Two of them were holding something. My heart jumped. I'm buggered, bandits, four of them, one of me, middle of nowhere. Shit! What do I do? I temporarily lost my cool, braked too sharply and slid across the road. I hit a rock with my front wheel, the back wheel spun round and slid off the edge of the road, dragging me with it. As the bike slid down the hillside, with my leg under it, I tried to keep my hands on the handlebars and my head up. I turned the left handlebar in, sharply, to try and dig it into the earth to slow my progress. I came to an agonisingly slow stop, balanced precariously halfway down the steep slope, with my leg trapped under the bike. I had to get away, run and hide, and think later. I kicked desperately at the ground and tried to heave the bike off me. Gravity was against me and it was too difficult. I kicked out again at the bike and looked up the slope. Damn it, they've got me.

As I was thinking this, four concerned heads popped over the rise. As soon as they saw me, squirming like a worm under my bike, they rushed down the slope and pulled it off me. One of them held the bike to prevent it sliding further while the other three all pushed me from behind, to get me up the slope and on the road. They then slid back down and joined their friend in manhandling the bike up. It was only when we were all safely on the road that they started jabbering away excitedly in Arabic and dusting me down. There was much backslapping, handshaking and general gesticulating, punctuated by many fits of manic laughter from me, before I brought out some water and cigarettes. I thanked them a thousand times for not being bandits and for helping me off the slope. After five minutes of admiring my battered bike we shook hands again. As they left two of them retrieved a pair of Hookah pipes from the side of the road and headed off, waving. I grinned sheepishly and waved thanks again. For God sake, pull it together. I blamed my over-the-top reaction to the crash on tiredness. Obviously.

I was determined to maintain the James Bond-like qualities of calmness and composure that I had just demonstrated during the previous incident. I dusted myself off, as they say, and continued on my quest. What else to do? Although I was a bit battered and the bike was still imitating an Australian marsupial, I somehow felt elated. It was a feeling I remembered well after successfully completing a parachute jump. I think it's called the vitality of being alive, the heightening of the senses. Whatever it is, I like it. I continued on for another 150 kilometres without incident and calculated that I was less than twenty kilometres from Kosti. Then my journey came to an abrupt halt. I drove straight into an army roadblock. The commander was livid and insisted on going through all my papers for an hour or twelve. With no explanation he told me, in no uncertain terms, which involved a lot of spitting, that I was to be returned to Khartoum. This is exactly what happened. I was escorted back by an army truck and found myself back in Khartoum. A round trip of 634 kilometres. I tried, as Africans say. Time to go to Ethiopia!

Ethiopia

The journey east from Khartoum, through Wad Madani and Al Qadarif, to the Ethiopian border was underwhelming, but the arrival in Ethiopia was the opposite. All my preconceptions were wrong. They were misconceptions. Ethiopia was lush, fertile and organised. The Ethiopian Highlands were verdantly green, spectacularly immense and the roads were tarred and well maintained. I had fallen for the media image of starving children, with distended bellies, swatting flies out of their eyes and mouths. I expected poverty, a raped, barren landscape, a ruined infrastructure with aid agencies and beggars everywhere. Before anyone jumps down my throat, I do realise that I was only there during a snapshot of time and I am fully aware that it would only take one year of failed rain to produce a humanitarian crisis. But, I realised it was not like that all the time. Climate and weather is all powerful in areas like this. Ethiopians are at the mercy of the Gods.

The other phenomenon that struck me most powerfully at the Ethiopian-Sudan border was how the people and the landscape change so instantaneously when you cross a border. After all, they are random man-made borders. It only takes a small amount of reasoning to realise that humans create natural boundaries, based on geographical features, whether they are massive mountain ranges, stretches of deserts or rivers. This of course creates a natural barrier between peoples and geographical zones. Still, I noticed it at most of the borders and it added to the wonder of the trip.

My wonder amplified as I entered the first major town in Ethiopia, Gonder. Just as in Sudan I had not expected to see pyramids, not in my wildest dreams did I expect to see full-blown castles, even in a city that has a name straight out of Lord of the Rings. But that's what Gonder had in store. Before this trip I could have undertaken extensive research into each place that I was going to visit, but I didn't, and in many ways I am glad. Ignorance sometimes unveils bliss. Gonder was a marvel. I wasn't aware, but it was the second largest city in Africa 300 years ago when it was the capital of Ethiopia for more than 200 years. After the conquest of Ethiopia by the kingdom of Italy in 1936, Gonder was further developed during Italian occupation. During the Second World War, Italian forces made their last stand in Gonder in November 1941, after Addis fell to the British six months earlier.

In my experience of twenty five years in Africa I had never really experienced towns like those I found in Ethiopia. Words ranging from hectic, bustling, vibrant and thrilling, to dirty, squalid, rundown and chaotic are those most often used to describe African towns. But the words landscaped, ordered, peaceful and even quaint can be used for the town of Gonder, without irony.

Of course the foreign influence was obvious as soon as I entered downtown Gonder, but it was still quintessentially an African city. Although Gonder is classed as a city, it has more of a feel of a compact town. The centre is set on the side of a hill. The main square features shops, a cinema and other public buildings in a simplified Italian Moderne style. All the buildings are painted in the same lemon yellow with light green shuttering and look wonderfully lively and crisp, bathed in the warm Ethiopian sun. The main square was in fact a mini roundabout, with blue and white tuk tuks pottering back and forth. On the verge of the roundabout was a small wooden shack, big enough to hold one man, painted light blue with a Pepsi logo on it. Above the logo painted in rough white letters were the words, Traffic Police. There was no sign of any traffic police but the flow of traffic was so sedentary that they were not needed.

I have to confess that my initial romantic image of Gonder was slightly marred by the fact that a lunatic jumped out into the middle of the road and pointed a pistol at me as soon as I pulled into the centre of town. I was not to know that he was the resident dribbling, break-dancing lunatic, who happened to own a wooden replica gun. All I saw as I rounded a corner was a wide-eyed man pointing a gun at me. I ducked down a side street to avoid death (always a good option if you wish to enjoy the rest of your trip), and once again wondered what sort of nuthouse town I had ended up in. Fortunately, I related my story to a local and he just laughed, brushing the incident aside with the comment, "Don't worry, that is Dawit, he fell off a rock at six and is not correct anymore." Not correct? That's an understatement; welcoming tourists with a realistic-looking gun. I wonder if he fashioned the gun himself, because if so, he had a future in carpentry, but definitely not with the tourist board.

After my initial fright I was directed to the Goha Hotel, which sat on a hill overlooking the city and the Castle of Fasilidas, which I was reliably told allowed camping on its rear lawn. This proved to be correct and I set up tent quickly before heading down to see the Castle and pick up some dinner. As I was walking down the hassle-free streets it suddenly dawned on me why I felt so comfortable here. The landscape had changed to one that I recognised, the landscape of my youth; Kenya and Swaziland. There were green trees, flowering plants, hedges and lawns! It was a visible, tangible sign of my progress south. I had battled the arid landscapes of Tunisia, Libya, Egypt and Sudan and, suddenly, no more sand. No more sand in my eyes, ears, throat and hair. No more sand sticking to my sweating body. No more sand to empty from my helmet, goggles and boots. No more sand weighing down my heavy bike jacket and trousers. No more sand sandwiches and sand water. No more sand blasting me day and night due to the ubiquitous wind that blows in all deserts. No more sand filling my tent and blocking up my bike. I felt sand-free, relaxed and elated, and treasured those few hours of wandering. I also needed a break from the bike and it was a pleasure to feel the muscles in my bum working once again, instead of the complete numbness brought on by long hours in the saddle. The weather was glorious and the people were friendly and unassuming.

The 'icing on the cake' of this walk was the complex of Fasil Ghebbi. I wandered around mesmerised by this fortress-like enclosure. It served as a home to Ethiopia's emperors in the 17th and 18th centuries. The complex seemed to be a mix of architectural styles, showing the diverse influences of Nubian, Arab and baroque styles. What surprised me the most was the scale. The complex includes Fasilides Castle which was as grand and spectacular as any I had seen in England. Spreading over an area of 70,000 square metres the site also included

Iyasu palace, Dawits Hall, a banqueting hall, stables, Menhewabs Castle, a chancellery, library and three churches. I learnt that this complex was a break from tradition. The Ethiopian emperors of old used to travel around the empire with their possessions, living off the produce of the local peasants and dwelling in tents. Emperor Fasilides ceased this nomadic progression through territories and founded the city of Gonder in 1636. He was also responsible for building seven stone bridges and forty four Ethiopian Orthodox churches in the Gonder district. The relative permanence of the city from an early age makes it historically important and was, deservedly so, declared a UNESCO world heritage site in 1978.

I marvelled at the atmosphere of Gonder and returned to my tent, feeling highly fortunate to be who I was, where I was. I sat outside and watched the sun go down. All people who visit Africa comment on how quickly the sun sets. This notion that the tropical dusk is extremely brief is true. With the sun having a nearly perfect arc through 90 degrees most of the year, it plunges vertically below the horizon and is lost in minutes. In more extreme latitudes it slides obliquely into night leaving the long period of twilight familiar in Europe and North America. As I witnessed this phenomenon first hand I also noticed something else. Gonder does shut down at night, unlike many African cities. How very civilised. All was quiet within an hour of darkness. Goodnight, Camelot of Africa.

I slept like a sand-free log and was ready the next morning to head off further south, to skirt down the east banks of Lake Tana to my next destination, Bahir Dar. Before heading off I managed to beg a shower from the hotel porter. To my surprise, on the floor of the shower room was a set of scales. I weighed myself and was unsurprised to find that I had lost six kilogrammes. If I continued at this rate I would weigh thirty eight kilogrammes when I get back to England. I should be a spectacularly emaciated sight.

The route to Bahir Dar is only 175 kilometres on what was

apparently a 'good' road. From past experience I knew that 'good' to Africans varied from a six-lane superhighway to a one-dog path, so was not holding my breath. The road was indeed top notch and I took the opportunity to set up my helmet camera, to capture some of the spectacular scenery. I rode steadily, singing Bob Marley songs in my head, which I am wont to do when I am feeling on top of the world. Ethiopia certainly felt like I was on top of the world. As I weaved my way down the mountain passes, patchworks of arable farming greeted me on either side, stretching up the steep mountainsides. Small thatched hut compounds were dotted along the valley floors and I could just make out the inhabitants, antlike, busying themselves in their yards, while children, goats and dogs scrambled around enthusiastically. Donkeys ambled aimlessly, fattening themselves on the green pasturelands. Compared to the skinny, bedraggled, sorry specimens I saw in Libya and especially Egypt, these ones were glowing with health. In fact the whole area seemed to have a glow, a sheen of growth and fertility. It was wonderful to see and I was elated. The children I infrequently met on the roadside whooped in delight when they saw me, jumping up and down and screaming, "Welcome, welcome!"

I was warned by a couple I met in Tunisia that the children in Ethiopia threw stones at motorbikes, and not just small ones (stones, that is). There must have been a stone-throwing truce when I rode through, because all that was thrown at me were big greetings and big smiles. When I did stop to hand out some sweets the children squealed with delight, their angular, noble faces breaking into toothy grins. They ran off down the mountainside to show their friends and family their treats, or maybe to hide behind a rock to eat them without having to share. I was loving every minute. I rounded a steep bend, the road winding down to a glistening river nestled far down in the valley below. I could make out a Dinky, toy-sized, white car crossing a steel bridge over the river. From the size of it, to the naked eye, I judged that I had a good fifteen minutes before I made the valley floor. The scale of the mountains in the Ethiopian Highlands is truly majestic. On my right side the rolling hills had broken into a steep jagged rock face, water glistening off its surface, while on my left the valley fell away steeply to green and khaki fields. The perfect road split these contrasting landscapes into two, snaking its way around all obstacles. It was so awe-inspiring I pulled over and double-checked that my helmet camera was functioning. I pulled in the clutch and continued freewheeling to avoid camera shake from the bike engine. I swept further round the bend and straight into a scene of unimaginable carnage.

A crowd of at least a hundred people were swarming the road. On the right hand side, in the shadow of a sheer rock face, a number of buses, cars and motorbikes had been hurriedly parked up. I pulled off and walked down the steep road to the rear of the crowd, craning my neck to see what the commotion was all about. To my absolute horror, a colossal, rusty DAF dump truck had obviously lost control on the steep corner and had careered into an Isuzu pickup truck. The livid scars gouged out on the tarmac marked the trajectory of both vehicles as they veered, out of control, off the mountainside. Both had rolled what must have been a dozen times and come to rest against a huge granite boulder, fifty metres down the slope. The front wheels and axle of the dump truck lay mangled, thirty metres from the body. Both trucks had evidently been fully laden with goods and people. Judging by the devastating scene before me there must have been thirty to forty people piled up on the fully laden dump truck, as is the norm in all of Africa. Bodies were lying where they had landed, spat out and crushed by the vehicles as they rolled. There were huge bundles of goods wrapped in blankets, plastic and rope, littering the mountainside. Shoes, torn clothing, cell phones and numerous personal belongings lay strewn around the area. I saw at least five bodies and others with injuries so severe I won't go into detail. But worst of all was the commotion around the Isuzu. A young man, about twenty, with a red Yamaha T-shirt, was lying trapped, squashed between the rock and the roof of the Isuzu pickup, only his torso visible. His eyes were open and staring straight ahead, vacant, in shock, but alive. I ran down the slope and joined the group of hysterical, shouting people surrounding him. The scale of the horror was so extreme they seemed unable to act. Without thinking, I gestured to the group on the mountainside below the truck to get out the way and gripped the edge of the truck, miming the act of pushing it over. I beckoned to others to help and it galvanised them into action. A group of about ten of us quite easily pushed the pickup off its side and it slid down the slope, bounced on to its wheels and came to rest in a small cloud of dust. I will never forget what happened next. The young man, free from the crushing weight of the truck, slid down the rock, came to a stop in the dirt, crumpled up on broken legs and a shattered body. He looked up, or so it seemed, dribbled some blood from his nose and mouth and took his last breath. It was beyond terrible.

Our small group was shocked into silence. I knew he was dead but checked for a pulse; there was none. I felt a powerful compulsion to keep busy. I hurried around for the next half an hour, helping whoever I could. We arranged blankets for the injured to stay warm and for the dead to be covered. Luckily this was not a problem as everybody in Ethiopia wrapped themselves in blankets. A tubby driver in a bright red Chinese Sinotruk offered to take the badly injured to hospital. He reversed the truck up to the edge of the drop, with much aggressive hooting and shouting at the thronging masses, and opened the tailgate. We busied ourselves with loading them up, which was awful, a scene out of a war zone. I have never seen injuries like that on people who are alive. With a great deal of co-operation and even more shouting, we brought some semblance of order to the scene and surprisingly, after about forty minutes a police car and ambulance turned up. I decided I had done what I could, and had to leave. As I got to the top of the hill and pushed my way through the spectating horde, onto the road, I looked back at the scene below me. No, it didn't look like a war zone. It looked like one of those mountainside plane crashes you see on news channels, when filmed from a helicopter. I rode off in a daze and only stopped after riding for a good fifteen to twenty minutes. I wanted to be far away from that grisly scene. But I couldn't be far away from it in my head.

The rest of the journey to Bahir Dar I did not notice, and can't really remember now. I spent the whole time re-living the past hour. Accidents like this happen every day in Africa. A combination of terrible roads, incompetent and reckless drivers and hopelessly unroadworthy vehicles are a recipe for what I had just witnessed. Add to this a pathological aversion to the rules of the road, often accentuated by alcohol or drugs and there seems little chance of this problem abating. You often hear it banded around that 'Life is cheap in Africa'. You try telling that to the traumatised people I saw at the crash site. Try telling that to the mother, brother or sister of the young man crushed to death on that mountain road. Just because death visits more frequently in Africa, it does not give us licence to use the word cheap when it comes to a life. If I was realistic about my personal quest, I had already nearly been killed four or five times and I was only a quarter of the way round. It was in this sober and grim frame of mind that I pulled into Bahir Dar, a beautiful city on the southern tip of Lake Tana.

Although traumatised by the day's events, I could still appreciate the beauty of Bahir Dar. The central streets were wide, clean boulevards lined with massive palm trees, their fronds throwing huge shadows of cooling shade onto the pavements below. These were neat and, unusually, were void of broken slabs. Splashes of white flowers sprung from the well-tended beds on the pavement edge. I drove round a small roundabout at the top of the main street, passing a high rise building, with neatly painted signs advertising Protection

House, Nyala Insurance and Dashen Bank. The traffic was primarily of three types; three-wheeled tricycles, blue and white as in Gonder; yellow Toyota taxis, and bicycles. The shop fronts were small, but neatly arranged and I had more than enough time to amble along, looking around as, thankfully, after my recent experience, the traffic was very civilised. I pulled up to a group of local boys who were quick to gather round my bike and poke it incessantly, I presume to see if it would bite. They were super friendly and I was pleased to ascertain that one of them, Alem, was fluent in English – well almost.

"I am really tired and need to find something to eat and a cheap place to stay," I asked.

"No problem, my friend. If you go to the way you coming before time, go over roundabout and you will be seeing Lake Tana. There is it a one cheap food there. There are many Hotels, like Blue Nile Hotel, Tana Hotel, Good Luck Hotel, Papyrus Hotel, Ghion Hotel… "

I stopped him in his tracks as I suspected he could continue listing hotels all day. "I don't want a hotel. I am looking for somewhere cheap, two or three dollars." He looked at me incredulously, so I added, "I don't have a lot of money; I just want a bed in a room, that is all." He answered with a line I have heard a multitude of times and still love.

"Ah, then you can be stay at the house of my sister. It is over this road behind the shop for selling shoes, yes, good!" he said, pointing to the opposite side of the boulevard. "I be take you there, with much pleasure."

"That's great," I said. "Jump on the bike." We went to the end of the boulevard, turned around and came back on ourselves. Alem tapped me on the left shoulder and we pulled down a small dirt track between two buildings. The town immediately turned into the Africa I am more familiar with; muddy, puddle-riddled tracks, with chickens and scrawny dogs running free. We stopped outside a small wooden gate, where Alem alighted and beckoned me to follow. We vaulted over a small stream which looked and smelled like raw sewage. We entered a small, dirt-swept quadrangle which looked like a miniature stables. There were eight rickety, rotting wooden doors, laid out in a semicircle each leading into a single room. Alem opened one of the creaking doors and showed me the interior. I squinted into the blackness. As my eyes adjusted, I could just make out a tatty, stained mattress, which had evidently suffered some major activity of a sexual nature and had undoubtedly seen better days. The springs sagged almost to the concrete floor, and in reality the bed resembled a filthy sunken bath and had the profile of a banana. A bare electric light bulb hung from the ceiling and a light blue plastic container, with the top hacked off, was sitting in the corner; finishing off the décor of the room with a flourish. The walls were stained with a variety of colours, most of them verging more towards the brown end of the spectrum. The whole quadrangle smelled of urine.

I turned round to Alem and said, "That's fine, I will take it."

He looked pleased and asked me to wait a few minutes as he disappeared around the corner, sliding in his sandals, in the mud, as he went. He returned promptly, "No problem, my friend, I will be taking you two dollars a night." He handed me a padlock, about the size of a small flattened grape, and an even smaller key, and pointed at the door. "For the room, for much good security," he announced proudly.

I thanked him and Alem disappeared, saying he would see me later. I unloaded my kit and put it in the room, realising that I had not even met his sister, if it was his sister, and whether it was even his room to rent out, more to the point. I rationalised the risk by arguing he hadn't even taken any money yet, so I decided to head off to Lake Tana, to feast. I packed up my little rucksack with my valuable paperwork and put the rest into the Fort Knox room.

As I walked from my accommodation through the slippery narrow back streets I realised what a façade many African city centres are. Glittering multi-storey buildings, swanky hotels with all the mod cons, and pristine high streets, quickly give way to sprawling, slum areas with not even the most basic amenities. The gap between the haves and the have-nots in many African cities can be measured literally by a space of a mere 100 metres. This was the case in Bahir Dar but not to the shocking extremes I was going to encounter in other countries further on my route. The face many city centres portray is merely a mask, covering the woes suffered by the many.

It depends on you, what face you want to see, and how deep you want to dig. It is often so much easier to take places at their surface value rather than stir up the grotty details.

No poverty, however, can take away from the pure power of the beauty of nature, and Lake Tana was up there. As I approached the 'marina', for want of a better word, the majesty of the lake revealed itself. The Marina was a series of six concrete slabs, about twenty five metres wide and four metres deep, leading down to the lake edge in a series of giant steps. There was row upon row of multi-coloured plastic chairs, numbering in the hundreds, laid out, facing the shimmering lake. All were occupied. On the left-hand side was an enormous, gnarled fig tree, its roots bursting through the concrete; cracking, curling and lifting the surface as it grew. Beneath the shade of the tree was a small, lopsided, corrugated iron hut, where two women, standing in a cloud of smoke, were busy frying up Nile Perch, Tilapia, and Sharptooth Catfish. Adjacent to them was an even smaller hut containing a man and a single rusty, paint-peeling freezer from which he retrieved cans of Coke, Fanta and gold coloured bottles of Castle beer.

I weaved through the throng and went up to the lake edge. My arrival had the same effect as a stranger walking into a saloon in a cowboy film. The chattering crowd fell silent and I felt a hundred pairs of eyes boring into my back. I was used to this. Openly staring is not seen as rude in many African countries and it quickly became evident that Ethiopians could easily win the 'Openly Staring Competition of the Year'. I did not mind one bit and just turned and smiled at as many people I possibly could. This had the desired effect as normal conversation shortly resumed. Through the centre of the crowd was a small gangway that led to a wooden walkway that stretched twenty metres over the water to a stilted café.

As I trundled over to the café, the immensity of Lake Tana stretched out before me. Lake Tana is, at eighty four kilometres long and sixty six kilometres wide, Ethiopia's largest lake and judging from the crowds gazing over it, highly prized. Great white Pelicans also followed my progress, their large, red upper and pale yellow, lower bills gliding through the water in search of fish. African Darters swooped around me and Perch splashed in the shallows. On the lake edge an African Fish Eagle launched out of a tree, its piercing cry echoing around the cove. Below, Storks and Ibis plied the lake floor for food, while a hundred metres out a hippo rose to the surface, expelling a great snort of air and water. It was an amazing place and I was looking forward to my first real Ethiopian meal whilst overlooking the splendour of Lake Tana. I sat out on the deck and a pretty young waitress with the world's whitest teeth came and took my order. I had no idea what I was going to get, as I couldn't understand any of the words. All I recognised was Injera, a traditional Ethiopian pancake type offering.

As I waited for my Ethiopian surprise to arrive an Orthodox priest in a traditional papyrus boat, shaped like a canoe, came gliding by, rowing serenely and steadily. He was obviously heading to one of the twenty medieval monasteries or churches that I knew were dotted around on more than thirty nine islands. He looked remarkably impressive. He was adorned in a red velvet hat, with a gold cross emblazoned on the front. His robes were bright green and yellow, and a red cape, with gold leaf motifs, fluttered in the breeze behind. He waved and smiled widely, shouting a greeting that disappeared in the breeze. I was struck by what a peaceful existence he must lead. Unless he got eaten by a hippo. The waitress returned, wiped the table rapidly with a cloth, and put down a plate the size of a car hub cap. Covering the whole surface area, and more, was an Injera, a large sourdough flatbread made out of fermented Teff flour. Ladelled on top of the Injera was what I had evidently ordered – Dulet, a spicy mixture of tripe, liver, beef and peppers. There were also a couple of splodges of an unidentifiable green substance, next to an unidentifiable puddle of brown stuff. It looked very daunting, and large. Injera would have served perfectly as sleeping bags for Ernst and Lena. The waitress stood looking over me, and seemingly had no intention of leaving, so I tore off a large piece of Injera from the edge, scooped up a hearty portion of tripe and beef, dipped it in some brown stuff and popped it in my mouth. Now, I am not the fussy type at all and will eat almost anything. I also know that some may feel I am insulting a national dish; that is not the case. It was simply that I was about to have one of the unluckiest introductions to traditional Ethiopian food that you could ever hope for. I was entering Food Poisoning City.

The first mouthful tasted disgusting. It was not so much the Injera, but the tripe and brown stuff. If you imagine cutting out a large piece of carpet underlay, covering it with sour milk and leaving it for a week; there you have Injera. Not too bad. But the tripe and brown stuff was toxic. I had had enough food from around the world to know that it was rotten, rotten to the core. The tripe tasted like it had been caught five years earlier, left out in the sun and then liquidised with a healthy dollop of raw sewage. (Yes, I know, you don't catch tripe.) There was no way I could eat it. The waitress was standing, smoothing one of her braids between two fingers, waiting for approval.

I swallowed as best as I could, smiling insanely and nodding. "It's good, Chokran, thank you, coffee please," I managed to splutter. She nodded approvingly and ambled off, shuffling her feet across the wooden deck boards as she went. My mind went into overdrive. I knew that if I ate this plate of food I would glow in the dark and be dead by the morning. At the same time I did not want to offend the waitress. I realised I was not at her house (which would be excruciatingly more embarrassing), but I wanted to respect the local food and people. I had also been brought up to always finish my food, and indeed, to refuse an offer of food in many African countries is an insult. I had three plans of action available to me:

1. Eat it. There was no chance of that. I had swallowed a healthy mouthful and could already feel the E-coli, Salmonella, Clostridium Botulinum, Bacillus Cereus and Campylobacter vying for space in my stomach.

2. Throw it in the Lake. I decided on this. I would have to do it surreptitiously, bit by bit. If I frisbeed the whole Injera, it could cause a suspicious wave that would definitely be noticed. Furthermore if it didn't sink, I would be spotted, as there are no stingrays in the lake that it could masquerade as. I picked off a healthy piece of Injera, looked around to check the coast was clear and dropped it into the water. The Lake erupted into a geyser of activity as every fish in Ethiopia attacked the morsel. At that minute, the waitress came around the corner and spotted the churning, bubbling commotion in the water. She eyed me suspiciously and plonked my coffee down. Off she headed and I continued with my task. The fish liked the food, but were not capable of acting sufficiently undercover, and so...

3. If I folded the Injera carefully, or even rolled it up and folded it, I was sure I could get it in my rucksack. All the filling and meat would have to remain inside, and hopefully would not dribble out too much as I made my escape. I tore off a smallish piece of Injera and left it on the plate. I placed a piece of meat on the plate and smeared a drop of sauce next to it. I was covering my tracks. The plate could not look spotless. Too suspicious.

Checking around, I loosened the drawstring on my rucksack and pulled it towards my feet, under the table and out of sight. I leant forwards over my plate, rolled up the Injera and its innards and quickly squeezed and squashed it into my bag. I managed it successfully. Like a Ninja. No one spotted me. I felt relieved and settled the bill with the suspicious-looking waitress, thanking her over-profusely and rubbing my stomach like some idiot. Then I dripped my way out of there. The obvious question is why I didn't send the food back. The only thing that stopped me was the niggling feeling that maybe traditional Ethiopian food is actually that bad. Ethiopians (eat with your right hand only, don't forget) don't use knives and forks. Injera is used to scoop up meat and sauces, and be eaten. I think I might prefer to eat my knife and fork.

I was ultimately proved correct though; the food I had was not representative of Ethiopian food. The food was rotten and I was about to have my worst night ever under African skies.

World's Worst Ablutions Experience

I have never been one for toilet humour; it's beneath me. (Sorry: crap humour.) On this occasion I will break my golden rule and tell you my worst ever toilet experience, which I suspect will never be surpassed in my lifetime. Bare with me. (Sorry again.)

I woke up at three o clock in the morning in a dreadful state, a state that David Livingstone would have been proud of overcoming. I was sweating like a man with only severe food poisoning could sweat. The cruddy mattress was soaked to dripping point. My T-shirt was stuck to me like a second, sweaty, dank skin. My hair was plastered to my forehead, salty sweat dripping into my eyes. I felt nauseous, dizzy and hallucinatory. My stomach was imitating a washing machine on rapid spin cycle, and my oesophagus promised to eject substances all over the room, by a process of reverse peristalsis. To put it bluntly, all orifices were out of control.

Stumbling out of bed I managed to projectile vomit into the corner of the room, narrowly missing the blue container I was aiming for. I staggered outside to visit the 'exterior boudoir', otherwise known as an Ethiopian long drop but was pipped to the post by one of the largest women in Africa. She 'rhinoed' past me, in a light green tent and green flip flops, making odd grunting noises as she rushed in and slammed the long drop toilet door behind her.

I stopped under the eaves of the corrugated iron roof, waiting patiently. By that I mean, I hopped around the yard, one leg raised and twisted oddly around the other, whilst clenching my bum cheeks. At the same time I had to concentrate on not throwing up. This was made increasingly difficult by the acoustic display unfurling in the long drop. She sounded like a fire hydrant. Africa's fattest woman had evidently eaten something more deadly than me. Between high pitched screeches and low moans, there emanated other sounds, from other regions. To put it bluntly, she sounded like she was taking off. It was too much for me, but as soon as she had completed her orchestral manoeuvres, I had no physical choice, so rushed past her and into the lion's den.

I was so ill-equipped for the occasion it was laughable. There were no windows and it was so dark I couldn't see me hand in front of my face. My only source of light was a tiny wind-up head torch, which flickered incessantly, and gave off a beam of light the width of a piece of spaghetti. I had to wind it up like a lunatic for at least a minute before achieving thirty seconds of light.

Rushing in to the toilet from hell, I realised I was also badly equipped for the levels of poo coating the floor. All I had on was a pair of fluorescent flip flops, a pair of boxers and a sweaty T-shirt. My flip flops became quickly inundated with waves of excrement. As the liquid oozed between my toes, I tried to calm myself. The daunting task of removing my shorts was the next hurdle. I hopped on one foot and managed to get one leg out. As I jumped, to transfer feet, I slipped and reached out to the wall to stop myself falling. The wall was slippery. My senses were reeling in the dark and I decided to check out the decor. A big mistake. As I scanned the walls around me, it became glaringly obvious that hundreds of people had died in this latrine. I scanned the wall with my head torch and was immediately transported into a John Carpenter film. There were brown streak marks everywhere, where people had clawed their fingernails down the walls; using the wall as one big toilet paper. As there were no windows there was also no escape route for the odours and I was retching constantly. I had to get this done. I successfully removed my shorts without dipping them on the floor and squatted down. I managed my business.

The horror was not over. I looked around for a hose, or jug of water (no toilet paper in these parts), when it dawned on me what the blue container in my room was for. Still in a squatting position, my left foot suddenly slipped away from me. I made a desperate attempt to stay upright, mimicking Road Runner when he goes off a cliff, my feet running on the spot, my arms flailing around like helicopter blades. It was to no avail. I fell backwards and on to the slippery, wet wall. I let out an involuntary scream, righted myself with difficulty, and made an instant decision. I had to get out and retrieve the container of water and clean up this mess. Clutching my shorts I ran out, wearing only my filthy T-shirt and sloppy flip flops and ran straight into Africa's fattest woman, my jewels in full view. She screamed and covered her eyes. I just pushed past her and carried on running to my room. I ran out into the mud yard (no way would that Chamber of Horrors be entered again), and started washing myself manically. Africa's fattest just ran away and was never seen again. After cleaning myself up, I spent the rest of the night in a fitful sleep of pure illness. When in doubt, when things are not going well, make an alternative plan. My decision was to move on to Addis, the very next morning, food poisoning permitting.

At eight in the morning I packed up in a daze of chills and dizziness, and clambered on to my bike with jelly-sick legs, but still determined to hit the open road. However, Bahir Dar was not ready to let me go without one more memorable and extremely surreal experience. I was about to be arrested for driving over a wet condom. Africa!

I pulled out into the main boulevard and headed down to the roundabout where I had spotted a sign for Addis the previous day. There was a massive ride ahead of five hundred and fifty kilometres, but it would do me the world of good. I was looking forward to cruising through central Ethiopia, up to the third highest capital in Africa, at 2,400m. Excitement was upon me as I rode down Fitawrari Gebeyehu Street and turned into the junction for Addis. A line of large rocks blocked off part of the road and I swerved to avoid them, following the other mopeds heading in that direction. As I straightened up the bike, a traffic policeman, straight out of a Persil Washing Powder advert stepped into the road and waved me down. The Ethiopian traffic police must be the world's smartest. There were two of them; one parked up on the pavement, casually leaning against his gleaming white Yamaha 750 road bike; the other, taller, slimmer one was approaching me, wagging his finger in the air, admonishing me for some, at present, unknown misdemeanour. Both were dressed in pristine white trousers, and white shirts with black epaulettes on the shoulder. Each epaulette was studded with two shining, five-pointed silver stars. Their hats were white with a black band running right around them and a white leather strap on the front. Both had white crash helmets hung over their handlebars. The look was finished off with spotless black riding boots, which had been polished to within an inch of their lives, and white gloves which stretched glistening to the elbow. You get the impression – bright white clothing in Africa, the dustiest continent on earth. I pulled over and he marched up to me, still waving his finger. Taking off my helmet quick-sharp and grinning like a loon, I dismounted, kicked down the foot stand and extended my hand in greeting, to this two-metre, moustachioed officer of the law.

Under arrest

"Hello Officer, I'm sorry, did I do something wrong?" He stopped waving his finger, broke into a friendly smile (washing powder, toothpaste; he could advertise both), and accepted my outstretched hand. In nearly perfect English, and now with a straight face, he announced, "Why are you driving like this? It is not good. Welcome, welcome, but we have a problem."

I waited. He nodded with his head, and gestured with his eyes, indicating back up the road, and said, without a hint of irony, "You drive over wet condom."

"I drove over what?" I said, not wanting to repeat the words, in case I had wildly misheard. I was also well aware that a crowd had gathered; par for the course throughout my journey, instant crowds. He repeated, deadpan, "You drive over wet condom. Come and look." I followed him back up the road, as did the rubbernecking onlookers and up to the line of rocks I

147

had swerved round earlier. A man was kneeling over in the road. We approached him and the policeman pointed down onto the tarmac. There was an eight foot condom, painted in bright red, spread across the road, with the words 'Practice Safe Sex' neatly scribed underneath.

Unfortunately, the tip of the condom had been driven over. There was a more-than-obvious, smudged, red wheel track leading away from the tip of the freshly painted prophylactic. It was obviously my tyre mark as all the other motorbikes here had wheels the width of biscuits. The condom painter stood up and they both stared at me, as did the crowd. I looked up to the condom painter and then to the policeman and struggling to keep a straight face, I said, "I am sorry, it was a mistake, I didn't see the condom, I only saw the last rock. The tip of the condom stretched further than the rock so I must have driven over it when I came around the corner. Sorry again."

I attempted to put it across to both of them in the most earnest manner I could muster. The policeman nodded, said a few rapid fire sentences, in Amaric, to the condom painter and said "Come with me," gesturing with his gloved hand back to the bikes. I followed rapidly behind as he strode off. The other, much darker-skinned, portly policeman was busy admiring the Ethiopian Flag sticker I had on the side of my petrol tank. On approach he pointed at the flag, looked at me, gave the thumbs up and said, "Ethiopia, good yes," grinning wildly. I nodded enthusiastically in agreement. At the same time I watched in mild horror as his partner jumped on my bike, bounced up and down, checking the shock absorbers and started the engine, revving it up while looking at us. A little cheeky, I thought.

When he suddenly pulled off, circled the roundabout and exited left, out of view behind a building I was more than freaked out. I turned to his partner and spluttered, "Where is he going?"

"No problem, he is good rider, very good, the most best on motor in Ethiopia," was his nonchalant reply.

I looked around at the crowd: no reaction. The portly policeman settled down on a stretch of grass at the side of the road, his shirt buttons bursting to breaking point as he squatted and then fell backwards on to the lawn. Luckily he had the foresight to have laid a few sheets of newspaper on the grass before he fell. He righted himself, straightened his hat, sighed and settled down to sending texts on his Zain network cell phone. The crowd slowly dissipated, no more fun here. I was left with the portly texter, while I built myself into a state of panic over the next fifteen minutes.

Interrupting Bahar Dar's finest law enforcement officer from his texts, I asked, "Do you think he is ok, maybe he has run out of fuel, maybe he has fallen off, it is a very tall bike. Maybe you can call him."

His answer was, "He is very top world rider, very, very good. Best in world. No signal on phone." So now he had been promoted to the best rider in the world, not merely Ethiopia. This recommendation gave me no comfort and after thirty minutes I was stressed. After forty minutes I didn't care if the bike poacher was Steve McQueen, there was no calming me down. In my mind he was, at this very moment being carted off to hospital (not literally, I hoped, I had seen ambulances in Ethiopia), and my bike was a mangled wreck at the side of the road, ready to go to the scrapyard in the sky. Well, that was it then, end of the journey, end of the road, literally. I had no funds to secure another bike. My dream of circumnavigating Africa through thirty four countries had cruelly collapsed after only six, and all because of a wet condom. Not cool.

As I spiralled into doom, after about fifty minutes I suddenly heard the sweet sound of my bike. Around the corner came the missing cop-bike-borrower, pulling up suavely in front of me and the now, sleeping policeman. He jumped off, gave me the thumbs up and said, "Very good bike, very much powerful," and followed up the word 'powerful' with the universal sexual gesture of pumping his fist underneath his other outstretched hand. Not very dignified for this area of the world, I thought. I turned around and said, "Listen here guys, this is ridiculous. I came to Ethiopia as a tourist, hoping to look around this historical and magnificent city and wallow in the culture, beauty and creativity of your people. Instead, I nearly die from food poisoning after my first Ethiopian meal and then nearly split my head open in my first Ethiopian latrine. Then I get arrested for driving over a wet condom. Then one of your police officers decides to kidnap my bike. This is no way to welcome visitors."

I didn't exactly say that. I said this: "Where did you go with my motorbike for so long?"

He replied, "I go to show my family, but it is far, far (gesturing with his hand, into the distance), out of Bahir Dar, very far, very good, thank you." He finished off with a megawatt smile and a handshake.

What could I say! Time for me to be chilled, wind down and go with the flow, as they say. I was enjoying our little meeting (now that my bike was back in my clutches, of course), and I was hoping they were enjoying it too. Africa always tells you when you are too uptight, and nudges you in the right direction, or whacks you, saying; calm down, other things are more important. Evidently the two policemen had enjoyed their afternoon and so had I. That's what counted. I was the first condom-smearing foreigner in Africa to smear innocently.

I was off at last, cruising out of the town, my mind free to roam, my bike skills kicking in. As I rode off I couldn't help wondering why the condoms were painted bright red. In my mind, the colour red, in that area of the anatomy only meant one thing, blood. Maybe, the problem was that if they had used white paint it would have blended into the other traffic signs painted in the road, 'Go,' 'Stop,' etc., and may have appeared as a command. Many moped riders attempting to fit condoms whilst riding would have led to chaos. As my mind wandered way past anything reasonable, I passed under a banner stretched across the road which was a huge red condom; with you know what written beneath it. As I made progress out of the town I noticed a truck with a huge sign board balanced on its flat-bed rear. 'Practice Safe Sex', a huge condom declared. I was right in the middle of Aids Awareness Week – Bahar Dar version. Good on them, superb. I hope it works. AIDS is a heavy-duty killer. Any efforts to eradicate it can only be applauded.

Open space, majestically formed landscapes, insane roads, and beautiful, welcoming people would be my next five hundred kilometres. Again, the sway of landscape, the awe of the natural and unspoilt, filled me with joy and adulation. I sang heartily in my helmet, Bob Marley never sounded so bad, but I enjoyed it. It seems like my highest and lowest points were to involve people, but my consistently high points always involved the natural world. Africa and I. Just the best feeling in the world. I felt at home, no other words could justify my electric mood. An eagle swooping for a desert rat, an owl flying out of a cave after being spooked, an impala vaulting a six-foot bush to evade death at the clutches of a lion; all were available in the film that is Africa. I was the luckiest person alive. I was to experience all the locations Africa had to offer; dune-filled deserts, tropical forests, endless barren plains, savannah, mountain ranges. You name it, but all with the added pleasure of seeing animals in their own domain. That included humans.

Not to sound callous, but my four years of Anthropology at the University of Edinburgh had taught me to look at things from a different perspective. I always wondered why I had spent four years at university, but it all became clear on my trip. When things got too tense or too heavy I had the capacity to step back and look at the situation from an anthropological point of view. Please don't get me wrong. I am not being condescending. In fact it was probably the opposite. It was my defence mechanism, my rational, controlled self, saying, "This is amazing, but I am way out of my depth." On these occasions I used whatever cover made me feel more comfortable; I am an anthropologist, no actually I am a film maker, no I'm an

Adventure Motorcyclist (notice the capitals to give the title emphasis and kudos), no I'm raising money for Save the Children, truthfully I am a teacher, actually I am lost and need directions for Addis. It was all of those and more. But it worked for me. What a life!

As I rode the perfect tar road to Addis, surrounded by a cathedral of mountains, I was free to think. That was a powerful aspect of my trip: the freedom to really think. The long periods of nothingness allowed my mind to wander free, and I found it exhilarating, liberating and uplifting. I realised that I was thriving on the challenge and loved the unpredictability of each minute, each day. To many people, a trip like this would be hell on earth. We are all cut from different material. If I was the wrong type of person I might focus on the negatives – the heat, the insects, the dangerous drivers and the other countless obstacles to overcome, including on many occasions the threat of real danger. To many, unpredictability is the ultimate nightmare. Humans tend to thrive on routine and order. I was the opposite. Not all of us ache to ride a rocket or sail the infinite sea. As a species we are curious enough about the world to watch its many facets on TV or to follow and indeed pay for a trip and cheer at the voyager's return. I have always wanted to be the voyager, the explorer – not the watcher.

Humans explore to find a better place to live or acquire a larger territory or make a fortune. But we also explore simply to discover what's there. No other mammal moves around like we do. We jump borders. We push into new territories even when we have resources where we are. Other animals don't do this. Other humans didn't either. Neanderthals were around for hundreds of thousands of years, but they never spread around the world. In just 50,000 years we covered everything. There is a kind of madness to it. Sailing out into the ocean, you have no idea what's on the other side. And now we go to Mars. We never stop. Why? For those trying to figure out what makes humans tick, our urge to explore is irresistible terrain. What gives rise to this 'madness' to explore? What drove us from Africa and on to the moon and beyond? What drove me back to Africa?

If an urge to explore rises in us innately, perhaps its foundation lies within our genome. In fact there is a mutation that pops up frequently in such discussions; a variant of a gene called DRD4, which helps control dopamine, a chemical brain messenger important in learning and reward. Researchers have repeatedly tied the variant, known as DRD4-7R, and carried by roughly 20 percent of all humans, to curiosity and restlessness. Dozens of human studies have found that 7R makes people more likely to take risks; explore new places, ideas, foods, relationships, drugs, or sexual opportunities; and generally embrace movement, change and adventure. Not incidentally, it is also closely associated with ADHD. Although I have always been hyperactive I would draw the line at saying I had ADHD. But if 7R is the so-called explorers' gene or adventure gene then I would like to think that I have it. A restless person may thrive in a changeable environment but wither in a stable one. As I cruised along on cloud nine, I realised that this one sentence summed me up, one of many of my problems.

I came down from cloud nine but the steep ascent I was taking up to Addis was taking me back there. The road became foggy and for the first time on my trip I began to feel cold. Not just cold but freezing. My fingers began to stiffen up and go numb, my teeth started chattering uncontrollably. My face burned from the cold air rushing into my helmet.

With a population of four million Addis is the third highest capital city in the world at 2,400 metres (8,000 feet). Addis was the coldest place I had been in so far on this trip and made me realise why I hated the English climate. Give me thirty five degrees and above every day of my life. I know it's not very fashionable but a vest, shorts and flip flops is the ideal to me. (Not on the bike.) Anyway, I knew exactly where I wanted to go in Addis because I had met an ex-South African mercenary called Lance in Sudan who had recommended cheap accommodation. (He must have been ex, ex, exArmy because he must have been knocking on the door of 63.)

"Check out Wanza Street bru, there's full-on cool places to crash out; the chicks are cool and the dop is cheap. It's a jol. Just tell them you know Lance the South African." I took him at his word and stopped at a street corner where four or five locals were comparing their mobile phones. I stopped and asked them if they knew where Wanza Street was. They all knew and one of them agreed to accompany me on the back of the bike to give directions. His name was Amare and he was dodgy as hell. Before I had a chance to protest he was on the back of the bike. He weighed about two kilogrammes so it was no problem for me, riding wise. Luckily his fingers were much heavier than the rest of him otherwise I might have been robbed. As he directed me to Wanza Street I felt something in my motorbike jacket pocket, a slight change in weight, or something, but it was enough for me to glance down and to my right. Amare quickly withdrew his right hand from my pocket but I got a good enough glimpse to be sure. I held my breath, leant forward over the handle bars and then pulled back quickly, head butting him off the bike. I looked back and saw him roll down the road, get up and stare at me in disbelief. I was glad he was standing. I only wanted him to be mildly stunned. I would have felt guilty otherwise.

I found Wanza Street without too much trouble and checked into a dingy but acceptable room. As I headed out into the street to search out some food I passed a group of Ethiopians waiting at a bus stop. I was horrified to see that the man at the front of the queue had another head growing out of the back of his neck. As I got closer I realised it was a growth of some sort. It was exactly the same size as his head and was splitting open at the base revealing livid red flesh underneath. It looked like a watermelon that had been dropped. It was horrific and I couldn't help thinking that no one should have to live with that.

I turned up towards the Bus Depot and, would you believe it, Carl was walking towards me. All thoughts of food dropped away and we headed off to a small roadside bar to have a beer and catch up. Wanza Street was extremely steep and it was quite difficult to stay upright on our chairs, even before a beer. Carl had also checked into the Wanza Hostel so we could relax for the evening and take in the sights. Fat chance of that happening. Three locals approached and asked if they could sit at the spare chairs on our table. We welcomed them but only had a brief stilted conversation as their English was extremely limited. They did however order a round of drinks, which I thought was generous. When they ordered a second round we accepted but made it clear that it was our last. We mimed out the fact that we were tired and they nodded in understanding. Carl called over the waiter and scribbled on an imaginary pad to show that we would like the bill for the first two beers. He returned promptly and handed Carl a bill for twelve beers and some food. It was the bill for the whole table's beers plus some greasy little snacks our table mates had been enthusiastically gobbling.

"You have made a mistake, we only ordered two beers," Carl stated, gesturing with two fingers (in a polite way, of course). "These guys bought the other beers and the food."

A short conversation ensued in Arabic and the waiter said, "You pay all table."

This was not going to end happily. I knew Carl well enough by now to realise that he had morals and principles, and stuck by them. "There is no way we are paying for them. They bought us the drinks. Bring us the bill for two beers and we will pay," replied Carl.

The waiter raised his voice, "You pay all table, now."

We were both aware that the bill only amounted to a few dollars but it wasn't the point. It was the principle. This seemed like an obvious scam probably involving the waiter. Sit down with foreigners, order loads and then claim a language misunderstanding. I was with Carl all the way. I knew Africans too well. They are exceedingly polite and manners are everything in their society. This was a set-up that the majority of Africans would frown upon. We stuck to our guns and the whole scene degenerated into a shouting match around the table.

"Let's go," I said to Carl as I stood up and offered the waiter enough to cover the two beers.

"Not good enough, you pay all!" he spat, pushing my hand away.

Carl stood up and we started walking down the road. One of the men grabbed Carl by the arm which was not a good move. Carl immediately swatted his arm off.

"Don't touch me," he screamed.

"We call Police," shouted the waiter. They all kicked off at Carl again in Amaric.

I walked off, calling Carl urgently. "Let's get out of here, this is no good. We are going to have big problems."

Carl ignored me and seemed intent on arguing, seemingly oblivious to the fact that they understood not one word of his French or English. I headed down the road and turned the corner in to the Hostel. I waited in the room for about ten minutes with no sign of the mad Canadian. I decided I had to head back out to see if Carl was alright. Thank God I did.

When I turned the corner it was like a scene from the Bruce Lee film *Way of the Dragon.* Carl was playing out the part of Bruce Lee's nemesis, Chuck Norris. He was standing in the middle of the road in Karate stance. He was surrounded by a group of police officers, dressed all in black and wielding batons. As they approached him, one by one, he expertly parried them off, without inflicting any damage. It was highly impressive and I must admit stalled my intervention. Eventually he was overcome by five or six officers but not without a massive struggle. They handcuffed him and threw him into the back of a police pick-up truck. Solitary confinement and bread and water for six months were staring Carl in the face. Time to help. I approached the group with my hands raised, in a placatory gesture. The obvious head cop approached me aggressively shouting in English, "Your friend is crazy-mad, he in big problem trouble."

I saw my opening. "Yes he is mad, a crazy man," I said, spinning my index finger next to my head to denote mental instability. My answer seemed to take him aback slightly and he muttered, "American, no good."

"He is not American, he is crazy Canadian. He needs a doctor to help his head," I said. I whistled and pointed to my head again to re-emphasise Carl's poor mental state.

"Please can I pay for all the drinks and I will take him to a doctor now, before it is too late." He stood in front of me, blocking out the other officers from view and said, "Give me thirty dollars, he can be go free." I knew when to lose the moral high ground and quickly and surreptitiously handed him the money. He turned and barked some orders. Carl was released and we were out of there, quick sharp. Could have been much, much worse. We returned to our rooms and tried to settle down but the adrenaline flow made it difficult to sleep. Eventually the three beers I had consumed won over and I fell asleep, dreaming of Ethiopian prison cells.

The following morning I headed off before daybreak, having said goodbye to The Canadian Karate Expert. My intention was to head to Lake Awassa in Central Ethiopia, camp and then push on to Kenya the following morning. It was 278 kilometres to Awassa and then 490 to the Kenyan border. I made it to Awassa with ease through meandering Great Rift Valley roads. My night was a lot more relaxed without Carl. He needed to calm down slightly or could come to a sticky end. Still, I agreed fully with his stance and knew that we would meet again. I looked forward to it.

Chapter Five
Bandits

'Success is not final, failure is not fatal. It is the courage to continue that counts.' Winston Churchill

'However long the night the dawn will break.' African proverb

I left Awassa, a beautiful town on the shores of Lake Awassa in the Great Rift Valley of Ethiopia, at 5am in the morning to try and make it to Moyale, which is the border post between Ethiopia and Northern Kenya. The morning was perfect, the sky was clear, and the air was as clean as you could ever dream. I knew that the Trans African Highway was in good condition all the way to the border, so was in high spirits and confident of good progress, and another amazing day.

The day didn't start all that well, however, as I had left my motocross boots outside the tent as I slept, and unbeknownst to me, ants had decided to move in and make the boots their new home. I decided to wear my leather boots for the day's ride, so I strapped the motocross boots to my kit bag, behind me, without noticing the trillion or so hitchhikers. I set off and after only a few minutes I started to itch violently. I ended up with ants in my pants, in my helmet, in my jacket and running around in my goggles like lunatics. I'm not talking about standard ants; I'm talking about steroid ants, which almost blocked my view of the road when they ran across my goggles. No wonder they are called Army ants, they certainly looked like they had Army issue boots on. All respect to their commanding officer, as they had managed to sneak up on me from the rear. When they decided to start biting me, it all became a bit much and I came to a sudden stop, jumped off the bike, threw off my jacket and brushed myself down like a lunatic. After dealing with the majority of the invading army with germ warfare (Doom Spray), I eventually made it to Moyale, a total distance of five hundred and seven kilometres. It was pretty good going and a beautiful ride, despite the fact that I was still getting rid of ants from various orifices seven hours later. The route was beautiful and I had the thrill of seeing Duiker, Dik-dik, and a stunning variety of birds, but once again, no people. The closer I got to Moyale the more the landscape changed from rich green, winding mountain passes, to flat-topped Acacia thorn trees, anthills and endless long straight roads with not a soul in sight.

Unfortunately, when I arrived at the border it was too late to enter Kenya so I ended up sitting in a stinking hovel of a room that cost me $2. It reeked of urine as usual, the bed was bought at discount from a medieval torture chamber, and the television just outside my room was on volume 1000 and completely distorted. It seemed like every local outside was drunk, and I kept popping out as I was paranoid that some inebriated guy might try to sit on the bike, and end up crushed beneath it when it toppled over. It was also about 30 degrees centigrade and like most African 'hotels' the portable fan had stopped working many years before and lay in the corner, a mangled, rusted mess. The room was sweltering. There was blood and other substances smeared all over the walls. I felt too shattered to venture out and celebrate New Year, but judging by the sound of the locals and the bullfrogs, they were more than making up for my lack of enthusiasm. It sounded like the local alcoholic was trying out his karaoke skills outside my room, with the population of Kenya cheering him on, but hey, good for them.

I felt ready for the next day, 1 January 2011. I had five hundred kilometres of tough road until I reached Isiolo, but nothing I couldn't deal with, with Co-codamol! I vowed to take it a bit easier as my tyre was even balder than the Pope now. Roll on tomorrow. Before settling down for the night I chased a moth around the room, a majestic fellow, the size of my hand, khaki-coloured, with two black circles on his wings. He reminded me of a WWI aeroplane, but was behaving more like a Kamikaze pilot, as he constantly divebombed and headbutted the flickering strip light in my hovel of a room. I managed to scoop him up in my hands, while he was disorientated from a particularly enthusiastic dive, and released him to the night.

As I returned to the room my mobile rang. I heard from my father that many schools in the UK were studying my progress and had done exhibitions on my trip. I had also been regularly featured in the newspapers. I tried to sound enthusiastic but it all seemed so distant and unreal, and somehow unimportant, but I knew that was a selfish thought and that I had become too focused on my own experiences. It was all too surreal for me, I suppose. I still found it hard to conceive that I was circumnavigating Africa!

The vastness of the landmass, covering more than three million square kilometres (12 million square miles), and the rich and complicated heritage of its indigenous people, with over 1400 languages spoken, are undoubtedly its most treasured assets, and I felt overwhelmingly privileged to be experiencing it. But, it was important to keep my eye on the goals. I must make it all the way round. Save the Children were counting on me, the film crew were counting on me and my family were counting on me. On a selfish and very personal note, there was such a fine line between success and failure. I didn't want to be "the guy who didn't make it around Africa," to my children. Don't ask me why it was so important, I guess it was simply because that was the goal I had set myself.

After a fitful night's sleep, I woke up stuck to my sheet and soaking wet. My ribs were aching and I had difficulty lifting myself off the bed. There was a metal bucket full of murky water in the corner of the room and I tried to shower as best I could. I had difficulty lifting my black vest off, and noticed that I had an angry purple bruise running from my upper back all the way around my side to the edge of my chest. I had no idea how

I got it. I had limited movement but did my best to wash most of my body with the rancid water. I didn't feel very clean but at least it woke me up.

I headed down the dusty road in the semi-darkness, to join the convoy of buses and trucks that was scheduled to leave at 7am, heading to Marsabit, a journey of two hundred and fifty kilometres, into the heart of Kenya. The reason for going in convoy was so that there could be some modicum of security against armed bandits, *shiftas*, who had been targeting vehicles on this stretch of road for many years. The border itself is split between two countries, the larger portion is in Ethiopia (the Oromo region) and the smaller is in Kenya (the Moyale region). There has been a long history of conflict in the area. The Human Right's Commission warned:

'Far from the eyes of the world the forgotten people of Moyale and Marsabit are dying from ethnic violence, local banditry and abuse by the provincial administration and international aggression. Murders, abductions, torture and rape and the disappearance of citizens are common occurrences. Insecurity and humanitarian need in this part of Kenya have reached staggering proportions.'

The road opened up into a mud clearing, the size of four football pitches. This was the Moyale bus station and was already springing into life. Women were busy lighting fires in upturned oil drums and stripping the husks off corns. The cobs were then placed in pyramid-shaped piles, ready to roast on the open fire. A group of children were folding pieces of newspaper into funnel shapes and filling them with peanuts to sell to the waiting crowds. Girls in brightly coloured dresses and matching headscarves wandered around with ceramic bowls on their heads, full of mangoes and bananas. Goats and dogs lay in the mud enjoying the first warm rays of the sun, or milled around picking at all the scraps left over from the previous day.

Young boys shouted their way around, with cell phone scratch credit cards pinned to pieces of cardboard, or with boxes full of small plastic bottles of cheap neon-coloured Chinese soft drinks, that looked as though they would make you glow in the dark if consumed.

A steady stream of less than roadworthy vehicles began collecting in the clearing, lining up one behind the other. At the front of the convoy was a lime green bus with SHUGAR painted in red letters on the side, and a huge Arsenal football logo painted next to it. The cab was decked out with fringed curtains and a sign on the windscreen stated, 'Deluxe Shugar Transport - Stronger, Faster'. It was the smartest of the transport options (except for the bullet holes down one side), and obviously the most popular, as a group of about fifty people were jammed up near the door, negotiating loudly for tickets. Sweating, shirtless men were perched on top of cattle and grain trucks, loading all sorts of produce wrapped in huge black plastic bundles. Mattresses, wardrobes and bicycles were hauled up the side of the trucks, along with live goats, their feet tethered together to stop them struggling, bleating as they were hoisted up the side with ropes.

While watching the convoy getting ready (which I could already see was going to take a long time), I spotted an AK47-wielding security guard standing outside the tiny, tatty Moyale bank. He was looking down at the ground, shuffling his feet in the dust that had collected on the bank step, looking less than alert for a security guard. I approached him to try and get some idea of the safety situation between Moyale and Isiolo, the stretch of unforgiving dirt roads and tiny scattered villages with a reputation for banditry. "Excuse me sir, could you tell me, is it safe to travel to Isiolo or is it still dangerous?"

He replied with a completely straight face, free of irony, "It is completely safe now; no one has been shot for three weeks!"

I replied, "Ah well, that's OK then, cool, no panic, relax, what's the problem, nothing to worry about, have a nice day, thank you Officer." Well, I might not have said that exactly, but I definitely thought about saying it. I love this continent, but it *is* chaos!

To add to the challenge of bandits, I knew from research, and from some previous travellers, what lay ahead. I knew that if one chose, it is possible to travel from Cairo to Cape Town completely on asphalt roads, *except* for this section. Not only is it a dirt road, but apparently it is a test for even advanced riders, if you want to progress at more than 10kms per hour. There is every sort of terrain from sandy stretches, to rock hard corrugations, to loose pebbles, to pile-ups of shingle, to potholes, mud, torrential rain, water-filled crevasses and burst rivers. Everything except snow! I was looking forward to the challenge of the ride, and became increasingly frustrated that the convoy preparation was dragging on so long.

I made my way to the front of the convoy and approached a soldier, who was standing in front of The Shugar Transport Company bus. "Excuse me sir, do you know when the convoy will be leaving?" I asked.

"If God is willing, they will move, in no more than one, two, three hours, maybe two," he replied.

I continued, "Is the road good to Marsabit?"

"Too good, but in the rain, too bad," he said, shaking his head, and furrowing his brow, as he stressed the word 'bad'.

"Does the road go straight to Marsabit, or do you turn anywhere?" I asked.

His reply wasn't too helpful. "You go straight, straight, until you turn." He then said that I should bring my bike up to the front of the convoy. During our discussion, a Land Rover arrived, with two English overlanders in it. They were tall, slim guys from the north of England and were wearing the classic gap year look; both were sporting long bushy beards (the equivalent of the beard for gap year girls being braided hair). I greeted them, but they were not over-friendly and I didn't even catch their names. We had a brief chat about the bandit/road situation and then I wandered to the back of the convoy to retrieve my bike and move up to the 'starting line'. As I returned to the bike, a familiar figure came into view, pushing himself through the crowds, to get to the snaking convoy of vehicles. It was my favourite wandering Canadian traveller/ photographer, Carl, who I had first bumped into in Egypt, then in Sudan, and here he was again, having just arrived on a bus from Ethiopia. After quick greetings, I said, "Carl, the convoy is leaving just now; I saw some English guys, and there are only two of them in the Land Rover. Let's go and see if you can get a lift to Marsabit."

We hurried up the column to their truck and, surprisingly, they were less than enthusiastic, but eventually agreed to give Carl a lift. Some people are strange. Carl went to the back of the vehicle to load up his rucksack, and I followed. "They don't seem very keen, hey," I said, quietly.

Stealing the words out of my head, Carl just shrugged, and replied, "Some people are strange."

I continued, "Look I'll try and keep with you guys, but if we get separated I will meet you in the main street in Marsabit." As we spoke there seemed to be some positive activity; everybody seemed to be loaded up and engines were being started. Suddenly, the policeman I had spoken to earlier waved us on. The three bearded ones headed off first, and I followed. We were off!

I made sure to stay far enough behind, so as not to get choked with the dust from the dirt road. After a couple of minutes I checked behind me. There was not a vehicle to be seen. So much for the armed convoy. I thought it might be sensible to keep the Land Rover in sight, and focused on my riding. There were women walking down the road with huge bundles on their heads, children in tow balancing buckets or water containers on theirs. Men were pushing bicycles, loaded to the maximum, some of them needing two people to steady the wobbling load. I passed a cart, full of petrol canisters, being pulled by a shattered-looking donkey, the owner hitting it frequently and impatiently to keep the momentum going. A sprinkling of huts covered the hillsides and children were playing in the bush and herding cows. After only fifteen minutes, the signs of humanity disappeared completely and we were left in the stunning African wilderness. The road was bad, sticky red mud in areas and teeth-chattering stones in others.

Everything went well until I came round a corner and hit a huge pile of mud and slid off the road. It was a minor accident, executed quite elegantly and in slow motion but I still nearly caught my foot under the pannier. The Land Rover stopped and Carl ran back, filming me as he approached. Through the camera lens he asked, "Are you ok?"

I laughed and said, "Yes I'm fine, but film my boot. My boot was buried in the mud, squashed under the pannier, where my leg could have been. Lucky.

The next prang was a lot more serious. I was riding in the track marks caused by truck tyres, between rows of shingle about eight inches deep. I hit a rock and immediately the handlebars were wrenched from my grasp and the front tyre bounced into the shingle. I immediately went into an out-of-control slide and knew the bike was going down, so I decided to bail off rather than get caught up with the bike. I pushed as hard as I could off the foot pegs and dived sideways, leaving the bike engine screaming as it slid down the road, smashing a pannier off, tearing an indicator off its mounting and bending the handlebars. I hit the road with a thud, landing on my side, and then followed the bike, sliding down the road before coming to a stop, in a cloud of dust. Instantly, I knew I had made an error, when I felt the burning pain across my back. I had forgotten to zip my jacket to my bike trousers and the jacket rode up to my shoulders. I was literally braking with my bare skin on the dirt road. The immediate pain and shock masked a worse injury. As I gathered myself together and fixed up the bike I realised that I was straining to breathe properly. I didn't realise it at the time but it was going to be six weeks of pretty constant painful riding before I would recover. I never did go to the doctor (where was he anyway?) but I had injured myself enough times to know that it was a broken rib, or at least a torn intercostal muscle. Laughing and coughing was to be strictly off the agenda!

The bearded ones were nowhere to be seen, so I continued on, gingerly I must admit. Neither of these accidents was important, but the next comment that Carl was going to make, when I caught up with the Land Rover was going to stick in my head, like glue, for the next seven months. After ten minutes of riding I saw the beard-mobile, parked up on the side of the road. Carl had apparently asked them to wait. He suspected something was wrong, as there was no sign of me, behind them.

I pulled up alongside the truck and said, "Thanks for stopping."

Carl looked at the bike and said, "What happened?"

"I came off again, injured my back and ribs and smashed up the bike a bit," I answered.

Without a hint of malice, Carl said, "You will never make it round Africa."

The comment hit me hard. Maybe it was because it was so direct, so matter of fact, so categorical, and made by someone I liked and respected. Maybe it was because I had some doubts at that point. Whatever the reason, it stung me more than my injuries, and as we continued down the heavily challenging road, the comment went round and round in my head. Those seven simple words, "You will never make it round Africa," uttered as an innocent, throwaway comment, were going to be a powerful motivator for me, for the next seven, eight, God knows how many, months. I felt upset that I had fallen, but I knew that I was where I wanted to be. As if to prove my point I soon made my way into the Marsabit National Park, which was a staggeringly beautiful experience. The majesty of nature quickly wiped my mind clean of any negative thoughts.

The park skirts the massive extinct volcano known as Mount

Marsabit. Here I was, driving through the foothills of rugged grandeur that fan out from its volcanic craters. Though born of volcanic fire, Marsabit is a cool, forested realm that completely took my breath away. As I rode up a rapidly steepening hill, the bike started skidding and slipping on the loose red soil, and I had to ease off and take it steady until I crept my way over the brow of the hill. The view that met me was incredible.

Crater view

On my right-hand side, thirty metres from the roadside, was the edge of a volcanic crater, so steep it dropped into a cloudy abyss. The rim of the crater must have stretched eight or ten kilometres and was completely cloaked in aromatic, moss-encrusted forests. I had to pull off the road, stop, get off the bike, and enjoy this. I took off my helmet, hung it on the handlebars, pulled out my water, took a good couple of swigs, poured some on my face and hair, and walked over to the rim of the crater. I sat on the edge of a rock, my mouth wide in awe at the vastness of this arena, when I heard a vehicle coming over the brow of the hill. It was the bearded ones. I watched them approach, and saw the eagerness on Carl's face in the back window, as he registered the view. They pulled up alongside me and Carl jumped out while the Land Rover was still moving. He skidded to a halt next to me and just said, "Wow! Wow! Wow!", and gave me a big grin and two thumbs up.

I replied, "Can you believe it. How beautiful is that?"

Bearded driver leant out of the window and asked, "Why did you stop here?" Some people!

As we continued on, I thought about a comment I once read, I don't know where, which went something like: "Too often I would hear men boast of the miles covered that day, rarely of what they had seen." Whatever it is, I suspected Carl and I were not going to be long-term friends with the bearded ones. Each to his own, I say. You can't click with everyone.

We eventually made it into Marsabit town, and Carl and I grabbed the first accommodation we came across, Jay Jays on the dirt road coming into Marsabit. It was clean and cheap, so quickly ticked both boxes. It seemed a peaceful town, nestled in a green valley, but I knew that Marsabit had had its problems, to say the least.

The Marsabit region is the eastern province of North Kenya and borders the shores of Lake Turkana. Ethnic clashes in Marsabit have been a common occurrence for years with raids and counter raids between the various communities resulting, in many cases, in death, injury and animal theft. These clashes escalated to what is now termed as the Turbi massacre of 12 July 2005 where ninety people were killed, property destroyed and over 7,500 people displaced. At least sixty eight children were orphaned due to the ethnic clashes. Out of the people that were killed, twenty two were pupils at Turbi primary school. The attack on the helpless children took place as pupils were preparing for morning class. As a result the school was closed down. Problems continue to this day, to be fickle, and it is still a very volatile area, to understate.

Partly due to this area's less-than-excellent reputation, and because I could not sleep because of my ribs, the next morning I headed off (bruised, scraped and indeed, slightly emotionally battered) at 6am to head to Isiolo. Carl, who had been abandoned by the bearded ones, under cover of darkness – no surprise there then – headed down to the bus stop to try and catch a ride to his next destination, also Isiolo. After what was becoming our ritual "goodbye/good luck/have fun, see you at the next place" speeches, we parted ways. I immediately got a puncture, when I hit the metal rim of a derelict bridge only a couple of kilometres outside the town.

As I laid out all my tools onto the red murram road in preparation for the repair, a pair of feet in sandals, made out of the rubber from car tyres, appeared before me and I looked up. Standing there was a young Samburu tribesman. He was wearing a brilliant red wrap and was adorned with long earrings and a variety of beads. He stood with one foot flat against the thigh of his other leg and was clutching a long thin spear.

I immediately rose and extended my hand in greeting which he ignored only to break into a wide grin, while slowly leaning his head forward in greeting. Throughout the fifty minutes it took me to fix the puncture he remained motionless, watching me, only breaking his stance once when I was having difficulty breaking the bead on the tyre. We both jumped up and down on the tyre like two demented rabbits, and I looked up at him, and the landscape, and where I was, and what I was doing and couldn't help smiling. Can this get any better? We eventually succeeded and he returned to his previous pose, not a bead of sweat perceptible on his body while I was soaked to the skin with the effort in the early morning heat. Having sorted the problem I thanked him by offering one of the two litre bottles of ice water I had. The only problem was that I had forgotten to buy the water and also realised I had no food either. He headed off over the hill smiling and waving as I returned to the town to get the supplies I had stupidly overlooked. Superb, army-like planning, it was not. Heading out solo into the wilderness on a treacherous road with no water or food! After stocking up with water, two cans of sardines and some stale bread I set off again. I immediately had two more punctures to deal with and when it came to my third puncture I ran out of patches, glue and spare inner tubes. It was extremely hot and I was not in the best of shape. As well as my ribs, which made riding on dirt corrugations a bit of a nightmare, the scrape on my back was burning from rubbing against my bike jacket and to add insult to injury I now had chafing between my legs from the constant sweating inside my bike trousers. I had to stop and regroup (if that's possible on your own). I pushed the bike to the side of the dirt road, put it on its stand, removed my jacket, unclipped one of the panniers and placed it under an Acacia thorn tree so I could have a small seat, away from the ants and insects that abound in that area. I was truly tired but elated.

I sat down in the shade, took off my riding boots, leant up against the tree and let my mind wander. I thrive on diversity and the more difficult things become the more my senses are heightened and the more alive and worthwhile my life seems. I think that is why this trip suited me so much. But the one thing that I never really predicted was how quickly I would have to adapt to different cultures. The most obvious point is this. If you are going on holiday for a couple of weeks to an unfamiliar country it is possible to adapt to the lifestyle, the customs, the food and the etiquette within a couple of days. But if you are constantly moving over borders then this adaptation becomes a roller coaster of changes, and one handshake and greeting that works in one country is an absolute failure in another.

This may seem glaringly obvious, but it is only when you are moving from one country to another in the space of a day that it becomes so crystal clear. Mistakes will be made but if you stick to the two most important principles universal to mankind, manners and respect, then you cannot go far wrong. The most important thing is to be open-minded about everyone you meet and every circumstance you find yourself in, and look for all the positives of the experience, while ignoring the negatives. Try and live for the moment, soak it up, dealing with the present circumstances, without worrying about your next step. Instead of complaining about a difficult section of road just embrace it as a challenge to be overcome. Instead of panicking at a police road block, take it as an opportunity to practice your humanity skills. Treat each day like a thrill, a privilege, a wonder and unique, because that is exactly what each day is. You will never repeat it.

On a trip of this magnitude it is not only the cultural adaptations that needed to be dealt with, however. The riding conditions are challenging to say the least and it is imperative to maintain concentration throughout the day.

I received an email from a Canadian rider, Pat, who had completed the Paris Dakar rally (the South America version) and was now planning to ride from Cairo to Cape Town in one hundred days. He heard that I had a lot of experience riding in Africa and wanted some advice on the road conditions, and my opinion on whether he could do it in that time period. I replied:

'Dear Pat, I am sure that it is feasible to do it in this time frame, bar visas and breakdowns, but don't you want to see the places you are heading through? I am not the right person to ask as I have never been into speed but please consider the following, if you are going to go fast. On the roads, you will come across sheep, goats, cows, donkeys, pigs, dogs, cats, wild animals, schoolchildren, carts, bicycles, car wrecks, wire, ropes across the road, potholes, swallow holes, burst rivers, landslides, collapsed bridges, cars without lights, closed gates, unmarked roadblocks, lunatic car, truck and moped drivers, all mixed up with rain, lightning, mud, sand, rocks and ruts. Add to this, flat tyres, mechanical and mental breakdowns and you might want to re-consider.'

Pat answered: 'Thanks, I think it may be 180 days I try for.'

As I was cooling down under the thorn tree, congratulating myself on the accuracy of my advice to Pat, a Matatu (a Kenyan Kombi taxi van) came roaring past and I caught a fleeting glimpse of Carl's bearded face squashed against the window. They disappeared out of view, only to return a few minutes later. Carl jumped out and said, "I got them to turn round when I saw you, what's up?"

I explained that I had another puncture and had run out of repair glue. I asked him to take my panniers and rucksack on the top of the Kombi, so I could deal with this tough section of the road just with the bike. We loaded up my gear on the rack and they spun off down the road. I freewheeled down to a village called Logo Logo and stayed the night with a local family who were gunrunning to Somalia.

The next day I fixed the flat and headed off. I went through a couple of tiny market towns including one called Merille. My tyre was still deflating slowly so I pulled in there to see if they could fix a slow leak. They started arguing and hitting each other over who would do the job and how much they would charge. I was tired from the tyre changes, from the tough road and from the injury to my ribs earlier on in this section as well as the extreme heat and just couldn't face this scene unfolding in front of me. I pulled away and carried on. I waved back to all the little children who were greeting me as I made my way out of the village. As soon as I was away from the village I stopped the bike and had another go at fixing the tube. All was successful and I headed off. It started to rain and what started off as a trickle rapidly escalated into a torrent of water. Within five minutes I was struggling to ride, so intensely heavy was the downpour. The lack of visibility was compounded by the fact that my goggles were completely scratched, and more than useless. If I took them off it was impossible to keep my eyes open in the sheeting rain. I chugged along at 30kms per hour, sliding from side to side in the slick red mud. Rivers of rainwater cut gulleys in the road surface, and I kept my feet down, paddling to keep my balance, but I fell often. Lightning flashed around me and the day became darker and darker under the black sky as the thunder rumbled about my head. My bike gear was soaked through and very heavy, and I began to shiver. It was quite a slog and after fifteen minutes I was shaking uncontrollably and starting to lose the feeling in my forearms.

Suddenly, a blue clearing broke in the black sky and within ten minutes I was riding in bright, strong sunshine. It was wonderful and lifted my mood. I felt the warmth of the sun coming through my visor and my gear started to dry off. I started to soak up the scenery; the flat thorny Acacia trees, dripping from the recent downpours, interspersed with gleaming sodden anthills, rainwater running in rivulets through the red soil and coming to rest in shining pools. The beauty and solitude of riding on this red road snaking through the Kenyan landscape made me feel, once again, like the luckiest man on earth. It was amazing, the effect that the weather could have on one's spirits, and mine were soaring. There is something about travelling, especially alone, where you get these flashes of feeling and emotion that seems to re-establish the harmony which once existed between man and the Universe.

Absolutely nothing could have prepared me for what was about to happen. I had no idea that the next thirty seconds were going to be the most important of my life and the next three days were destined to be the most difficult I had ever faced. It was to be an experience that would live with me forever. I came round a sweeping bend in the dirt road, keeping to the left hand edge which was a little bit higher, as the centre of the road was still waterlogged and difficult to negotiate. On the right-hand side of the road was a small hill with the scar of a footpath running up its centre. The path caught my eye and I followed its route up the hill. At the top of the hill, standing under the shade of a tree were three men. I was surprised that there was anyone out here, as I had not seen any sign of villages for a long while. I quickly raised my right hand off the accelerator and gave them a wave. Instantaneously, one of the men swung his right arm up from his side, and before I even realised it was a machine gun, he fired. I heard nothing, but within a split second the back of the bike bucked away from me, slipped sideways and I was off. As soon as I hit the mud and slid a short distance, I was up. I knew exactly what had happened. I was so shocked I went into what only can be described as auto pilot: instant survival mode, surprising myself actually. I scrambled to the bike, picked it up faster than I had ever done in my life, slid on to the seat, pulled in the clutch, and pressed the electric start in one manic but fluid motion. The bike started immediately, I kicked the gear aggressively into first and was off.

Only then did I glance back over my shoulder to see the men, running towards me at high speed. I turned immediately back to the road and concentrated on keeping the bike upright, while keeping my body low, accelerating and fish tailing as the tyre tried to find traction on the slippery surface. I waited to be shot in the back. I knew it was coming. There was no way he would shoot me off the bike and then not follow it up. He meant to kill me: there was no doubt about that. I looked up and the next bend in the road was an impossible fifty metres away. The bike felt strange, heavy and uncontrollable. That was it then, I was done for. I gritted my teeth, stopped breathing and just rode. I was suddenly aware that I was rounding the corner and incredibly, would soon be out of sight! Nothing had happened. Where were they? I kept riding, I couldn't believe it. Where were they? I kept moving until I had covered a couple of kilometres before I dared look back. An empty road, this is unbelievable! I rode for another five minutes. The last thing I wanted to do was to stop, even though it was obvious that the bike was badly damaged. I drove straight off the main dirt road, continued into the bush for a hundred metres and fell off the bike. My hip hit the dirt first, directly onto a stone, which made me grimace, and I came to rest behind a small group of trees and shoulder-high scrub. I lay there for a minute, then slowly removed my helmet and placed it next to me on a small pile of thorn twigs, which kept it out of the mud, and gave me some 'illusion' of orderly thinking in this insane situation. I tried to control my breathing. I looked all around me to see if I could be seen from the road, and if there was anyone about. All seemed safe for the moment, and I took a deep breath, turned my neck, rubbed an itch on my shoulder with my chin, and there in front of me was a tortoise, ambling past. He looked very relaxed and calm and had a fixed grin on him as he sauntered his way through the savannah. I said, "Hello tortoise, how's it going? You look pretty chilled out." I couldn't really decipher his reply but definitely noticed that he turned his head, and possibly winked in encouragement, before lifting his leg shakily and making his next step towards home. I think we connected. Well, he cheered me up a bit, anyway. Right, time to pull myself together.

I immediately turned my attention to the bike. It didn't take a second to assess the damage. The aluminium brake callipers had been shot away and all that remained was the cable. The tyre was completely shredded and I had been riding on the metal rim. There were at least ten broken spokes and a bullet hole in the swing arm about 30 centimetres from where my leg was positioned when I was shot at. The mounting for the pannier was also smashed and I had added another broken indicator to add to my sick bike's ailments. This was the least of my worries. I was alive! I also didn't feel any pain despite falling directly on to my already injured ribs so decided I had to get further away while I still felt strong physically, even though I was definitely not mentally.

I made my way to the main road and quietly peered out in both directions to see if all was clear. It was. My heart was thumping and I was feeling nauseous and slightly dizzy. I started the bike and made my way onto the road. I set off, but it immediately became obvious that there was no way I was going to ride more than five kilometres an hour. For some reason the wheel was buckled and was dragging to the right making it almost impossible to keep in a straight line. My progress was agonisingly slow and I slipped and fell my way through forty torturous kilometres in over six hours. I knew in my heart that even this snail's pace was going to come to a halt sooner or later. The bike was taking a beating, and I could hear the remaining spokes pinging as they broke. I have no idea what I was thinking about during this time. All I was aware of was a strong desire to get as far away from the shooting as possible and to find someone to tell. I really needed to speak to someone. I felt very, very alone.

As it started to get dark and the bike became more difficult to ride, and with no settlements in sight, I had no choice but to find somewhere to sleep for the night. I knew that night time in central Africa always takes you by surprise, as if someone turned out the light. All people who visit Africa comment on how quickly the sun sets.

Luckily, I quickly found a small depression behind a termite mound which was large enough to obscure myself and the bike from view. I put a rock under the bike side stand, so it wouldn't sink in the mud and crush me while I slept. That certainly would add insult to injury!

I settled down on the mud next to the bike, feeling physically shattered but mentally I was spinning and couldn't switch off. Everything started to sink in and my brain went into overdrive. I knew I was not going to be able to sleep. Weather factors made doubly sure of that, as within fifteen minutes it started to rain heavily. Although I was underneath an Acacia thorn tree, it provided very little in the way of shelter. I had no choice but to sit there, soaking wet. I had given Carl everything I needed now; my tent, sleeping bag, food and water. Well, at least I wouldn't be short of the last one.

As the night progressed it became colder and colder, and the nine hours I spent there felt like fifty. I wrapped myself up in a ball and put my head inside my jacket using my breath to warm up my chest. It rained all night. Africa can get very cold, especially when you are wet, alone, stressed, injured, without shelter and have just survived a shooting at the hands of Kenyan bandits; trust me on that one.

As soon as there was the first glimmer of light, enough to see the road ahead, I jumped on the bike, shivering uncontrollably, and was off again, happy to be doing something constructive. Unfortunately, the bike was very ill by now and I could only ride at a walking pace, paddling with my feet to stop the bike slipping over. After ten painful kilometres all the spokes finally snapped, the chain came off and the wheel lurched to the left side and came to rest twisted under the bike.

I slid into the mud and lay there for a few seconds. My ribs were aching badly now, making breathing a concentrated effort and I had grazes on my back and shoulder, both of which were becoming raw from the friction with the wet, heavy bike gear. I was also starving, which was a small thing, really. I quickly snapped out of this 'feeling sorry for myself mood' as it would achieve absolutely nothing. At least there was no danger of laughing, which would have hurt my ribs even more. Keep going, make a plan. I felt like crying actually, but didn't. Right, nothing for it but to walk.

I dragged the bike to the edge of the road and left it there. I walked on as quickly as my ribs would allow me and, thank God, after only an hour's painful trudge I rounded a corner and came across a wooden bridge spanning a river.

I made my way onto the bridge and there, spread out on the rocks, on the river's edge was an array of colourful clothes, drying in the sun. People! Fifty metres down on the opposite bank was a woman in a bright purple headscarf, squatting over the water's edge, rubbing a garment vigorously in the shallow water. I was so happy to see someone, I shouted out to her, a little desperately, I suspect. She could tell that I was highly distressed and pointed me up the road. Apparently I was just outside a village.

I rounded the next corner, passing through a canopy of bamboo hanging over the road, where a digger driver, in blue overalls and covered in grease and sweat, was fixing some engine parts in the mud next to his stricken JCB. I gave him a breathless, garbled explanation of what had happened to me. Titus put his hand on my shoulder and said, "I am very sorry my friend, this road is full of many bad men."

He explained that he was working for the Chinese road construction company, Wu-Hi, who were building the new tar road, and that all the road workers carried guns because of bandits. Apart from all the obvious economic benefits of a good road network, Titus said, "The new road will stop bandits one hundred percent, even more than one hundred percent. The bad people don't stop fast-fast transport." A bit late to help me, but a good idea indeed.

He also made it very clear that I was 'a very mad Mzungu' for travelling alone. I couldn't argue with that one. Pointing up the road, he told me that there was a Catholic Mission up on the left, past the primary school and that he would take me there. He said that the priest would help me out.

We headed up there and Titus rapped on the wooden door which was adorned with a tacky-looking statue of Jesus on the Cross. It had been spray- painted gold, obviously in situ, judging by the streaks of gold paint on the door. This was immediately opened, and we were greeted by an elderly, portly German priest with a biker's style goatee, and a warm open face. He had bandages on both arms from his wrists to his elbows, and a hacking cough that suggested he would fall down dead any minute.

He invited us in, closed the door, and offered me a seat in a small, sparse kitchen. I slumped down in the plastic chair he motioned me to, put my elbows on the blue and white chequered plastic cloth that covered the wooden table, and fell apart. I think it was because I was in a building, an enclosed space, with people I trusted. I finally realised that I was safe and the tears began to well in my eyes. I put my forehead on the wooden table, hid my face in my hands and tried not to crack up. I struggled to tell them what had happened, but I think they understood immediately that I was traumatised, and they did not interrupt me once, or try to push me for details. The School Matron made me a cup of tea and gave me some porridge on a pink plastic plate. Her name was 'Beryl in the blue and white plastic apron with the huge smile', and she radiated concern and optimism, at the same time, if you see what I mean. Every time I came to a problematic part of the story she went, "Eee-shee! that is toooo bad, these pee-pool are no good!" while shaking her hand in the air. If I came to a more positive part of the story, like escaping the bandits, she would howl, "Owww-oooo! God is on your side, for sure!" Beryl had such a positive effect on me that I began to calm down.

Unbeknownst to me, however, during our conversation either the priest called the police, or one of the villagers, and they turned up at the Mission along with two army trucks. It was the last thing I really wanted. My intention was to try and organise a truck, get the bike on it and get to Nairobi for repairs. I wanted to be busy, constructive and progressive and put this incident behind me as soon as I could.

That was my psychological defence mechanism. Just get moving again. That was not going to happen now. I looked out of the window. The soldiers were filing out of the truck like some demented swat team, in front of the crowd that had now assembled. As they jumped out of the rear of the vehicle, they proceeded to fall over like dominoes into the muddy road. It was obvious that they were roaring drunk. They insisted that we drive back the 40kms to "find the guilty ones". I couldn't believe it; it was two days ago on a hill in the middle of nowhere. I really didn't expect the gunman to be standing there on the hill shouting and waving, "It's me! I shot the guy on the motorbike!" but realised it would be more problematic to say no to the soldiers, as they were obviously making a show of

179

helping me, and I didn't want to offend them by ruining their little exercise in the bush.

It goes without saying that the whole operation was pointless, as they wandered around aimlessly, crouching in the bush like some sort of low budget war film, whilst lurching forward every now and then when they lost their inebriated balance. They eventually gave up after forty minutes with the leader declaring categorically and quite obviously, "They are gone!" We headed back, but not without first sparing me a guided tour on the way back of different locations where people had been attacked. They stopped at a crude, white wooden cross stuck in the sand at the side of the road, and told me this was the site where a Chinese road surveyor had been shot in the head three weeks earlier. They seemed to love the whole saga. I disliked them all at that point. I know that they were only trying to help but to them it was a joke. They kept saying "Mzungu, Mzungu" and making machine gun noises. I just wanted to be away from them. It was too recent and too raw for me to be joking about yet. But I still had to make the official police report so after picking up the bike, the army dropped me back in the village. Getting my hands on a police report was going to prove to be a hilarious and protracted affair but it lifted my spirits greatly.

I was led down a dirt path, through the brush by two young boys, following a slippery track running next to a small stream, and then through a small banana plantation until the trees cleared into a swept, open courtyard. In the centre of the clearing was a small mud hut, with a thatched roof and a small broken window. There was a black and white rusty bicycle leaning against the hut, behind which sat a small black mongrel making a concerted effort to eat his own foot.

Titus knocked on the door and went in, sticking his head back out a few seconds later to usher me in. I bent my head down to get under the door, and after my eyes had adapted to the dark, I made out a police officer sitting behind a rickety desk, tapping a pen on the surface. Chief Inspector Obama (not President yet), the head of the Logo Logo District Police, stood up and gave me a warm handshake, while offering me a chair. He was a tall, angular man whose stern face and business-like manner, I quickly realised, belied his gentle nature. He offered me a cup of tea, and gave me a dry police T-shirt to replace my sodden bike jacket. I felt myself welling up again. What the hell was wrong with me? I thought I was supposed to be a hard core motorcycle adventurer!

Before getting down to the official business of the police report, Chief Inspector Obama explained the situation in this part of Kenya. He was very apologetic about what had happened to me and hoped that, "this event does not remove your pleasure of Kenya." He was very proud of Kenya and his face lit up when he spoke of his village, twenty kilometres south of here. I liked his enthusiasm for his country and I liked *him* a great deal. Apparently, however, the northern part of Kenya was a serious problem. (I was beginning to suspect as much.) It seemed that it was a hotbed of Boran Shiftas, bandits who move around the vast empty areas between the northern border of Kenya and the town of Isiolo, eighty kilometres south of where we were now. Added to this, there were apparently Somali training camps spilling in to Kenya, and frequent violent clashes with the Kenyan Defence Force. The remote villages dotted around the five hundred kilometre stretch were also involved in long-standing ethnic clashes. Their hobby was to undertake cattle and goat-rustling raids into their neighbour's village. This inevitably led to shoot-outs, as this area of Kenya has the highest ratio of guns in the country, which were apparently spilling in from war-torn Somalia.

"Furthermore," explained the Chief Inspector, "this road from Moyale is the worst in Kenya and, I have heard, maybe the worst in the world. In the rains it is only mud, and in the dry season it is just too bad. Very bumpy and many, many holes. Cars and trucks can go only slowly for all the year so it is easy for Shiftas to attack. I think, more than four hundred have died in this area last year."

Whether he was exaggerating about the road and the number of people killed, I don't know, but I do know I felt very relieved, lucky and elated to be alive. I asked him, "Do you think that they knew I was coming?"

He replied immediately: "No, if they had known by cell phone, they would wait in the road. It was just too unlucky. They see you, and maybe think, Mzungu, alone, and maybe some dollars."

I queried, "But why would they shoot me off the bike and then not shoot me when I was riding away. They were very close by then?"

He said, "I think he finish the bullets, guns are cheap but bullets are expensive." I leant back on the chair, put my hands behind my head, wincing from my rib injury, and let out a long sigh. I think I had had, what you could proverbially call, a very close shave.

Chief Inspector Obama got up and came over to me, surprising me with a sudden loud laugh, as he patted me hard on the back. He then asked me a question that I would be asked many, many times again during this expedition: "You are lucky man, but why do you do this? White men are crazy. Where is your wife and children, your family? You are a strong man, but why must you do this?"

I laughed, but had no answer for him, as I didn't have one for myself either.

Luckily he needed no reply as he continued, "I am happy to meet you, but you are crazy; now we make the report."

Chief Inspector Obama wrote more slowly than anyone I have ever met, ever, in my life. This was not because he struggled with the English, because he didn't, it was because he just wrote more slowly than anyone on earth. It was almost impossible to see the pen moving and was quite fascinating to watch. After an hour it became less fascinating, and I started following the paths of the cockroaches around the walls, until they disappeared into the thatch roof. After about eleven hours, no I exaggerate slightly, maybe two, he finally said the words I was hoping to hear. "It is finished." I sighed quietly with relief and thanked him for his time.

"Now I will read it to you," he said enthusiastically.

"Of course, no problem," I replied, slightly less enthusiastically than him, I must admit. He proceeded to read the statement out loud, slightly faster than his writing, thankfully. Once he had finished he handed it to me and said, "Read it, to check." I said it wasn't necessary as I trusted him, but he insisted. I was finding the whole rigmarole quite hysterical, but managed to stifle it, as I did not want to offend someone who had been so helpful and friendly. Credit where credit is due. It was the neatest report I had ever seen in my life, by far, ever.

My next mission in the village was to arrange a truck to transport me and my battered bike to Isiolo where I hoped Carl and everything I owned would be waiting for me. Chief Inspector Speedy Writing Obama informed me that George, the head fixer of the village, had told him that I couldn't catch a truck tonight, because the driver was too drunk to walk, let alone drive, but that he could leave tomorrow for Isiolo, where I may be able to get help with the bike. I heartily agreed that this was the right decision. Although I was pleased that this had been organised, in the back of my mind I knew that once the bike was fixed I would have to return here, where I left off, to continue my circumnavigation. It suddenly dawned on me that not for one second during the last two days had I entertained the idea of giving up. All my focus was on the next stage. I was pleased with myself, my frame of mind, and on top of that, every kilometre I covered also meant more money raised for Save the Children. Why let the small matter of a shooting scupper my plans. In fact, I realised that I was more determined than ever to cover the fifty thousand kilometres plus, and soak up all the challenges, experiences and wonders that thirty four African countries would throw at me. I had met so many incredible people already. The experience of getting to know someone like Sami Osman, the Scottish Libyan tour guide, or Ashraf, the magnificent felluca boat captain in Egypt, or Carl, the donkey riding, Jesus look-alike Canadian photographer in Sudan, to name just a few, far outweighed the negative experience of being shot at by a bullet-scarce, bandit idiot!

I went to sleep in a small hut George the fixer had organised for me, staring at the beautiful clear blue sky through the open door, listening to the crickets, feeling shattered but somehow elated. What was next? What incredible view, what interesting person, what amazing life story was around the corner?

The next day I felt buoyant and ecstatic to be alive and it was with patience and humility that I waited the three hours until the truck was loaded and ready to go. The journey to Isiolo was spent on the top of a bumpy truck, balanced on a five-inch-thick steel girder. My posterior was completely numb and for three hours I felt nothing from the waist down. The only time this changed was when we hit particularly vicious pot holes and I was jettisoned a foot in the air. Upon landing I tried to cushion the fall with my bum cheeks. It was not entirely successful as I had lost a lot of weight. My coccyx and spine were jolted beyond happy. I was partially disabled and bent in two when we hit the outskirts of Isiolo.

My torture was interrupted by a group of children running next to the truck shouting up to me excitedly, "Jesus is waiting for you, Jesus is waiting for you, you come quickly, Jesus is here." They followed the truck for over a kilometre until we pulled into a dusty, noisy taxi rank and parked up. I jumped down into the dust like a sprightly 200-year-old and was immediately surrounded by children grabbing my arm and pulling me down a side road. As I began protesting I looked down the dusty road and could just make out a vision. It was Jesus walking towards me, except he was wearing Timberland sandals, grey shorts and a moth-eaten grey T-shirt. Carl! I had never felt so happy to see someone in my life. He ran up and gave me a massive hug. "I thought you were dead."

I felt a lump rising in my throat and struggled not to cry. I couldn't really speak and mumbled, "Let's get the bike off the truck and get organised. Where are you staying?"

"Just around the corner, but what happened to you?"

"Let's get away from these crowds and we can talk." I was struggling to hold it together. I organised the payment to the truck driver and a group of about fifteen helped us manhandle the bike into a courtyard where Carl had a room booked. Once we got into Carl's room, I collapsed onto the bed and started crying. With impeccable timing Carl pulled two ice-cold beers from somewhere and handed me one. At the same time he put his arm around my shoulder and said, "Man, it's good to see you, I have heard so many stories, I didn't know what to believe." I told him the whole story and it was incredibly cathartic. He listened quietly, nodding at the right times like a top class shrink. When I had finished he filled me in on his experiences over the last two days.

"I came here on the Kombi van and waited in the main street for you to arrive. When it was getting dark I started asking the cars coming in if they had seen a big white guy on a motorbike. A taxi driver told me that you had been shot in Merille. I didn't want to believe it so stayed all night on the pavement looking for news. It was terrible. I heard that you were dead, then, no you were alive, but naked on the side of the road, having been beaten and had everything stolen. I heard so many stories but by the second day was beginning to lose hope that you were alive. I was planning on dropping all your things in Nairobi and contacting your father with the terrible news. I didn't want to leave but my girlfriend is arriving in Zanzibar tomorrow morning. I am so sorry, but I had no choice."

"Don't be absurd Carl. I can't believe you waited this long. Thank you so much." We hugged again, then settled down on our mattresses. I looked up at the white ceiling and fatigue began to envelop me. My head began to swim. As soon as my emotions take over I try to block them in the best possible way, by planning. I blocked out the last two days by focussing on my next move; how to get to Nairobi, find a workshop to rent and fix the bike. I tried to ignore my aching ribs and traumatised thought patterns and eventually fell asleep.

The next day we set about finding a truck to Nairobi. Isiolo was like a one-horse cowboy town without the horse or cowboys. Really it was a one-goat African town but it did have the tumbleweed rolling down the dusty main street. The people of Isiolo were helpful and friendly but very odd-looking. Many of them were extremely thin and hyperactive, with green teeth and saucer-sized eyes. This was all down to Chat, the flowering plant with amphetamine-type effects that I had come across regularly from Sudan onwards. It seemed like Isiolo was the centre of Chat as most of the male inhabitants would have put a cow to shame with their chewing habits.

A flash flood suddenly hit the town as we headed into the centre and Isiolo quickly became a river of mud and litter. A group of green teeths tried to push and pull my bike on to the top of a bus but it was destined to failure. They were sliding around in the torrential mud-covered street with no inkling of teamwork. They were all buzzing in their own little worlds. Even if they had co-ordinated their movements, the piece of cotton they were trying to lift the bike with did not have a hope in hell. After much gesticulating and the odd lashing out they gave up. Luckily a less-Chat-affected truck driver came past and offered us a lift to Nai-robbery, sorry, Nairobi. We leapt aboard and were off. I had counted my chickens too soon. The driver was high on Chat and after two hours of chewing like a camel he began negotiating corners on two wheels, giggling manically. We hung on for dear life and miraculously made it to Nairobi. The next three weeks were spent repairing the bike, my ribs and my confidence before I headed off to Tanzania.

Tanzania

Tanzania was another trip altogether. I know Africa. I know what to expect and I am rarely surprised. I am not bragging, just stating a fact. My pleasure and excitement in Tanzania was mainly lived through the reactions of Shaun, the director from Diesel Films. It often takes a visitor to the place you love to make you realise how mind-blowing it really is. Things that you take for granted are suddenly pointed out by a complete stranger and you have the privilege of living the thrill again, through them. In a cynical way, I was intent on Shaun going through the same experiences that I had, no matter how harsh. To that end I was determined that he would not live his experience safely, from the comfort of a plush hotel room. Luckily he was open to my suggestion that he experienced what I did and stayed where I stayed. I had no need to worry that the trip would be an anti-climax; it was more radical than even I could have hoped for. The agenda for Tanzania was to capture some seriously beautiful footage and to film a seriously corny second advert for the laser eye surgery company whose name I refuse to mention. We managed both, spectacularly successfully, but not without some dramatic interruptions.

I met Shaun in Arusha, like many African cities a weird combination of the modern, the archaic and the traditional. Accommodation had been sorted before Shaun's arrival through a New Zealand overland truck driver called Mark. He was based at a workshop in Arusha that looked and felt a lot like a maximum security prison. The route to the site was set off one of the main Arusha streets but quickly degenerated into a rutted dirt track. There were local bars and street restaurants that were shabby but atmospheric. It didn't bother me at all but Shaun felt uncomfortable. The entrance to the truck stop was a twenty-foot high wall surrounded by barbed wire and exploding concealed mines (made up the last bit). It was highly intimidating. Colditz security step aside. The entrance was not one, but two steel gates that looked as though they could survive a tank attack. Once inside the compound we were met by a number of rabid, steroid dogs who made it clear that they would tear you into pieces if you misbehaved. There were all the classic, clichéd, tough dogs; Dobermans, Alsatians, Rottweilers, Pitt Bulls and Boerbols. I loved them all and they loved me. Dogs can immediately suss out dog lovers. When we arrived Mark was busy re-spraying one of the trucks, so pointed out our accommodation and went back to work. (A no-nonsense, hard-working Kiwi.) Shaun seemed fairly surprised that we were sleeping in a metal shipping container but took it in good humour. Mark told us that the dogs could stay with us to counter burglars and terrorism. Only an Israeli SWAT team could make it over the defences but it was great to have the dogs around. We settled down in our container but not before noticing that our roommates were rats, as large as the largest rats in Large Town.

As we lay there in the dark, I could feel Shaun's tension, and truth be told, I wanted to laugh out loud, but held it together. These things never bothered me. Nor did the fact that it was like sitting in an oven. What did bother me was when we woke in the morning, one of the dogs had eaten one of my motorcycle boots. I couldn't blame him, or her (let's not be sexist). If you are a dog, the combination of high quality Italian leather and a cheesy odour must be an irresistible snack. I waited to see if any of the steroid dogs burped up a sturdy boot sole, but it was not to be. Our plan, after our peaceful, siege-mentality evening, was to head towards the Ngorogoro Crater. What beautiful names African places have; a bit like Pratts Bottom, Effingham and Cockfosters, to name a few of the romantic places I live near in the UK.

Before the crater, we were heading to the plains below Mount Kilimanjaro to film the second advert for the laser eye surgery company that I won't mention by name (cue: spit on the ground like Clint Eastwood). Whereas the Egyptian advert was based on the classic Egyptian scene of the Nile with sand dunes and camels, this advert would be the classic East Africa scene; Kilimanjaro, Acacia thorn trees and wildlife. During the drive to the location, past the smaller but no less impressive Mt. Meru, Africa threw one of its massive shocks at us. Shaun decided to film me from the back of the truck that Not-So-Tall-Kiwi-Mark had kindly agreed to drive. I positioned myself about twenty metres behind while Shaun took up position with his HD hand-held camera. Just as we were preparing to shoot, a battered black Mazda hatchback came racing up behind us and Shaun waved to me, indicating that it was 'no go' for a while.

Without hesitating, the car swerved past us on the asphalt road and sped on. No sooner had he overtaken us when the smooth tar road changed into a rutted, stony dirt surface. In full view of us all and to our absolute horror, the driver began to lose control on the loose surface. The back end of the car started fishtailing at over one hundred kilometres an hour. I knew instantly that there wasn't a hope in hell of him recovering. The car slid violently sideways and flipped over into a vicious roll. It must have rolled five or six times before it hit a mud bank on the fringes of the road. There was no stopping it and the impact changed the trajectory. The Mazda flipped up onto its front and started rolling over end to end. During the first flip, the instant it hit the mud bank, a young woman flew out of the window, somersaulting through the air and landed like a rag doll in the bush. The car continued on its aggressive assault, flipping over two more times before settling on its side in the dust. It was a complete wreck from every angle. The roof was crushed, the lights were ripped out and smashed, and both sides were dented beyond recognition. A snapped-off door lay against a thorny tree and a wheel disappeared into the distance. It was the most horrific crash I have ever seen, and I have seen a fair few in my twenty years of living in Africa. I knew that they would both be dead. My immediate reaction was to tell Shaun and Mark to wait by the truck and I would go and check out the situation.

As I approached, expecting the worst, I was flabbergasted to find that both were alive. The woman had a nasty, livid gash on her forehead and her clothes were torn to shreds. Miraculously, she was sitting up and seemed fairly coherent. Even more shocking was the driver. He was sitting in the mangled wreck crushed in around him, but was on his mobile phone! It was absolutely incredible. He was acting as though he had just suffered a puncture. I realised that in both cases they could be suffering from shock and that it was distinctly possible that they had serious internal injuries. As I was formulating a plan to help the young man out of the wreck a bus pulled up and people began pouring out to help. At this point I took the easy way out. I am a little ashamed to admit it but I decided to retreat and leave it to the fifty people or so who were thronging around.

I rushed back to the truck and said, "You won't believe this guys, but both of them are alive. Let's get out of here." Neither of them argued but we were all shell-shocked and we abandoned filming and carried on towards Kilimanjaro, lost in our thoughts. Violence in any form, whether mechanical or manmade, takes some time to recover from. Although I didn't know the victims I hoped that they would recover fully. After all, everybody has parents or children that would be affected by any tragedy.

The sombre mood continued until we arrived at the stunningly beautiful scene of the advert. Everything went like clockwork. The lighting was perfect, the scenery as magnificent as one could imagine and, as if things couldn't get any better, a dazzle of zebra ran straight through camera shot. (Yes, that is the wonderful term you use for a group of the stripey beasts.) All was perfect apart from my mumbling and insincere attempts to say, "Wearing glasses and lenses really held me back. But now, thanks to laser eye surgery I can take on the biggest challenge of my life. Just go for it, don't let poor vision hold you back." It was the weakest script I had ever come across. The marketing manager of the laser eye surgery company I was representing (cue: spit on the ground) should be shot. Or at the least, ridiculed to death. Just like I have been by my friends. If I have to hear "Just go for it Spencer," once more, in answer to one of my questions, I might become mildly violent. It took me about a thousand takes to get the advert right, between bouts of hysterical laughter. Actually, I lie. In fact I got worse and worse and ended up sounding as wooden as Arnold Schwarzenegger saying, "Back to the chopper." I think Shaun had eventually given up when he said, "That's great, it's a wrap." He didn't say that but it sounds professional. Mark, who was holding the light reflector (I don't know the correct term), was also creasing up. Superb fun.

Our next destination was the Ngorogoro Crater, the most spectacular and surreal wildlife spot on earth. The crater is a World Heritage site and for good reason. It was formed three million years ago when a huge volcano collapsed in on itself. It is now the world's largest, inactive, intact and unfilled volcanic caldera in the world. It is truly spectacular and must be one of the places where the term breathtaking was coined. The sides are 600 metres high and the ground area inside the crater is a staggering 260 kilometres square. The amazing thing about the crater is that it is a unique, almost isolated habitat containing over 25,000 large animals. A side effect of the crater's steep walls is that, in effect, it is a giant enclosure where few animals come in or out. This leads to significant inbreeding as very few new bloodlines enter the ecosystem.

It is a truly unique place and our journey into it was made all the more spectacular due to the fact that we were allowed in before any other visitors, at five thirty in the morning. Unfortunately I was not allowed to take the bike, as I would be eaten by a lion. It was too good an opportunity to miss so I jumped into the truck and we began our descent. The early morning mist swirled around the base of the crater giving the impression of a totally prehistoric almost alien scene. Over the next half hour the sun slowly burned its way through the mist. It was like the curtain rising on the most spectacular animal show imaginable.

During one incredible hour we saw hippo, elephant, hook-lipped black rhino, wildebeest, zebra, eland, oribi, wild dog and warthog, to name just a few. Coming to a small gorge with a river running through it, Shaun decided he wanted a shot of me driving the Land Rover through the water. He jumped out of the truck and positioned himself on the other side of the gorge. As I waited for the thumbs up I spotted a flickering ear in the undergrowth about a hundred metres from Shaun. To my horror I realised that it was a lion. There was little I could do so I decided to just leave it and follow through with the shot. After picking up Shaun on the other side I pointed out the lion and he went whiter than a white man painted white. And not without cause as almost immediately the lioness leapt from the bush in a full-out hunting charge. Still, we were all alive and headed off to our campsite for a braai (barbecue). I cooked up a pretty decent meal and as darkness took over we sat around having a cold beer. Unbelievably, a huge bull elephant strolled into the campsite and lumbered past us, almost within touching distance. It was a superb bonus to the end of the day. We slept well and the next morning it was time for me to say goodbye and head off on my own once more. Malawi, here I come.

Chapter Six
Where the Malawi Are We?

'If you wish to travel, travel light; unpack all your envies, jealousies, unforgiveness, selfishness and fears.' Glenn Clark

I would rather wake up in the middle of nowhere than in any city on earth.' Steve McQueen

Malawi was one of the few countries that I visited that is landlocked. It was not a massive detour from my planned route and I had heard so much about the beauty of Malawi that I had to see it. I was not to be disappointed. As I entered through the northern territory, with its capital Mzuzu, I was met by steep, winding mountain roads with lush tropical vegetation. The road surface was almost pristine asphalt (the Chinese?) so my concentration levels could ease off slightly. I could soak up the beauty of the mountain sides, dotted with picture-perfect homesteads, nestled in verdant green, thick vegetation. This was interspersed with palm groves, bubbling rivers and mini waterfalls. The road swung eastwards and far below me, glimmering on the horizon, I could just make out the shimmering shape of the Lake of Stars – Lake Malawi. The weather was perfect and as the altitude dropped it became warmer and warmer. I was thrilled to be heading down to the shores of this famous lake, one that I had heard so much about.

As is my habit, when emotionally buoyant, I began singing Bob Marley at the top of my voice. I was ripped from my reverie by a sudden, intensely loud bang and a ripping and grinding of metal. I immediately lost control and started careering across the road, towards the steep cliff edge on my left. I booted the gears downward, pulled on the front brake, then the back, and slid sideways. The back wheel bucked outwards and upwards and before I could do anything the bike was sliding down the road on its side. I was following hot on its heels and knew it would be instant mortality if I went over the edge. The incredible thing about this split second accident was that I actually had time to think, 'Have I just been bloody shot at again?' as I was sliding to my doom. Fortunately, the foot peg clipped a pot hole, the handlebar flipped sideways and became embedded in the road surface. The bike came to a halt and I slid into the fuel tank with my boot and then my knee cap. It was instantly painful but I was overwhelmed with relief that we had come to a stop. I jumped up and instantly hopped as my right knee gave way. I looked around for any sign of people with sub-machine guns; nothing, so I flopped down next to the bike wheel, gripping my throbbing knee. I glanced down to my right and noticed the chain had snapped and had wrapped itself around the rear wheel rim. So that's what the bang and grinding of metal was. I could not believe my accident was so mild and my injuries so superficial. In thirty years of riding I have never broken a chain and it was one of my biggest fears.

When travelling at high speed I had often envisioned the chain snapping, flying through the air and ripping my leg or head off. Ok, I know the chances are slim, but it is possible. I sat there and tried to calm my breathing. I pulled off my bike trousers where I lay, and examined my knee. There was a scratch as small as a mosquito bite. Thank God for my padding. I couldn't put any weight on my leg so it was with extreme difficulty that I managed to lift the bike upright. I spent the next forty minutes repairing the chain lying down on the tarmac. Once done I had to hop around to the left side of the bike and try to get on. It took me three or four attempts because my leg refused to bend. Once on the bike, with my leg finally bent, my knee decided that it would produce its own heart beat and it was quite a struggle not to faint. I wouldn't like to be kneecapped by the Cosa Nostra, that's for sure.

I continued on for a good hour until I could almost feel the presence of Lake Malawi. My knee felt like it had ballooned so I made the decision to stop riding for the night as soon as I could find a suitable place on the shores of the lake. I continued on for much longer than I should have. I suspect that it was because I couldn't face the pain of straightening my leg, which I would have to, if I was to ever dismount my bike again. Eventually I saw a sign for Kande Beach and turned left onto a sandy track through a palm plantation. The bike slid on the sand and the pain shot up my leg, with each jolt. After a kilometre or so I came across a very strange setting that was not at all to my liking. A group of about fifteen local guys came running up to me smiling and waving. I pulled up on the bike. I was very pleased to see them and said, "Hi guys, listen, can you please help me hold the bike while I get off. I fell off the bike today and I have hurt my leg."

They jostled for positions to help support the bike, shouting, "No problem, no problem!"

With difficulty I dismounted the monster. I hobbled over to a piece of driftwood lying next to a small ramshackle grass hut. The hut was full of rows and rows of wooden carvings. I picked up the piece of wood and placed it under the foot stand of the bike to stop it sinking in the sand. I took off my helmet and shook hands with various cheery characters, thanking them for their assistance. I looked around me and noticed what I can only describe as a fortress looming out from the trees ahead of me. "What is this place?" I asked?

"It is the Chincheche place for tourists," replied a tall, very dark guy. It seemed from his demeanour that he was the main man. "This is where the backpackers and big trucks stop. My name is Cisco 59," he said, smiling widely and slapping himself on the chest. "Come and see our shop, we have T-shirts, jewelleries, carvingies and boat trips."

"I would love to Cisco 59, but my leg is killing me. I will come and look tomorrow; I am staying a few days. Sorry."

"No problem, we see you around." said another, whose name was apparently Mr Fantastic. I continued, "Can you just help me push the bike into the backpackers, it's difficult on my own in the sand."

"Sorry it is not possible," said Cisco 59. "It is only for foreign people inside this place."

I was pretty shocked but said, "No problem, I will see you guys tomorrow." I said my goodbyes, grimaced and pushed the bike up to a huge set of double wooden doors. I knocked and it swung open slowly. It was like knocking on the portcullis of an ominous-looking castle. A short, squat American of about fifty, in red surf shorts and some ridiculous white sunglasses, appeared round the fifteen foot door. "Hi man, welcome to Kande. Awesome bike," he said scrunching up his face to reveal long yellow teeth. "You'all be wanting Reception. It's on the right over there, where that hot woman's walking," he said, pointing. I thanked him and made my escape (as fast as my basket ball knee would let me) while he closed the huge gates. I checked in and found a square of grass to put my tent. I do mean a square of grass. Let me briefly describe the interior of this fortress.

The whole resort was surrounded by a semi-circular, ten-foot, solid metal sheet fence stretching all the way down to the beach front. Within the confines of the walls were a beach bar, a small shop for essentials, an internet café, and a truck park and repair area. There was a campsite set out in tiny squares, with inches between each tent. For those a little bit more monetarily flush there were five rondavels available for rent. Three overland buses were parked up; Oasis, Dragoman and The Pink Ladies (a Swedish tour group). Everywhere I looked there were drunken teenagers flirting their socks off. (Figuratively speaking as socks would have looked odd with bikinis.) There is no denying that it was well organised, but to me it was hell. Firstly, because I am too old for that flirty malarkey and secondly, because I am a bit of a loner. Most importantly was the fact that I felt it was a bit like a corral or laager that had been set up to fend off the locals. The Us and Them mentality did not sit well with me so I decided to head to my tent, rest up my leg and leave the next day. I spent the whole night listening to giggling, inane conversations amongst bespectacled, braided Germans about how to solve the complex problems of Africa. There was also the inevitable vomiting emanating from various bushes. I woke up at six with a throbbing head and knee, so decided to hobble down to the waterfront for a swim.

A hundred metres from the 'resort' and the atmosphere changed completely. Lake Malawi really is the jewel in the crown, a body of stunningly large freshwater, fringed by beaches of golden sand. I sat on the edge of the water digging my feet into the already warm sand. I looked out over the vast expanse and recalled what I had recently read on Wetu about this amazing lake. It is worth repeating. As a teacher I sometimes feel that statistics and facts speak for themselves:

'Lake Malawi came to the attention of 'foreigners' just over 150 years ago when it was 'discovered' by Dr David Livingstone. Scientists are undecided as to how long it existed before Livingstone wandered up to it but have given the absurdly inaccurate estimate of between forty thousand and two million years old. The Lake is the ninth largest in the world and visually there is no telling it from the ocean. This is no surprise as it is 52 miles wide and 365 miles long. (Hence also the sobriquet, 'the calendar lake'.)'

As I sat there with waves breaking onto the golden beach and specks of islands on the horizon I couldn't help but wonder if Livingstone had assumed he had reached the Indian Ocean. The lake is also astonishingly deep, more than 700 metres, plunging well below sea level. This reflects the enormity of the natural faulting of the Rift Valley, which is the origin of the Lake. It's an inspiring place to witness. I stood up and walked gingerly into the water up to my waist. The water was luxuriously warm and crystal clear, with thousands of tiny cichlids flashing around me in the shadows. I lay on my back and stared up at the equally blue sky, not even a wisp of a cloud was to be seen. My knee was also enjoying the buoyancy of the Lake and I lay there totally relaxed and pain-free for about fifteen minutes. Until the shark bit me. Don't be ridiculous, there are no sharks. No: I was interrupted by the vague sound of voices echoing through the water. I looked up. It was Cisco 59, Mr Fantastic and his posse, twenty metres down the beach, also wading in the shallows. I motioned to them to swim over but Mr Fantastic nodded in the negative and waved me over to them. I swam up to them, stood up and said, "Don't tell me; apartheid in the water."

They burst out laughing and Cisco said, "Spencer, it is no go area. No mind, we are going fishing on that island," pointing to a rocky outcrop, a good kilometre away. "You come with us?"

"I would love to," I replied.

"We will be swim over, I don't think it is possible for you," he said, shaking his head.

"I don't think it is possible for you," repeated someone called Cheese On Toast. Although it was totally light-hearted I rose to the comment, saying somewhat arrogantly, "I will beat all of you, I will get there first." This caused much hilarity and discussion.

Cisco countered, "This is good, we can try. It will also be these two brothers," he said, pointing to two identical skinny, shy boys. I estimated them at about ten. "They are Fish and Chip." Ok, the race was on. I was in the lucky position that I have been swimming for as long, and also almost as much, as I have been walking. I feel as happy in water as out. But I suspected they would not be a pushover, having been born next to the Lake.

It was a much longer swim than I had envisaged and my knee was aching to buggery before we had even conquered the halfway mark. But I hung on in there. I can proudly report that I had the unique experience of swimming to an uninhabited island on Lake Malawi with Cisco 59, Mr Fantastic, Cheese On Toast, and Fish and Chip trailing in my wake. I pulled myself up onto a rock and was followed shortly by a muscular teenager with mini dreads. The others scrambled up over the next few minutes and we all sat in the sun catching our breath. After a moment the little dread leaned over and patted me on the back, "Very good, very good."

I thanked him and said, "You must be Mr Quick." They laughed. "No, my name is "Good Morning Good Night."

"OK, if that's the case, call me Spanner." They never called me anything but that for the next two days. We stayed on the island for the whole day, fishing successfully, netting about twenty fish. They were small but there was enough to go around. We jumped off overhanging rocks and had underwater distance swimming competitions. It was a superb day and these guys were the reason I stuck around; more than to get my knee healed and despite the backpackers.

As they were leaving and I headed back to my tent, Cisco 59 said, "Spanner, I will make T-shirt for you, all your countries you travel." I thought it was a great idea and quizzed him "How long will it take you and how much?"

"No, no, I will finish tomorrow at four and no charge." I scribbled down the ten countries I had been through already and the twenty five I had left, plus the website, *www.africa-bike-adventure.com*.

We parted and I went back to my tent to contemplate the day's events. What a way to live. The Malawian guys were great and I loved their sense of humour, especially with the nicknames. I was no stranger to odd names as my parents' gardener in Kenya was called Jesus Christ Mercedes Benz. I also knew an Intelligence who wasn't the brightest, a Beauty who was a moose and a Health Inspector in Swaziland called Virus Magagula. The difference was that these were their real names, not like the joker Malawi boys. I wondered if the rest of Malawi was going to be as beautiful and the people so welcoming. I hoped it wouldn't be trampled by tourism all the way down the Lake edge. I took a painkiller and slept like a log on valium, my body pleasantly tired from the two-mile round swim and eight hours of sunlight on my back. Difficult to feel better.

The next morning I felt invigorated and went for an early morning walk down to the beach front. It helped loosen up my knee and when I returned to my tent, I felt strong enough to think about leaving and heading down to the capital, Lilongwe. I persuaded myself that it would be better to wait another day. I liked the idea of another day of rest and recuperation and another instalment of the Nickname Boys. I had to wait for my T-shirt and it would be too late to leave by then. (My excuse and I'm sticking to it.) A Croatian girl (she had an 'I am Croatian' blouse) approached my camping area and said, "Sorry, are you Spencer?"

"Yes, why's that?"

"There is a man outside the gates who wants to see you."

"OK, thanks a lot."

I headed down to the mega swinging doors and out to the grass hut shop owned by the Nickname Boys.

They were all there sitting in the shade and were extremely happy to see me. "Spanner, I have your shirt. It is good, top class, number one," stated Cisco 59 confidently. He went into the hut and came out with a flattened piece of brown paper in his hand. "Here," he pronounced, pulling off the paper in a flourish. He held out a black T-shirt with white writing. On the front was the outline of Africa with my website address curved over the top of the continent and my name curved beneath the Cape of Good Hope. He spun it round in the air. On the back were all 35 countries listed.

"That's fantastic Cisco, thanks very much. Let me give you some money. It must have taken ages to do that."

"No, it's for you, for nothing. I come visit you in Swaziland or the United Kingdom of England, thank you."

It was a touching effort he had made, but honesty must prevail. The artistic execution was dreadful. It seemed as though Cisco 59 had designed it blindfolded in the dark. The outline of Africa 'only just' looked like Africa; it seemed as though it had melted in the African sun. My website and name were heavily lopsided, so much so that the web address spread up the left sleeve. Both looked like they were written in Tippex. The countries on the back were in a random order and at least ten were misspelt. It was obvious that Cisco had been too enthusiastic with the font size. The country names got smaller and smaller as it dawned on him that he was running out of T-shirt. Many names were smudged.

It was for these reasons that I loved this shirt. I did eventually give Cisco 59 $10, because he was poor and very nice and didn't ask for it. The next morning all the crew were there, helping to push me through the deeper sand ruts. They accompanied me for the kilometre to the main road running next to me. The guys took turns jumping on the back for a brief respite and when I reached the main road they cheered, "Spanner, Spanner." One of the better exits.

I continued down the southbound road with the lake on my left-hand side. Because of its rich harvest the lake plays a massive part in the economy, as do most waterways and water sources worldwide. With more species of fish than any other fresh water lake it was no surprise that I came across fishing villages scattered all along its shores. But what surprised me most was the lack of tourism. For a country with such a reputation for kayaking, sailing, snorkelling, water skiing, luxury lodges and hotels, it seemed exceedingly localised. There were still long stretches of totally uninhabited lakeshore with golden sand lapped by crystal clear waters. This theme continued for two hundred kilometres through Nkhotakota and on to Domira Bay where I headed west towards Lilongwe. I nailed the 350 kilometres from the Nickname Boys to Lilongwe with ease and headed straight to the Lilongwe Golf Club where I heard camping was cheap.

As I pulled in I was shocked to see a vehicle I recognised. It was an elderly German couple who I had met on the Egypt to Sudan ferry. I had a brief chat with them. They told me that on the infamous Moyale to Isiolo road in Northern Kenya (where I was shot at) they had flipped their overland truck on its side on a slippery corner. They were unhurt and managed to scramble free of the wreckage. To add insult to injury, as they were contemplating how to upright the truck, a car came round the corner sliding at high speed. It rammed their truck and sent it rolling over into a ravine. They waited two days for help to arrive. They then flew the truck to South Africa for repairs and then re-commenced their trip, but this time heading northwards. (Not short of money then.)

More importantly, they confirmed that Ernst and Lena had also come to a sticky end on the same road. Well, Ernst had. Apparently he had hit a pot hole, flipped the bike and broken his leg. He was airlifted to Switzerland to undergo emergency surgery. I hate know-alls but I never thought they would make it through that stretch. Lack of riding experience + extreme terrain + copious Schnapps = Injured Ernst. I don't wish injury on any one and I hope Ernst is one hundred percent recovered, but due to his behaviour he certainly deserved it more than Lena did. Also her nightmare trip was over.

Moçambique

After organising my visa for Moçambique I embarked on a mammoth two-day ride from Lilongwe to Vilankulos on the east coast. The flag sticker of Moçambique that I bought at the border was interesting. The national emblems were a red star, a hoe, a sheaf of corn, a blank book, a sunrise and an AK47 assault rifle! I understand they all represent the history of the country but it's a bit odd to feature a killing machine on your flag of national unity. That aside, I rode 1,215 kilometres in 22 hours and 34 minutes and saw no AK47s.

I slept for one night (well, four hours) in the bush. The entire journey was undertaken battling the chaos of African road works, which are unlike any other. There were no road signs warning of non-existent bridges, diversions, huge craters, stricken telegraph poles, metal rods and general road building materials, surface changes, giant trucks, ravines, workers in the road, people, animals etc etc. Every corner was a potential death trap. I kept my wits about me despite constant dust blinding me, lorries trying to kill me and owls flying in my face.

I was only twenty kilometres from the coastal resort of Vilankulos when I came round a long, smooth corner hitting 120 kilometres an hour. A white Scania bus was hurtling towards me in a cloud of dust, hogging most of the road. On my left-hand side three women with bundles of textiles strapped to their heads were negotiating the hard shoulder. I had a tiny corridor of space with which to squeeze through. I accelerated past the startled women and missed the bus by inches. I was engulfed in a cloud of dust and could see nothing. I kept my line and accelerated further. As I hurtled out of the dust cloud a brown and white goat sprang out of the undergrowth. I hit it dead centre and it disintegrated into pieces, splattering the front of the bike and covering my visor and jacket with blood and lumps of goat. I am exceedingly partial to a fine goat curry but this was a less pleasant serving. I swerved heavily but managed to keep upright. There was no way I was going to stop and see how the goat was; it was obvious. There was also no way I was going to stop and clean up. I wiped the blood from the visor with my glove and continued on for a couple of kilometres.

I pulled into the bush, out of view from the road. I knew from experience that if you hit an animal in a rural village, you escape as fast as possible. This may sound morally irresponsible but it is inevitable that the exact goat you hit will be the prize-winning village goat. No, it will be the Chief's favourite goat that was given to him by his favourite dying brother. It will have won Goat Awards throughout Africa and the world. It would be a very sacred goat, an almost mystical, once-in-a-lifetime goat with superpowers. You would end up embroiled in a compensation claim that would end up with you handing over your motorbike, your money and promising that your wife would be sent over to the Chief for Christmas.

On a graver note, I knew that I was exceedingly lucky that I had not run over a person. That is a moral dilemma on a much more serious level. There is a distinct possibility of being stoned and beaten to death by the villagers. If there are witnesses (more importantly, people to help the injured party), it is vital to try and escape to the nearest police station and hand yourself in. If there are no witnesses, or helpers, it goes without saying you have to stop and help.

Luckily, I only had a goat to worry about and I didn't worry much. I had a brief clean-up, removing pieces of goat from the bike and then headed on to Vilankulos. I pulled up at a beach-front bar, inspiringly called The Beach Front Bar. I walked in dressed from head to toe in black, with a Darth Vader helmet splattered with blood. I must have looked like an alien mass murderer and expected the locals to start fleeing in panic. Instead I received a few side glances from some drunken locals and nothing more. I ordered a beer and sat outside on the concrete veranda. The beach was undoubtedly stunning but was covered in layers of rubbish. I took off my bike gear and walked down to the water's edge to wash my face. On my return I cut my heel on a broken bottle. My right leg had been really unlucky recently. I sat down, wrapped my foot in tissue and put it up on the concrete wall. I pulled out a pack of cigarettes and lit one. A local guy of about twenty walked over, helped himself to one of my cigarettes, lit it with my lighter and walked off. He sat down with his three friends and grinned at me. I was stunned into silence, but then my blood began to boil.

I got up and went over, "What the hell do you think you are doing. You can't just help yourself to my cigarettes." He said something in Portuguese and shrugged his shoulders smugly.

Defeated but not placated I went back to my seat. The anger rose in me. I sat there contemplating what to do, knowing I should leave it, when the cigarette thief rose and ordered more beers. After he sat down I waited a few seconds, went over, took his beer off the table and went back and sat down. My heart was pounding. What a stupid thing to do. I steadfastly ignored them and robotically stared out to sea. They had a loud animated discussion for what seemed like five minutes and then all burst out laughing. The cig thief got up, came over and extended his hand. I took it, we shook, he shook his head, laughed and returned to his seat. Job done. Maybe they thought I was brave or mad and had already killed someone that day. I didn't stick around to find out. My exit was not exactly 007. I hobbled out on my cut foot and stiff knee, a helmet in one hand and a blood and mud soaked jacket in the other. I gave them a nod which they all reciprocated and I was gone, on the bike in a painful flash. I felt good but childish. Oh well. Accommodation and then another massive ride to my homeland, Swaziland!

And talking of being childish, whenever you stop in Africa you will be surrounded by young people and smiling faces. One such group was the 'football team' I greeted by a small village. The goalie is second on the left.

Swaziland

Swaziland is my country and the most beautiful country in Africa. This is a compliment indeed when you consider that even when I see the shape of Africa on a map my heart literally starts racing. I have been lucky enough to have travelled to more than one hundred and ten countries in the world including forty of the fifty two countries in Africa. I am convinced that Africa is the most vibrant and unpredictable. It is also jam-packed with dysfunctional and off-the-radar people who are a pleasure to meet. Africa doesn't just get under your skin; it soaks you with its atmosphere and fills your senses to bursting point. Africa is my drug and Swaziland is the pinnacle. Embarrassingly, I have to admit that when I came over the border and saw the stunning, emerald green, rolling hills – no, mountains – of my homeland I stopped the bike, kissed the ground and shed a few drops of water from my eyes. I have always felt my happiest in Swaziland so it was ironic that on this occasion it would be the saddest visit of my trip.

I decided to stay my first night with Danny Dlamini, a Rasta friend of mine since childhood. He lived in the mountains of Pigg's Peak in the north of Swaziland. The next morning I planned to ride to the capital Mbabane and see my brother Simon and his daughter and one of my best friends William Rudd. The visit to Danny was great. He was pleased to see me and I was reminded why I liked his company so much. He was extremely soft spoken and kind and there was an aura of calmness and serenity surrounding him. The relaxed atmosphere was accentuated by the stunning surroundings. His house was nestled at the base of a rolling green mountain, close to a crystal clear, pristine river that meandered slowly through the valley. His house was small but spotless.

Unusually, for Swazi houses, his house was set on brick stilts and was made of packed mud, painted bright blue. The interior was decked out with reggae posters and quotes from the

Bible. The walls were painted red, gold and green and his Spartan possessions and ornaments were artistically and neatly arranged around the house. It definitely stood out amongst the thatched mud rondavels that peppered the mountainside. Danny was a wood carver and, as we had done fifteen years earlier, we sat in his yard discussing life. As before, Danny whittled away constantly at pieces of wood to produce masks and statues of raw beauty. I loved my brief visit with Danny but I was excited to get to Mbabane. I left his therapeutic manner and surroundings reluctantly, but not before I acquired a nickname for my bike. "You be careful on that Burning Spear," Danny shouted after me.

My next visit went just as well. By pure luck I turned up at my ten-year-old niece's school while they were on lunch break. She had no idea that I was in Swaziland and thought I was fourteen thousand one hundred and sixty two kilometres away (as the crow flies), in England. Within seconds I spotted her sitting with a group of girls under an Acacia tree. I drove the bike up next to her and turned off the engine without removing my helmet. I just said, "Hi Ysa." For a split second she looked confused, then incredulous and then just collapsed in tears. I couldn't take my helmet off fast enough to hug her as she shook uncontrollably saying, "Uncle Spencer, Uncle Spencer," over and over. It was a wonderful moment, one of the highlights of the whole journey. I spent a wonderful few hours with her catching up on a ten-year-old's worries in life. I love her so much and we are very close.

My next visit was not so good. I drove up to the Mbabane Golf Course Road to William's house. As I turned the corner into his road I saw someone in the distance. It was William, who from a distance hadn't aged at all in fifteen years. As I got closer I realised it was an impossibility as this boy was about fifteen whereas Willie was forty two. There was no doubting it. I jumped off the bike and said, "Hi, are you by any chance Willie Rudd's son?"

"Yes, that is me," he said smiling.

"Hi, my name is Spencer. I am one of your Dad's best friends. Sorry, what's your name?" I asked, extending my hand.

"My name is William Rudd," he said proudly, taking my hand.

"Listen William, I have travelled all the way here on a motorbike from England. I haven't seen your dad for ten years. I want to surprise him. Is he around or at work?"

"My father is dead, he passed away three months back," he said sadly, staring at the road.

My heart sank. I said I was so sorry and we passed a few more awkward moments. The connection that we had both just established had been severed. There just seemed no point in telling him how much I liked his father, how we had toured South Africa together, how much he made me laugh.

I suspected Willie had died in a car accident as they are so common in Swaziland, but I had to ask: "I am sorry to ask you William, but what happened?"

"He was sick, his chest. He had pneumonia."

"That's terrible, he was too young. I am really sorry again."

I rode off feeling devastated. In different circumstances I would probably have got to know William Junior well. But it was not to be. I felt so sad. I also knew that 'pneumonia' in Swaziland is another way of saying AIDS. Forty percent of Swaziland is infected by AIDS, the highest rate on earth. My good friend William had become a victim.

My next visit was worse. I was reeling from the news about Willie when I pulled up to my brother's house. I knocked on the door and heard a noise inside. No one answered. I waited and waited and knocked again. I sat on his lawn and looked out at a wonderful mountain vista. After about twenty minutes he opened the door very slightly, stuck his head out and uttered an unenthusiastic "Hello." He looked terrible; so ill and gaunt and much older than his forty five years. It was evident that I was not going to be invited in so I cut my losses and agreed to meet him in town at a local pizzeria, Porto Fino. He didn't turn up. My brother and I have a history that is too complicated, painful and personal to bring up. I have issues but he has more than National Geographic.

After that initial meeting I decided to leave the next day. I had looked forward to seeing my brother since leaving England, but it wasn't to be. And so it was that I reluctantly left Swaziland, the only country in the world I would go to war for. It was more beautiful, more organised and the people more friendly than I ever remembered. How many emotional ups and downs can you stuff into two days? I felt wretched and hollow riding to the southern border with South Africa. I couldn't think straight and was wrenched between two emotions; stuff it and ride off as fast as possible and get on with the task at hand, or go back and see Simon and Ysa again. I think I made the right decision. I turned round and drove the eighty kilometres back to Mbabane to visit Ysa. I did not visit Simon. I sort of understand why he didn't want to see me but he is my only brother and I love him. I hope we can sit down and talk one day.

I crossed into South Africa having left two people I love dearly and a country I never wanted to leave. I would not finally stop until I was fourteen thousand one hundred and sixty two kilometres away (as the vulture flies). Being a human means you often rely on your relationships with others to gain happiness. I was not happy at that point.

Chapter Seven
Shipwrecks and Skeletons

*'Too often I would hear men boast of the miles covered that day,
rarely of what they have seen.'* Louis L'Amour

*'To get to know a country you must have direct contact with the earth.
It's futile to gaze at the world through a car window.'* Albert Einstein

Now I have another dilemma. I risk offending someone else and after this book comes out I might have no family or friends talking to me. My girlfriend is South African but I have to say in all honesty that South Africa was a bit of a disappointment. I know South Africa well. I have lived there and travelled widely. I have always loved it. But something was different. It was not the landscape, which doesn't generally change and which is universally accepted as one of the most diverse and breathtaking on earth. It was a tension hanging in the air that seemed to have intensified since I lived there. I am not getting into politics, but the past has not been swept away completely and the present is getting suspect to say the least. Almost all the people I met during my 'race' through the centre of South Africa were superb but a tiny minority were arseholes.

I say 'race' because for the first time since Libya I hit 'white line fever' and managed to cross South Africa in two and a half days. It was beautiful but my mind was elsewhere. After a brief stay in Cape Town it was time to turn around; literally. I had made it half way. It was time to keep the momentum going and face the radical west coast roads. I suspected the next half of the journey would be even more insane than the first and I was going to be proved correct! I left Cape Town in superb shape mentally and average shape physically. My ribs had ached ever since the 'mishap' in Kenya. My right wrist had problems. Repetitive Stress Injury is the official term. I prefer 'knackered wrist from riding eight hours a day for six months lunatic syndrome'. It could have been worse. I could have been shot dead in the wilds of Kenya. A little physical pain was not a problem as long as I could finish this mammoth task. As if to prove my intent I covered 562 kilometres from Cape Town to Springbok in seven hours and sixteen minutes. The journey started through the lush mountains and valleys of the Paarl and Ceres area famous for their fruit and wine respectively. Exquisite landscape and perfect roads led rapidly to drier harsher, hotter and more desolate terrain as I headed further north towards the border with Namibia.

I turned up in the weirdest town in the world – Springbok. I talked about a one-horse town earlier but this was a no-horse town. I felt like I had doubled the population just by turning up, so quiet were the streets. This place was stuck in the fifties. I spotted a prefab building that advertised 'Best Motel'. I am sure it was the best motel... at that address. I knocked on the door with a sign 'Reception-Owner Hettie Le Roux' and it was opened by the scariest double act I have ever seen. It was a mother and daughter duo. They looked identical and the daughter hovered behind her mother, mimicking her movements. They looked like a two-headed beast. They both had dark, severely short, army-type haircuts and floral dresses. It looked like two men in drag. The floral dresses only added to the image. They must have bought them from Rent-a-Tent, they were so obese. Two female wrestlers who had let their fitness regime slip, maybe ten years earlier; that's what crossed my mind. The mother said, "Yes?" whilst giving me a wilting look.

I put on my biggest smile and said, "Do you have a room for tonight?"

The 'Worst Landlady in South Africa Award Winner' without a moment's delay said, "It's 150 Rand and you pay before you go in." She scowled and considered spitting in the dirt in front of me. I pulled out the money for fear of a beating and handed it to her.

"You can't stay tomorrow because we have a bus coming. Your room is around the corner," she said harshly, pointing around the building like a demented loon. I thanked her and as I turned to go she said, "No drink, no drugs, no women."

I replied, "No worries, that's OK. Thanks for trying. I will look around town later to see if I can find any." No, I didn't say that. I said, "No, of course not. I just want to have some food, sleep and head off in the morning." As she pointed out the room and handed me the key she responded, with a wag of her finger, "No stealing; everything is on the inventory."

I assured her that I had no intention of pocketing her knives, forks and salt cellars. (I was too scared.) The room was not exactly homely. It was a long metal container with metal beds bolted into the walls on either side. They folded down and were held firm by thick metal chains. The mattresses were thick, extremely hard and covered in slippery blue plastic; a bit like an incontinence mattress or the type you find in British Police holding cells (not that I have witnessed that first hand of course, someone told me). There were overhead lights that shone down on each bed which made it look even more like an interrogation chamber. There was a cooker, fridge and a draw of utensils. In the centre of the room was a table with eight chairs. She had obviously made a great effort to add her personal charm as there was a solitary plastic flower in a mug in the centre of the table. The walls were plastered with hundreds of different rules; no weapons, no graffiti, don't leave the fridge open, wash and clean up after eating (including yourself), no visitors, no talking, no laughing, no noise, no fun, etc. etc. It was an odd place but very clean.

I slept well but had a nightmare. I had been kidnapped as a sex slave by the landlady for her and her slightly slimmer, five-hundred kilogramme daughter. I was surprised I slept so well, especially as the chains rattled every time I moved on the bed. I also found out quickly that if I moved too enthusiastically inside my sleeping bag I would slide across the mattress and be jettisoned unceremoniously onto the floor. Maybe the chains were some of their instruments of torture. I packed up quickly and departed before they had a chance to get their chubby clutches on me.

My aim was to cover the 317 kilometres into Namibia and on to Fish River Canyon, the second largest canyon in the world. That should be far enough away from Mrs Hettie La Roux to sleep comfortably. I estimated that with a smooth road and an easy border crossing I could arrive at Fish River in under five hours. The border crossing was a formality but I didn't add Mother Nature into the equation. She was about to teach me a serious lesson. The journey was through pure desert with no signs of habitation.

It started as most desert journeys do with high temperatures and low winds. The road was excellent and there were no traffic or animals to negotiate. But within a space of ten minutes the wind whipped up into a massive squall. I was being blown all over the road and a serious accident in the middle of nowhere was a distinct possibility. At one point I was leaning so far into the wind that I looked like a speedway rider. Suddenly the wind changed direction completely and it took all my lack of skill to stay upright. At that point I stopped the bike and hunkered behind it for a good half hour until the wind had dissipated enough for me to negotiate it. I continued on slowly, my neck aching from the effort.

Just as I was beginning to flag I spotted a sight that made me grin. Once again someone had arrived in 'nowhere' before me, albeit by bus, hitching and airplane. It was Carl. He was curled up at the only junction in the road for 300 kilometres. He looked absolutely hilarious. His massive bushy beard was sticking out sideways from his face, making it very clear what the prevailing wind direction was. His eyes were covered in sand and he was squatting behind his rucksack to try and get some relief.

"What the hell are you doing here?" I laughed as I pulled up.

"Thank God you have arrived, Spencer. I thought I might be here for the rest of my life. I was dropped here six hours ago and haven't seen a single person!"

"Why here, it's in the middle of nowhere?" I asked.

"This is the turn-off for Fish River Canyon and I wanted to see it."

"Me too, jump on and we'll go." Easier said than done. I already had a 'sausage' army kit bag on the back of the bike, plus two tripods and a rucksack, oh and a tent bag. Now I had to balance Carl and his bath-size rucksack on top of this mound. By the time we got balanced Carl was about three foot higher than me. It looked like he was in an observation post. All of this in desert winds. We weaved along gingerly but there was more to come. Namibia decided to throw in a flash flood. It was one of the most spectacular weather phenomena I had ever seen. Within seconds the bone-dry, dusty desert road turned into a raging torrent. Not only was the road a fast flowing river but other rivers were coming in from all sides joining up to create one bubbling, swirling mass. We were soaked to the skin and progressed at less than ten kms an hour. I kept my feet firmly planted in the water, sliding wildly from side to side. After twenty minutes it was gone, soaked up by the desperately thirsty land. After fighting this route for eighty kilometres we came to a camp site where the guard told us we had gone the wrong way. We were at the hot spring resort of Ais-Ais. Fish River Canyon was 70 kilometres in the other direction in a place called Hobas. It was a superb end to the day and we camped up to recharge for the next assault across the Namaqua desert. Hopefully in the right direction this time.

The next day we did the two-up balancing trick again and made it to the Canyon by noon. It was not a disappointment in any way. The Fish River has carved itself deep into the plateau but was now dry, stony and sparsely covered in drought-resistant plants. The gigantic ravine is 160 kilometres long, 27 kilometres wide and 550 metres deep. It was astoundingly impressive and even more so because Carl and I were alone to appreciate it. Like many before and many to come, we screamed as loud as we could to hear the echo. It was as clear as day. The enormity of the place was a humbling sight and made me feel exceedingly ant-like and insignificant.

Escarpment photo shoot

We camped up and the following morning parted ways. Carl managed to get a lift with a truck and I headed off towards the Angolan border. It was a trouble-free massive 1,424 kilometres with a two-night stop and quick TV and newspaper interviews in Windhoek. On the second day in Windhoek I met up with Carl again. The sand dunes on the outskirts of Windhoek were amazing. Diesel Films had decided to hire a pick-up truck so that Carl could film me doing some desert riding. They had also agreed to pay Carl, which was a bonus as he was running out of dosh. Our only problem now was to find a driver. No problem. Or so we thought. A French guy called Michel who we met at the Cardboard Box Backpackers offered to drive. It turned out that he could not drive at all. It was an absolute nightmare. Not only did he turn right when he was supposed to turn left, he went round the roundabouts the wrong way. We could have dealt with this if the rest of his driving had been passable. Unfortunately he may as well have been blind. Michel was worse than any driver on this continent so far, and that was saying something. There was no saving grace in his driving. We careered off the road frequently and sent various cars spinning off the thoroughfare. As soon as we ventured off-road he was completely out-of-control; bouncing off this rock, slipping on that dune. As a passenger it was a no win situation. If you said something to him about his appalling driving, he would forget about driving completely. He would give you full attention to try and answer your misgivings. Michel would turn to you as if you were having a discussion in a bar. All thoughts of driving were forgotten until we were rocketing up a mountainside out of control. It was impossible, 100% impossible, to film. As soon as Carl had a steady shot the truck would slide sideways, almost hitting me and ejecting Carl, followed by a "Pardon." We gave up quickly, valuing our lives more than some decent footage. I paid Michel to go away, not for the footage we had captured because there was none. The relative serenity of this journey was to be in complete contrast to the absolute anarchy and insanity I was about to face. See. All is relative.

The insanity was on hold for one more day as I rocketed towards Swakopmund. It was a decent enough place but was so German it made Borrusia Munchengladbach sound like an English village. People spoke Afrikaans, Oshiwambo, Damara, Ovambo, English and various snippets of other languages. All spoke German. The tourist kiosks still sold flags of German

South West Africa and various other red, black and Swastikary (new word) type stuff. It was all very suspect. Not wanting to fall into the German colonial trap, I ordered a Bratwurst, some sauerkraut and a Stein of Lager from an eighty-year-old plaited blonde woman called Helga. She threatened me, which was a sign to leave. She said, "I like you very much, Ja!" It was enough for me and I headed offski. Time to leave Germany and head into Angola, Ja!

The Skeleton Coast was incredible and up there with the weirdest atmosphere that I had ever witnessed. There was only one road that followed the coast so it was impossible to get lost. For hour after hour after hour I motored along with the endless Atlantic Ocean crashing onto the shore on my left and the endless Namib Desert stretching out on my right. It was the flattest desert I have ever been in (now that I am an expert). It was so flat that I started coming up with childish addresses; Michael Flatley, Flat Four, Flat Avenue, Flatington, Flatville, Namibia. You can tell that I had a lot of time to think. Without exaggeration it was so flat you could see the silhouette of ants against the horizon. A Smartie would have been a hillock. An M&M would have been a hill and a piece of Toblerone, a pyramid. You get the point.

The landscape was harsh, desolate, windswept, shipwreck-strewn and truly incredible. The Namib Bushmen called it 'The Land God made in Anger'. This is spot on. The weather is angry. Dense ocean fogs and winds blow constantly. Rainfall rarely exceeds 10 millimetres and the climate is intensely inhospitable. The name derives from the whale and seal bones that used to litter the shore. Nowadays, the skeletal remains of more than 1,000 ships litter the coastline and give a different poignancy to the name. They were all caught out by the fog and vicious rocks. It lends for an amazingly depressing, yet inspiring scene. I slept on the world's flattest piece of ground and the next day headed through to the Angolan border. The time of chilled 'tourist' riding was well and truly over.

Chapter Eight
The Unknown Border

'The Horror! The Horror!' Heart of Darkness, Joseph Conrad

'I dislike feeling at home when I am abroad.' George Bernard Shaw

U p to this point I had spent one hundred and sixty seven days attempting to circumnavigate Africa by motorbike. After riding down the East coast, I had turned round at the southern most point of the continent and had now travelled through sixteen countries and covered 31,050 kilometres. Whilst it's almost impossible to have a dull moment on this continent, I'd now stumbled upon the two most exciting, confusing and visually stimulating countries so far: Angola and the Democratic Republic of Congo.

As if to confirm this I was writing, sitting in a gloomy, filthy room in the centre of the capital, Kinshasa, while in the streets riots were going on over police brutality. Taxi drivers had gone on strike and were blocking the main roads. Two policemen had been shot dead and I feared that the ever-present armed forces would want revenge. But more of that later.

I entered Angola through the Santa Clara border with Namibia but only after having waited fourteen days for the visa, being relieved of my HD camera by thieves (which I was to regret sorely when I saw the beauty that Angola had to offer), and lastly, having been rolled on by an extremely obese man while I was sleeping.

The Santa Clara border was very similar to most African border posts and they are not too pleasant an experience. They generally consist of one main, bustling, chaotic street full of money changers, prostitutes in garish shiny dresses and ludicrously over-applied neon lipstick, teetering in the mud in high heels amongst the petty thieves, pickpockets and food sellers. The 'ladies of the day and night' heavily favour leopard print miniskirts and vests which more often than not reveal one or both of their breasts, whilst they swig enthusiastically from litre bottles of Castle Milk Stout, becoming more unstable on their feet as the day wears on. It makes for a very classy sight as they slip and slide in the muddy streets.

Although most borders have some sort of bank, the illegal money changers trade openly and in fact the customs officers and police often point them out as they are all in cahoots. I knew I was going to be delayed at the border for a few days because I was waiting for a letter of introduction into Angola from Save the Children. I knew it was absolutely impossible to get into Angola without this letter so I set off to find some accommodation for at least a couple of nights. I spotted a badly painted red sign on a soggy mud-covered piece of cardboard which promised 'Bar and First Clas Acom dation'. That seemed like my kind of place and price range! I sloshed down the muddy side road and sure enough there was 'Happy Hotel'. (I would hate to see a sad one.) The bar was a small hut with three broken blue plastic chairs, a white plastic table, a battered table football game, and the loudest music I have ever heard blaring from two massive distorted, broken speakers hanging on the grimy wall. The speakers were obviously prized possessions as they were both encased in metal boxes which were bolted to the wall. Below one of the speakers was a torn poster extolling the virtues of Guinness. It showed a man holding a bottle of Guinness to the sky, with the biggest grin and cheeks I have ever seen. He looked like he had attempted to swallow a Frisbee. Underneath his picture someone had scrawled, 'Be a man, drink Gunnes.'

The serving counter was a small cage in the corner of the

room with an iron mesh from floor to ceiling. There was a small hinged hatch at waist height, where the drinks were obviously passed through to the eager, thirsty customers (all three of them, if it was packed full). I approached the bar lady who was slouched over the peeling, brown lino bar counter, her fat cheek squashed against the counter, one eye open, watching me as I approached. There was an overpowering smell of urine and it was difficult not to gag but I managed to shout over the million decibel music, "Excuse me, kind and welcoming patron, do you by any chance have an air-conditioned bedroom with en-suite bath, TV, satellite dish, bar fridge, complimentary white towels and chocolate on the pillow? Oh, and petals sprinkled on the bed cover so a weary but friendly traveller might rest his aching bones." No, I didn't really say that. I said, "Do you have a room for one night?"

In response she managed to let out a massive sigh, and with huge difficulty lifted her hand, and with her fat thumb pointed down the alleyway running next to the bar. I thanked her kindly and made my way around the back where there was a brick building with four filthy rooms. The only way from the bar to the rooms was over an open sewer, which had spilled out onto the road and was now mixed with the red mud in a huge stinking slurry lake. Someone had laid down wooden pallets between the buildings, so that you could jump from one to the next, but unfortunately these were submerged, so were of little use. At least they had made some attempt to keep up the high standards of the establishment. I peered through one of the broken, louvered windows and through a large gash in the mosquito netting. The room was fine; just a bed and a tiny frayed mat, but was not too dirty and perfect for me. I sloshed my way back through the sewerage and approached the caged hyperactive barmaid once more. "I would like a room for at least two nights please," I grinned enthusiastically.

Giant woman looked up in slow motion, adjusted her very unflattering wig, pushing it back off her forehead like it was a baseball cap, yawned widely and slowly and said, "You pay now and put bike in bar for make safe." She stood there looking at me, waiting for a reply, while she attempted to hide her whole finger up her nostril.

I replied, "No problem madam," and reached down to the zip in my lower trouser leg to retrieve my money. I settled up for two nights and returned to the bike, wheeling it into the small bar area. When parked up it allowed very little room for any customers, but no one seemed to mind, and I was happy because the bar entrance had a sturdy sliding metal door, and a slightly less sturdy lock which would at least give me some peace of mind while I slept. Also the room was not visible from the street which was a bonus. (You see, dropping my guard again; it would only end in tears.)

Sloth woman stated, "Put bag in room and lock, do not carry, the thief will steal off you." (Excellent, so there is only one thief in this town. I will look out for him.) After sorting out the gear and locking the room I headed off to find somewhere to eat, but instead found myself running back to the room after fifteen minutes, clutching a raw fish and being pursued by a group of enthusiastic prostitutes. I don't think it was the fish they were after, but by the look on his face, sticking out of the newspaper wrapping, the fish was also worried. I managed to shake them off with sign language about how my genitals were not in a good shape; smelling, diseased, almost falling off, etc, until they got the point and I headed back to cook up my culinary find on my portable camping stove. I tiptoed through the mud around the side of the bar, went round the corner, looked up, sighed and said out loud, "Oh, for God's sake!"

The front door of my room had been kicked in, the lock was smashed and lying on the concrete floor, although I have to admit that did not surprise me, as an anorexic mouse would have been able to prise the padlock off. I felt like an idiot. I didn't need to go in to the room to know that my bag was missing. It was an obvious set up and I could not believe I had

221

taken Sloth barmaid's advice. She was undoubtedly involved, but I knew Africa better than to expect any luck with quizzing her, or trying to get my things back in any conventional way.

I walked out on to the main road and sat on the pavement. My head was swimming as I had lost everything that was important; my passport, wallet, bike papers, driving licence, bike keys and the HD video camera with which I was documenting my trip. I had also lost the memory stick with the Namibia footage on it. For some reason I was not angry, just worried. It's amazing how these border towns seem to be the most lawless areas, but it's mainly because the police are fully involved in all the scams and all they want to do is make a living in a very harsh continent. After all, being a policeman, especially in a difficult environment, is only a job to most, and not a calling. People worldwide fall into the trap; trust a doctor, dentist, judge, priest, happy hotel owner, etc but to be cynical the fact of the matter is behind the titles we are all human beings with the same frailties, vices and needs. We are all animals and life is very hard in Africa. Animals need to eat, and we are an animal, that's the bottom line. I just felt stupid and naïve that I had become another victim of 'Africa Tax'.

I was sitting on the pavement thinking these thoughts, and trying to come up with a plan of action, when down the road came Carl, my bearded, Canadian, Jesus look-alike friend, who I was destined to bump into on numerous occasions on route. What a relief. I liked Carl more every time I saw him. He had a positive, optimistic outlook on life, and a steely determination that I admired. Carl looked hot and worn out, his long hair sticking in clumps to his cheeks, sweat circles staining the underarms and chest sections of his torn grey T-shirt. He was weighed down by a green rucksack, camera tripod and his 20 kilogramme beard. When he saw me he looked just as happy as I felt, and broke into a wide grin.

I quickly filled him in on what had just befallen me and we made a decision that many stressed men have made throughout history. We must discuss this over a beer, it is vital. We went to a fly-infested shebeen (bush bar), to have a beer and formulate a plan. Carl went to the bar and ordered two Nova Cuca beers, picking up two beer coasters from the next table before he sat down. These mats were necessary to cover the opened beers, as they prevented flies from committing suicide in our beverages. After a couple of Cucas, it was eventually decided that we would spread the word amongst all the prostitutes that we did not expect the camera or money back, but if they could find all the other things we would give $200 to whoever located the items.

Surprise, surprise, the very next day, two dodgy-looking characters turned up outside Happy Hotel in a battered Peugeot taxi which was covered in rust and red dust. The passenger jumped out and approached us. He was only about twenty years old but had obviously had a bad accident involving either fire or boiling water. He had severe burns over his entire face and arms. His skin was a creamy pink colour where he had been burnt, and his hair grew in patches. He tapped his hand on the table to get our attention further, and got straight to the point. "I know this man with your bag, I take you there now to get it, but you give me money."

"I will give you nothing until we see the bag and check what's inside," I replied.

He scrunched up his nose, tried to look hard, which wasn't difficult, and said, "It's Ok, let's go!" Like absolute lunatics, we agreed, and jumped in the back of the battered car, our hearts thumping as we left the border and headed out into the bush.

Like many cars in Africa, the interior was minus most of its fittings, including the window winders, the handles and most of the dashboard. The seats were ripped and collapsed, with dangerous-looking springs sticking through the torn upholstery. The back windscreen was completely shattered and seemed to be held precariously in place by a large sticker, which said 'Snoop Doggy' on it. It was difficult to see where we were going, as the windscreen was covered in mud. There was only one windscreen wiper, which had obviously not worked since the seventies, and would have been useless anyway, as it was on the passenger side. The driver leant forward, peering through a small gap of slightly cleaner windscreen to see where he was heading. Great, if we didn't die in a car accident, we would probably get mugged when we arrived wherever we were heading. We drove in silence for about fifteen minutes until they turned off the main track. We bounced along a bush track, just wide enough for the car, the thorn trees scraping along the metalwork on either side, producing a dental unfriendly screech. They pulled up outside a corrugated hut, erected under the shade of a massive Acacia tree in the middle of nowhere. The driver jumped out, pulled his cell phone from his shirt pocket, spoke for a few seconds, before leaning his head back into the car, and stating, "He is coming."

After what seemed like an age, another car pulled up, a red Mazda pickup, and a very dark Angolan in a baby blue tracksuit and oversized white sunglasses approached us, clutching my rucksack. Carl got out and I gestured to the thief to get into the car. He reluctantly got in, and handed me the bag across the seat. My mouth was desert dry as I checked to see everything was there. I couldn't find the bike keys. I quizzed him on this, and he pointed to the zip on the side pocket.

As soon as I felt the keys in my grasp, I blurted out, "No way am I giving you any money," and jumped quickly out of the car. He sprung out of the other door and immediately pulled out a vicious-looking wooden handled machete from a cloth bag he was carrying. I have no idea what possessed him, but the moment he saw the machete, Carl screamed at the top of his voice, raised his hands high in the air, like some demented ghoul, and ran at the machete-wielding, gay-looking thief. Instantaneously, the tracksuit-wearing thug turned and ran as fast as he could around the building and into the bush, with Carl on his tail, his eyes wide and beard burning (OK, not the last bit). The taxi driver who had brought us here, skidded off in a cloud of dust and was gone. I was left standing there alone, wondering what had just happened. Carl came back seconds later, out of breath, slapped me on the back and said, "Let's get the hell out of here!" We ran to the middle of the main road and stopped the first car we saw, driven by a startled-looking, middle-aged man in a Rolling Stones T-shirt.

Without explaining we jumped in and I said, "Drive, please drive!", and he pulled off, looking scared stiff. After I had explained to him as best as I could what had happened, we lapsed into silence. After five minutes or so, Carl and I looked at each other, at exactly the same time, and burst out laughing, through fear, adrenalin and relief. Carl whistled loudly, widened his eyes and raised his eyebrows; that set me off in fits of laughter. The driver gave us strange looks from the rear view mirror. We were alive and I had my bag: the trip could continue. Is this insane or what! Excellent! But we were not destined to be on our way, until a few other minor hiccups had been dealt with.

On the last night, before crossing the border, I offered to buy a few drinks for Bongani, a Swazi/Namibian I had befriended and who had been very helpful during the days I was stuck at the border. He turned out to be an intelligent man with an amazing general knowledge and we had forthright discussions on a favourite subject in most African countries, the corruption of the government, army and police force. Unfortunately the intelligent conversation was short-lived, as he was unable to hold his drink, and became progressively more unsteady. One of his eyelids started collapsing, and his elbow kept slipping off the white plastic table, as he tried to prop up his head in his hands. Eventually I could not understand a word he was saying, and I don't think he could really focus on me anymore, as one eye was completely closed, and the other kept rolling back into his head. I knew it was a long way to his homestead, so I offered to let him have my small inflatable camping mattress, so that he could sleep it off on the floor of my 5-star room. During the night he decided that he was definitely not comfortable enough, scrambled off the floor and proceeded to lie on top of me. As riding with broken ribs is not ideal, I managed eventually to roll him back onto the floor, not without considerable effort as he made Pavarotti look like Slimmer of the Year.

Later in the night he was snoring loudly so I deemed it safe to pop to the toilet. When I returned he was snuggled up in my bed with only his head sticking out of the sleeping bag, making super comfortable cooing noises in between grunts. This was too much for me and with some hippo-herding tactics I learnt in Swaziland (not really), I managed to 'coax' him out of the door. This was not a simple task and he ended up stuck in the doorway upside down, his neck folded into the floor with me trying to push his legs and exceedingly generous midsection over his head. I eventually braced my back against the wall and with my foot managed to roll him into the corridor. So after this uneventful, peaceful night I found myself in Angola.

A terrain that is rich in oil, diamonds, iron ore and copper, plus a measurable hydroelectric capacity, Angola has the potential to be one of Africa's richest states. Instead, the more common reality is a nation of shattered infrastructure and devastated towns struggling to feed a desperately poor and eternally uprooted population. Despite this, I came across the most resilient, helpful and friendly people I have ever met in Africa.

My first aim was to get to the city of Lubango and I was not disappointed. Although it was a shanty town of massive proportions it had two hidden gems. The city is overlooked by a spectacular mountain that easily rivals Table Mountain in Cape Town. Perched on the top is a statue of Christ reminiscent of that in Rio. In its shadow live the warm, welcoming people and I spent an excellent evening on the streets eating goat kebabs from a rusty, cut-in-half, oil drum barbecue. I sipped on local beer, my eyes streaming from the smoke, as I tried to catch the conversations of those circling the fire, their faces lit up momentarily by the flicker of flames, as the fat from the goat dripped on the open coals. Cars hooted, taxi Kombi vans creaked down the potholed road, with young boys in stained tatty clothes hanging on the sides shouting for business, whilst the drivers patiently edged through the thousands cluttering up the road and negotiated the massive potholes. It was an excellent evening before I headed off the next morning at 6am to my next destination, Huambo.

Formerly known as Nova Lisbon (New Lisbon), Huambo has an estimated population of over one million. It was once renowned for its stunning, well-tended expansive parks and attractive colonial buildings and was briefly touted as the country's capital-in-waiting. But this was not to be because civil war arrived in 1993, and a gruesome 52-day siege reduced the city to little more than a pile of pock-marked bullet holes and shell-ridden rubble. Although Huambo is taking its first tentative steps to recovery after a twenty year brutal war, it now presents a vista that is remarkably surreal.

Many of the buildings have no front but are inhabited by families getting on with their day-to-day domestic life as if it is completely normal. I watched families having dinner, children playing in their rooms, women cleaning, and televisions and radios blaring (for some reason many Africans enjoy playing both at the same time at ear-shattering volumes). It was like peering into life-size dolls' houses. I felt a bit like a voyeur but eventually realised it was completely normal and acceptable and when people in the houses caught my eye they waved and smiled, greeting me loudly in Portuguese.

From Huambo my next mission was to get up to the capital, Luanda. The roads turned out to be excellent and the countryside extremely beautiful. I was lucky to travel through the rainy season (yes, really!) as the vegetation was lush: so green it almost looked like computer graphics and the road was bordered by shimmering lakes of crystal clear water.

Scattered all along the route were small children, in ragged shorts or naked, fishing and swimming, or proudly displaying their catch for sale at the side of the road. They jumped in the air waving their hands, clapping and screaming as I went past.

At one stage the vegetation changed and the asphalt surface turned into a mud road, an implausible red colour, which made the puddles look fluorescent orange. Lining the road was a massive Eucalyptus forest, the heady perfume smell of the trees even more powerful from the rain pummelling their leaves. It was a spectacular experience made even more special by the fact that on this stretch of road humanity had disappeared and there was not a single soul or vehicle around.

Things were made a little more difficult as the rains caused the glue-like red mud to stick to my tyres, making them instantly twice the size, and I inevitably fell off four or five times. This only added to the experience and fortunately the tumbles were more comical than a problem. I found myself lying on the ground completely caked in mud and laughing out loud at my position. Struggling up I found I could not see!

Sitting on my bike looking bemused, my goggles masked in red murram. Hot springs anywhere?

Democratic Republic of Congo

In Luanda, the capital, I once again found the Angolan people to be welcoming and had no problem wandering out at night to experience what the city had to offer. My biggest regret was my lack of Portuguese, but the sheer enthusiasm of the locals to try and break down this communication barrier made this a very special experience for me, and up to this point it was unequivocally my favourite country in Africa.

This was in sharp contrast to what I was going to find in Kinshasa, the capital of the Democratic Republic of Congo. The area was made famous by the exploits of Henry Morton Stanley to track the source of the Congo River which led to the manic interest of the insane King Leopold of Belgium and subsequently the Scramble for Africa in 1878. From this point onwards DRC probably suffered more than any country in the world. But I still had to get there to see it for myself.

Instead of taking the 'traditional' route to Kinshasa through the border of Matai, I decided to take a gamble and test myself by taking a secondary road through such exotic-sounding villages as Manuela de Zombo, Banza Sosso and Ngidinga. My Michelin map (I had no GPS throughout the trip) marked it as a passable road but not in the rainy season. Unfortunately, my map was more than six years out of date and would prove to be not such a reliable friend. However it proved to be a remarkable decision, as I was thrown into the centre of a tropical jungle with no cars, bicycles, people, electricity or buildings of any kind and to be honest, no road. What Michelin called a road turned out to be a track with ruts metres deep, rivers and puddles as high as my waist and bordering the path in a thick wall, the lushest tropical forest I had ever seen. Tarzan would have been proud to hack through it but it was so dense there is no way he would have been able to swing from tree to tree. The sounds of the forest were deafening, created by the monkeys, birds and many other creatures lurking in the undergrowth.

It was a punishing ordeal for me and the bike and a test for the most experienced rider. I fell often, getting caught up in the dense undergrowth or slipping in the mud, and was drenched to the bone with sweat, my vest glued to my skin, and my bike trousers beginning to chafe and rub in uncomfortable places. This was the hardest ride of my life and I had to change my maxim 'from border by border' to 'day by day', to 'kilometre by kilometre' and eventually to '100m by 100m'.

Hard going in DRC

The first day I covered thirty kilometres in eight hours, at times having to hack a path with a machete. This was totally draining as I had to park up the bike and cut through twenty metres of tangled branches, lianas and dead wood that had taken over the route. I then had to retrieve the bike and negotiate the track, paddling with my feet to stop myself from falling over. It must have been thirty degrees, but I had to keep my protective gear on to prevent myself being cut to shreds. I kept slipping and getting snagged on branches until I eventually got the bike through. I then had to repeat the process over and over again. Obviously this was not the thoroughfare my optimistic mind had conjured up when studying, what I now realised, was a seriously out-of-date map. On the second day I managed forty kms in nine hours, and on the third I completed a hundred and twenty. I felt incredibly proud of my achievements as I had to work really hard to gain ground. For the first time I really felt I deserved the rather pretentious title of Adventure Motorcyclist rather than just a tourer. This was compounded by the fact that the border was really just a clearing in the jungle with three dilapidated huts, one of which I assumed to be the official hut, judging by the bent flagpole outside it, sporting a filthy, half-torn Democratic Republic of Congo flag.

I removed my helmet, wiped the sweat and flies off my face and out of my eyes, and approached the customs, reaching into my rucksack for my passport. The official, in a ragged dirty, dark blue uniform with torn lapels, was asleep on a grey plastic school chair. When he woke and saw me, he nearly fell over backwards and his eyes widened in astonishment.

I queried, "Is this immigration?"

In Pidgin English he asked, "How do you come here, where are your friends? This road is finished. How do you come here?" I pointed back in the direction I had come from and said, "I am travelling alone, from that direction."

He was astonished, stood up, looked me up and down, whistling at the same time, and told me, in French, that no foreigners had been here for four years. He informed me that even the locals don't use this route. "It is finished, this road bad road, no good." I felt great. Loved that comment.

I think he may have been a bit out of touch with border procedures, not surprising really, considering the heavy traffic passing through, and he spent a full five minutes studying my passport upside down. When it came to getting an official stamp in my passport that was just wishful thinking on my part. The border guard stationed himself behind his desk, and motioned to me to take a seat, pointing to an upturned breeze block with a piece of hardboard balanced on top of it. He made a futile attempt to appear organised, fiddling in the two broken drawers of his desk, and shuffling a few papers around. He eventually pulled out a stamp with a flourish, but it was not to be, as the ink had obviously dried up on the cracked pad many years earlier.

I eventually made do with some unintelligible scribblings by the official, but not before half-heartedly arguing that I would not be able to get into the next country without a stamp. I realised that it was futile and cut myself short. I thanked him for his help, gave him some leftover corned beef and a handful of chillies. He shook my hand enthusiastically and said, "Merci beaucoup, Monsieur Le Blanc, et bon chance, bonne journée."

He followed me out to the bike, whistling again when he saw it, and proceeded to look at himself in the rear view mirror, pulling all sorts of, I presume, tough/sexy faces, while holding on to the handlebars. I drank a litre of water, trying not to cough it up through laughter, as I watched his poses. I kitted up, shook the guard's hand again, and headed off ,waving and laughing to myself inside my helmet. I wondered if he would still be sitting there, in four years' time, still on the government payroll, patiently waiting for the next lunatic on a motorbike to pass through. I was in adventurers' heaven and I sang Bob Marley songs at the top of my voice until my tunelessness started annoying me. After a tough couple of hours' riding, where I had to maintain exhausting concentration, I finally emerged from the jungle and reached the junction that freed me from this punishing path, as it miraculously turned into the asphalt road leading to Kinshasa. I felt euphoric.

My mood changed completely as soon as I hit the outskirts of Kinshasa. It was undoubtedly the hottest, dirtiest, most unsafe and least friendly place I have ever had the displeasure of driving into. As the jungle gave way to sprawling shanty towns, I stopped at a scrappy, one pump petrol station, manned (or womanned, if it bothers you) by a large woman, in a torn Esso uniform which revealed half her grubby bra. I asked directions to the centre of the city but was met with a blank expression, as though I was mad. No wonder, as I subsequently found out that it was going to take me two more gruelling, boiling, traffic-jammed hours to get into the centre and she had probably never ventured that far in her life.

Kinshasa has an estimated twelve million people and is incredibly poor. The majority survive by selling what they can on the streets, like small, 200 gram, plastic bags of water. The whole city is covered layers deep in these bags (the inventor of plastic has a lot to answer for). Others mill around holding twenty pairs of sunglasses in each hand in some octopus imitating act, while others carry an exceptional number of baguettes on their heads and are armed with a knife and a tub of margarine.

Jostling for space are the food sellers, offering chicken in peanut sauce, fish wrapped in palm leaves, and caterpillars and crocodile meat (the oysters and caviar of Kinshasa's culinary scene), or chikwange – the leaf-wrapped blocks of fermenting cassava paste that to the uninitiated resembles warm carpet glue. That is being overly polite and even my culturally adapted taste buds struggled to keep chikwangwe down when being watched enthusiastically for a reaction. Then there are the fruit, mobile phone, cigarette and soft drink sellers, again balancing ridiculous numbers of products on their heads. Needless to say all the brands are fake (Raybon, George Amani [sic] etc). Sellers have all sorts of demonstrations to show you how genuine they are, varying from displaying the 'original' sunglasses case as proof, to burning the lens with a lighter to show you it is real glass, etc.

Standards do drop though, believe you me. One particularly enthusiastic salesman tried to sell me a pair of sunglasses with one arm missing. Do I look like Van Gogh? I also had a less-than-normal thief, halfway inside my rucksack, before I noticed a slight tugging on my shoulder. He had managed to completely open one of the zips on my rucksack and was just about to relieve me of my belongings when something must have got snagged. I turned round to confront him and he just fell into the road and rolled around laughing manically. He had obviously lost a few marbles as he was filthy beyond normal standards and was dribbling. There were three Algerian UN troops standing on a corner, smoking cigarettes and ordering coffee from a street seller standing behind his two-wheeled portable stall. They just looked over and shrugged. They had seen it all before and worse, I suppose. I transferred my rucksack from my back and strapped it to my front. That would be the last time I would ever have it on my back.

Adding to the mayhem were the ubiquitous yellow and blue taxis and mini vans, careering around with their sweating human cargo, bouncing along the potholed roads. On every street corner were the Cheges, or street children (named after Che Guevara for some odd reason), who are feral and intimidating; demanding money and calling you 'Le Blanc' or worse if you don't oblige.

Seated on rickety wooden stools dotted around the city street corners were the money changers who were always well-fed women (I'm being polite), in bright floral dresses with huge wads of Central African Francs, a thousand of which might buy you a soft drink.

Everywhere there was French and Lingala simultaneously machine-gunning out of hundreds of mouths as people tried to make their lives heard. Among all of this were the occasional fat cats with brand new American 4x4s, immaculate suits, mirror-shiny leather shoes, Ray-Bans, (the right spelling this time) and mobile phones, scornfully ignoring the masses surrounding their trucks trying to sell their wares.

Finally, pushing, jostling and dragging themselves around the capital were the disabled and deformed, and the cart pushers with their unfeasibly heavy loads, muscular bodies and shaved heads glistening with perspiration.

It was a scene at the port that distressed me the most. I went to check on tickets for the ferry to the capital of Congo, Brazzaville, which was visible on the opposite bank of the famous river, when a scene unfolded in front of me straight out of a horror film. The disabled traditionally travel on hand or foot-pedalled tricycles (depending on the nature of their disability) across on the ferry and load up their wheelchairs to snapping point with goods to sell for a meagre profit in Brazzaville. In the past they were allowed to travel free but this privilege has been taken away as they are suspected drug runners.

However, the police refuse to physically touch them or search them as they are believed to have special powers. So the disabled have been forced to run the gauntlet of beatings as they disembark. A man with hideously shrivelled legs was dragging himself across as the police beat him about the head with batons. It was so vicious that his eye immediately split, and swelled to the size of a tennis ball. Others had their heads split open with rifle butts while the lucky ones got away with a few whippings from cut-off pieces of heavy duty hosepipe wielded by these despicable police. It made me feel nauseous and I could not stay any longer to find out about my ticket. It was too much for me.

I left the port and headed back to my room. As I rode, it suddenly dawned on me that I had been here a week and hadn't seen a single tourist. The only foreigners I had seen were members of aid agencies and they could only be seen fleetingly, passing by in 4x4s – they never walked in the street. The UN presence in The Democratic Republic of Congo is the biggest of any country in the world with 20,000 permanent troops, along with UNICEF, World Food Programme, WHO and Save the Children, to name just a few. They keep their lives completely separate from the day-to-day goings on of the country, hearing it secondhand from radio, TV or sources while they travel from one secure compound to another. A member of Save the Children did not see the irony when I suggested walking to a nearby café and he replied, "No, no we must drive, the children are dangerous!"

The only people you meet on the street who are not locals are the news reporters because DRC is obviously a hotbed of news. All the negative things that people want to dwell on, will happen here. I was lucky enough to meet up with a Reuters reporter. It was not surprising that we bumped into each other really, because he was the only European out and about apart from me. I was sitting at a roadside café with Yves (I'm sure he was the reincarnation of Marc Bolan from T-Rex or possibly a famous ex-American wrestler). By the way, before you get delusions of grandeur the roadside café consists of a tatty Primus beer umbrella with rain dripping through the rips in it, a couple of upturned beer crates sliding in the mud for stools, with a less than sane waiter serving beers which he had undoubtedly put through quality control (down his oesophagus), to make sure he was only serving the best.

As we enjoyed an ice cold Primus, and didn't enjoy two less-than-acceptable samoosas a strange situation unfolded before us. A brand new Silver Nissan Patrol 4x4 drove past us with a number of children hanging off the back and sides. Within a matter of seconds hundreds of Cheges or street children descended on the vehicle, bringing it to a standstill, not unlike a swarm of ants bringing down a dung beetle. Small children were hanging on to the bumper and lying in the road, directly in front of the wheels, so there was no chance of the occupant moving off unless he wanted to decrease the population of street children by at least ten. Eventually the crowd parted and a slightly older boy, maybe seventeen, made his way to the driver's window. In a surreal scene the hundreds of children were singing the popular football chant 'Ole Ole Ole Ole' while the head of the gang negotiated with the driver for 'tax' to continue his journey. Yves informed me that this was a perfectly normal routine. If the children spotted a really smart car, or a celebrity, or a minister they descended upon it in this manner and the driver was always forced to pay his taxes.

The public stood by and watched until the gang leader had negotiated a price – he then motioned to all the others and they disappeared into the side streets as quickly as they had arrived and the driver continued on his way. Can't really imagine this happening in Kent, UK, where I started this insane trip, but then again I was 30,000km away and things were very, very different out here!

Ever since the beginning of this trip I vowed that I would make every minute of it count and soak up the experiences. Following this motto I tried to get into Somalia and Darfur in Sudan to see exactly what was going on, but it turned out to be an impossibility to get visas. In the same vein I made sure that I consciously did not avoid any of the less reputable areas or ones I was warned about. In fact for strange reasons I can't even explain to myself, I actively sought out places I had been warned against. I met some of the nicest people in such locations, ghettos, shanty towns, whatever you call them. On the flip side I also found myself in some sticky situations – police checks; attempted bag thefts by the resident dribbling lunatic; confrontations with armed drunk soldiers and hundreds of other magically memorable experiences.

Whilst on the subject of resident dribbling lunatics, in my experience of travelling in Africa it seems every town or village has its resident lunatic. These people are accepted in the community and when they approach, mumbling to themselves, "I'm not mad; the voices in my head tell me that I'm not," or something along those lines, people just shrug their shoulders and say, "Oh, he's mad." I am all for them being part of society rather than being locked up, as long as their madness does not involve murdering visiting motorcycle adventurers, obviously!

Although I have befriended a number of resident lunatics during thirty years in Africa, one particular gentleman sticks in my mind more than others; the resident lunatic of my hometown, Mbabane, in Swaziland. He was called 'Touch Everything'. He used to wear a baseball cap with all his possessions stuck underneath it in a weird balancing act; matches, cigarettes, a pen, a few small children, etc. Touch Everything, as his name implies, touched everything he walked past; trees, lampposts, walls, etc. But by far his favourite thing to touch, was women's bottoms. (A good choice of target, I think, if you are going to be a mad man who touches everything!) If he went past a woman and missed her bottom he would walk a few paces and stop, looking confused. His mistake would slowly register on his face, as he looked up to the heavens for inspiration. Then he would quickly turn back and chase the escaped posterior until he had success. He was harmless and everyone accepted his behaviour, although he did get a few light-hearted slaps around the back of the head, and some sharp words from the local women. All the locals looked out for his wellbeing however, and tourists were often pre-warned about his behaviour, so that they didn't overreact, which could possibly lead to problems for Touch Everything. One thing's for sure, Touch Everything was never going to be the governor of The Central Bank, but at least he was free and happy and, most importantly, part of a community.

To get back to the point, Kinshasa has its fair share of resident lunatics, and I had bumped into a fair few mentally challenged folk. I was busy watching one such fellow, a Rastafarian trying to cross the street, talking to all the cars as though they understood him, probably preaching as often seems to be their calling or conviction in life. His appearance was extremely bizarre. He was covered from head to toe in strips of different coloured plastic bags, including his hair and he looked like a massive pom-pom.

As I watched him conversing with various makes of car (not the occupants), a battered Nissan with a smashed windscreen, no ears – sorry, wing mirrors – pulled up beside me with four heavyweight men inside, all of whom made Idi Amin look like an anorexic primary school student. The front seat passenger pulled out a card saying 'Police'. It was flashed at me so quickly it could just as easily have been a voucher for McDonalds, or a photo of his mother. He then snarled, "Le Blanc," and demanded my passport. (I instantly twigged what was going on; it was a con I had luckily heard about a few days earlier from one of the Save the Children staff.) When I said I did not carry my passport with me, he quickly raised a handgun to his chest just above the height of the door, sufficient for me to see it, and then lowered it again. Simultaneously, the back door opened, and he stated in English, "You come to the police station now, white man, so we can make report."

I quietly and calmly said, "I would not get into your car even if you were four topless Swedish blonde girls looking for a motorcycle adventurer to party with." No, I didn't really say that. I told him that I would walk up to the British Embassy, and that they could follow me there to make an official complaint, because there was no way I was going in their car. I think they realised that I was going to prove harder work than they had anticipated and they swore at me in various languages, while the driver spat out of the window onto the road next to me, like all hard men feel they have to do, and sped off.

Once they had disappeared out of sight I leant over and put my trembling hands on my knees and gasped in huge lungfuls of air. No matter how streetwise or brave you think you are, it is difficult not to be shaken by the threat of a gun. All of this on the main High Street in the city centre. Another normal day in Kinshasa. I would continue my journey and hoped that things improved for the citizens of a beautiful land that was systematically plundered by The Mighty Leopard Mobutu Sese Seko for thirty years.

The next day I psyched myself up and paid my second visit to the hellhole that is the port of Kinshasa. This is the only gateway to Congo – Brazzaville, just visible on the opposite bank of The Congo River, and consequently is a heaving bottleneck of disabled people, crawling, dragging, and pedalling their way back and forth with goods. Conjuring up visions of palm trees and holidays this area is known as The Beach. It was not to be, of course. This visit was no better. I was immediately halted at an eight-foot rusted gateway by a border guard with blood-red eyes and a vicious demeanour. He didn't bother with the niceties and immediately spat out, "Donnez moi l'argent!" (Give me money.) I refused and an argument ensued amongst a group of 'customs officers'. I stayed completely silent and tried to put on a steely expression but probably succeeded in looking more like I had a severe case of diarrhoea. Eventually they let me through the gate.

Immediately upon entering, I saw a group of about fifteen blind people, with cardboard boxes sellotaped to their backs, with the sellotape strapped round and round their torsos like the early stages of a mummification process. They were in a 'train', each one holding on to the box of the person in front of them, literally the blind leading the blind. This was not strictly true as the leading vendor still had one eye but had a serious cataract covering it. He managed to stumble through somehow.

A disused railway line crossed the road and a group of four men were trying to push a disabled man in a wheelchair. The wheelchair was so overloaded with goods, all that was visible of the man was the top of his head sticking out amongst various boxes. The horrific thing was the helpers were also disabled; arms missing, legs withered and distorted into gross positions, while alongside them a mountain of a border guard was not helping. He kept hitting them with a stick, spitting and screaming at them at the top of his lungs to unblock the road. Once again I felt nauseous but had to ignore it and get on with my mission of finding a boat.

A small pockmarked man with one foot twisted completely in the opposite direction to normal, in filthy flapping sandals made from strips of car tyre, hobbled over to me and introduced

Charly Boy, Nigeria

Four on a bike, Burkina Faso

On the way to… !!

Trade boats, Ghana

Smoking man, DRC

Future Dakar Rally rider, Senegal!

Friendly policemen, Congo

Above: motorbike brigade, Mali

Left: muddy High Street, DRC

Below: my next bike

himself as Guillaume Faustin. Guillaume was a handsome man of about thirty, who despite his tough existence had a warm, open face. I trusted him immediately. I also liked the way he went straight to the point, no beating around the bush (or jungle). He stated said that for $20 he could get me through the rabble, as he knew the procedures and the customs officers. Guillame worked tirelessly, dragging himself from one official to another, dripping with sweat, but never hesitating, calling to me, "Come friend, follow friend." He managed to arrange all my bike paperwork, visa checks and ferry ticket in under two hours. I was so grateful for his help, I gave him a manly hug, and it was decided I would present myself at Customs promptly at 7.30am the next morning. Guillmaine said he would meet me, so that he could help me get the bike on to the ferry before all the disabled vendors descended on the port ramp.

The next day I was unable to make my appointment with Guillame as the bike conked out. I felt bad about that, and vowed that I would find him before I crossed the river. Even though he had been paid, I wanted to thank him again. As the bike was not going anywhere today, I accepted an invitation to visit a project set up by Save the Children. I was so glad I did.

The project was a refuge for street children, girls only, and was in the slums of Kinshasa. We made our way through the rain-soaked filth, the tyres of the Land Rover sliding from side to side as we negotiated the tight gaps left between the millions of street vendors sloshing their way through the garbage-filled streets. To reach the refuge we had to cross a stinking, open sewer trench and the Land Rover lurched off the edge of the impossibly narrow concrete crossing and was stuck.

I forewarned the driver that it was impossible to get across but he insisted and the inevitable happened. Within the blink of an eye, the vehicle was surrounded and swamped by people begging for money; well, offering to help for money. The driver handed out of a number of 500 Franc notes (30 cents) through a small gap in the window, and immediately about forty people

241

bounced the wheel back up onto the verge and we were across. They all followed, banging their palms on the windows, and pushing their faces up against the glass, leaving stains of sweat and dirt imprinted on the glass. We slowly edged forward and made it to the crèche, rushing in through a tunnel of people jostling and pushing us in the mud. We came to some large iron green gates which were immediately opened by a beautifully presented Congolese woman in traditional dress who remained incredibly calm, almost serene, in the face of the crowd.

We pushed against the gates to try and prevent the crowds coming in, as people started falling in the mud and filth. Eventually we got it closed and she quickly pulled a massive rusty bar across to secure the gate. We were in! Madelaine introduced herself with a large grin and graceful handshake, offering immediately to show us around. The refuge consisted of a tiny kitchen with a microwave, a two-hob stove and an assortment of battered, chipped, bent and broken crockery and cutlery stored in a wall cupboard with no doors. "This is where the girls have cooking lessons," she proudly announced.

In an adjoining room was a small classroom with a blackboard and about ten broken desks. Opposite this, across an open, swept, concrete courtyard, was an empty small hall. There was off-white paint flaking off the walls, and mildew, mould and water dripping off the ceiling. In the corner was a wooden chair with a sad-looking, mangled, electric fan balanced on it, the plugless cord draping on the floor. A number of blankets were strewn around. This was where more than forty girls slept every night. Next to this was a tiny room, the size of a larder with eight children in white aprons. They were squeezed in, listening intently to a bright-faced young teacher demonstrating how to hold scissors. This was where they were taught hairdressing. I asked Madelaine what the biggest problems were that these children faced. She said many were tortured, raped, beaten or accused of witchcraft, and found themselves on the street and most were now prostitutes.

Save the Children refuge

I asked her whether the smaller children (the girls ranged from 7–18) were not influenced into prostitution by the older girls. Madelaine stated, shockingly, that it was the opposite; that the younger ones were the prostitutes! She said that some of the older girls had gained some working skills, and some self-respect, and had managed to stop selling themselves. It was a desperate, dark situation, with Madelaine providing the only light of hope and safety to many of these children. She impressed me even more when I asked, "Can't you lock the girls in at night?" She looked me directly in the eyes and answered, "If I lock them in at night, then this is a prison. But it is not a prison, it is a refuge. If I want them to come back every night, there must be the trust."

Although Madelaine was doing an incredible job, I passed some girls lying on benches, with the stony-faced blank looks more normally associated with war survivors. I greeted them but there was no answer and no glimmer of light in their vacant expressions. Maybe humans can get too damaged to repair. I hoped not. What hell for these children. I felt extremely depressed and a bit sickened by myself that I was there with my camera, insensitively snapping away. What right did I have to come and examine their lives? But at the same time it was remarkable to meet these selfless volunteers, who worked so hard to give these broken children some semblance of a normal existence. We think that poverty is only being hungry, naked and homeless. The poverty of being unwanted, unloved and uncared for is the greatest poverty. I felt pleased that I had chosen to raise money for Save the Children and privileged to see where some of the money was going. These volunteers on the ground were inspiring and made me thankful for the work they were doing with the money I was raising.

The next day I woke up feeling gloomy and pensive. Whilst stuck in Kinshasa waiting for spares for my bike, I had got into the routine of going to the internet café every morning. This café, with a grand total of two computers, was on the 30th June Boulevard, which is Kinshasa's main thoroughfare. It was only a five-minute walk from the centrally located apartment I was staying in. Luckily, a Save the Children employee, Glenn, and his Congolese wife, Antoinette, had offered me a room for the duration of my stay in Kinshasa. They lived in a complex which was surrounded by high walls and a huge iron gate manned by two security guards. On my walk from the complex I passed a small, scrappy grass verge on the Boulevard corner where I always met a small street boy of about six years old with a sweet little face and a slightly droopy left eye, à la Forrest Whittaker, a torn Madonna T-shirt, filthy green shorts and flip-flops. He always politely asked me for some money. I made a conscious decision before I left on this expedition that I would not give money to anyone, because you have to set a precedent early on, no matter how callous it sounds and how difficult it is.

I knew from previous experience that giving money to people in public in Africa immediately singles you out more than ever, and you will be surrounded by thousands of children, permanently pushing, shoving and shouting for help. I know it is sad, but you become a small beacon of hope, if only for a day, and if you succumb, it becomes almost impossible to go out. I struggled with this moral issue throughout the trip, and my personal selfish worries were put starkly in perspective on this walk.

I was feeling pretty down about the bike problems and my lack of progress, as I walked past the street children once again. 'Forrest' was always polite and not pushy and because I was wallowing in my self-pity, I didn't notice him walking next to me, almost running in fact, to keep up with my strides. I felt a tug on my shirt and looked down next to me. He said nothing, but looked up at me, imploringly. His nose was running and he had a brown, dirt stain on his hair, where he had obviously laid his head down to sleep the night before. I felt a stab of sadness and hopelessness, and reached down and brushed the dirt from his hair. I said to him, "Attends! Attends un moment!" and headed down the road to the nearest street vendor. I bought him some cheap Chinese chocolate from a vendor wearing a David Beckham shirt and bedroom slippers. I wrapped a small amount of money around the sweets and approached Forrest with my hand outstretched. When he looked down at his hand, it dawned on him what I had given him. His face slowly contorted into a grimace and he burst into a flood of tears, his shoulders wracked with emotion, his face collapsing with grief and thanks at the same time. I was so taken aback I gave him a big hug, but had to walk off, as I was being watched, and I could feel the tears welling up in my eyes. I wanted to hug him some more and say it would all be OK, but that's only in films, and it was not going to be OK. It was soul-destroying, and had a real effect on me. I decided to go for a walk to clear my head and wandered around aimlessly for a half hour. I eventually made it to the outskirts of the city. I turned down a wide boulevard with a derelict grassy area running down the left hand side of the road. Set on the 'lawn' was a funfair of sorts; rickety, rusted swings and slides and a dodgy-looking dodgem track. All the cars were occupied, but the strange thing I quickly noticed was that everyone was driving extremely carefully and politely, making great efforts to avoid one another! The absolute opposite to their driving ethos on real roads and, let's face it, not really the point of bumper cars! What a strange world we live in.

This quirky scene wasn't enough to stop me thinking about 'Forrest' though. Life was so terrible, for so many. I didn't know how I felt at that moment. It was a little bit like I was being a reporter when I wrote my journal, and blocked out my emotional reaction to what I was seeing on the trip. I didn't understand why I was reacting like this, but I felt like I had put myself in a little bubble to protect myself. I was confused about what I was doing, why I was here. I feel like a voyeur of poverty, a privileged fleeting visitor, on a $7,000 machine, imposing myself on these people.

I didn't even know how to feel. I knew I was raising money for Save the Children. At this moment it doesn't make me feel good. I knew I would be the first to circumnavigate Africa. It didn't make me feel good. I know I would have a book and a DVD out of this. It didn't make me feel good. I knew this experience would change me forever. But was it important? No. I felt like a fraud. I was being so self-centred and couldn't shake off this feeling. Maybe all would become clear, but I doubted it. All I knew was, that this was the furthest thing possible away from a holiday that I could ever imagine. I had psychologically given myself a 'job'; to film, write, observe and 'get round Africa', to protect myself from the futility and helplessness I felt. The only thing I knew for sure was that I was exactly where I wanted to be, and where I wanted to be for the rest of my life: AFRICA. Why I was here was another question altogether. I was not looking for some great epiphany of why I was in the world or what my purpose was. I have never been that way inclined. I realised that I was irrelevant to Africa; Africa did not care if I was here or not. But Africa was not irrelevant to me and I hoped I would find out something about this continent that would sort out my confused mind. Instead, I was more confused than I had ever been.

Maybe that's the way it was always going to be. The humanity of Africa is so complex and confusing, and that is where the magic maybe lies. Nothing worthwhile is easy. Africa is not easy, but why has God decided that it should be so difficult for the people who live in it. Did he have to go that far? Only He Knows.

Chapter Nine
Crossing the Congo River

'I cried because I had no shoes, then I met a man with no feet.'
Helen Keller

What did the Democratic Republic of Congo have before candles?
Electricity

Whenever you go somewhere, you meet it as if it were alive, which of course it is. The rainforest outside Kinshasa is the loudest thing you will ever hear, like trains, planes, a city or a subway. How apt, actually, to also call a city 'the jungle'. Every sound that is made by the vegetation; giant trees, tree-sized vines, groaning, as they rub against each other, is also made by creatures. Every being was chattering, talking, whistling, and singing. Everything was in motion – slithering, sliding, jumping, falling, hopping, ambling, crawling and flying. The vital difference between the two jungles is that one is the pure sound of nature and all its animals, whereas the other is the despairing sound of only one animal, the human being. I had escaped into this rainforest, an hour out of the city to get a breather from the claustrophobia that is Kinshasa, and to gather my thoughts on tackling another fifteen countries.

I had found sixteen days in Kinshasa a real eye-opener. For the first time in my life, I have witnessed real undiluted poverty, where people have got absolutely nothing. For some reason it is so much more striking in an urban environment. In rural areas, people may be in rags, but I always feel to be in that environment is much more dealable with than the filthy, hot, emotionless, cramped city scene. In the jungle I felt calm and remotivated. I headed back to Kinshasa with my batteries charged and my joie-de-vivre reinstalled.

After two more days of problems with the bike, which I won't bore you with, I finally arrived at the Kinshasa port to get the 10'oclock ferry and continue my journey around Africa. It was 11 May, and the next day was my birthday. A new country on my birthday, and Congo-Brazzaville, of all places. How many people can say that!

The crowd at 'The Beach' was the same heaving, broken mass of bodies, crawling, scrambling, and limping. The ferry was a huge flatbed lump of rusting steel, which took four hours to fill. It was almost indescribable. I drove my bike on past the masses and tried to find a space to put it. People were pushing and shoving, and I was eventually forced into such a tight space and knocked off my feet so many times, it was a miracle I didn't topple over with the bike. Next to me was a tricycle, which had been fashioned with broken pieces of wood into some sort of makeshift cart. The driver of the cart was half a man. Although he had no legs he seemed to have shrunken into himself, so that he just looked like a chest, head and arms. His passengers consisted of a middle-aged man with cataracts, so bad that he was completely blind. His eyes were a deep milky white and as if that was not enough, both his feet were splayed out, one facing completely backwards, and the other one curled up on itself in a twisted, distorted ball.

Next to him in the same box (yes, box) was a young man, maybe eighteen, whose legs were pencil thin and completely useless. The worst thing about the whole scenario was that this 'box of broken people' was the norm. There were rows and rows of these tricycles tip to tail; people numbered in the thousands. As more and more people crammed on I was squashed up hard against my bike with absolutely no room to move. The man next to me was selling soft drinks, which I helped pass over my head, in a conveyer belt method, to whoever was calling out for them. A customs official was pushing his way around the ferry hitting people indiscriminately with a piece of hose pipe. Suddenly, out of the corner of my

249

eye, I saw something scurrying beside me at high speed, and glanced down between the masses of distorted legs, boxes, litter, sweat, cloth, goods etc. There was the smallest man I have ever seen in my life, so grossly disfigured that both his legs were bent double, glued to his back, and he was as thin as a pool cue. He was making his way through everyone's legs balanced on his hands. This is the life he had; down by people's feet in the filth, unnoticed, uncared for, and kicked from one dusty section to another.

After three hours and no sign of the ferry's engines firing up, I started to feel claustrophobic and like I was having a panic attack. It was impossible to even shuffle my feet back and forth without bumping into another passenger. I have never been good in enclosed spaces and large crowds, and this was both, to the extreme. My heart rate started to flutter, my breathing became erratic, and I literally had to concentrate on inhaling, then exhaling, and trying to keep my breathing regular. I tried closing my eyes but it only made matters worse, it made me realise how incredibly loud everything was. It was hellish; thousands of disabled and deformed people crammed onto a boiling hot steel hulk, all shouting and screaming at the tops of their voices. I felt guilty that I felt trapped in a horrific film. After all this was no film, but for these people, day in, day out.

I opened my eyes and standing in front of me was an incredibly dark man with his hair shaved, wearing a red and black Angolan T-shirt, with one of the sleeves ripped off. He had a nasty gash running from the centre of his cheek to the edge of his mouth which reminded me of The Joker in *Batman*. He extended his hand to me. As soon as I took it, he started laughing manically, with the crowd looking on in interest. It's difficult to hide when you are 6ft 4ins, the only white person, and on a huge multi-coloured, flag-covered motorbike. Another passenger with a mangled right arm told him to leave me alone. I said, "Thank you, but it's no problem," but as I spoke, The Joker turned and tried to punch the other passenger in the face.

Luckily, it was a wild swing, and he missed completely, losing his balance in the process and bounced off a number of passengers, before sliding down between them. He immediately scrambled to his feet, leapt all around the ferry, stepping on and punching people indiscriminately, until two customs officers came on and dragged him off the ferry. The passengers all started cheering, and I suspect by their reaction, that this was a regular occurrence, and that he was a well known 'mentally challenged' passenger.

I decided to try and keep to myself, and just stared at the floor or at the dials of the bike. I regretted this feeling because it was not my normal travelling ethos. As James A. Michener said, "If you reject the food, fear the religion and avoid the people, you might better stay at home." I wanted to talk to people, but I also wanted to scream out and cry in despair at the difficulties so many African people have to face.

My thoughts were interrupted by the young man with the withered arm, who had tried to help me earlier. "Hello, my name is Albert, where are you going?" he asked in English, extending his good hand.

I was pleased he had spoken to me, and I gripped his hand, smiled and said, "I'm going into Congo, and then on to Gabon and Cameroon."

"You travel alone, where is your wife?" he queried.

I said, "My wife is in England."

He looked confused, pointed at my bike stickers, and said, "You go to all these countries alone?"

I replied, "Yes, I have been through sixteen African countries on this bike."

He whistled, turned to the crowd around us, his slim face breaking into a wide smile, and said in French, "This white man is very strong, he is going around all of Africa, alone."

This comment had the effect of galvanising the crowd into a flurry of questions: "Why are you doing this?" "Where do you sleep?" "Are you not scared of wild animals?" "Have you seen any evil spirits in the forest?" "How do you fix the moto?" "Is your wife angry?" "Where are your children?'' "Are you blessed with boys or girls?" Albert duly translated every question fired at me, and my responses. I speak French, but didn't tell Albert, as I was enjoying the rapport with this happy, enthusiastic man, and I suspect he was enjoying his role as translator. He embellished my answers, liberally, and had the crowd animated, laughing, whistling and arguing goodnaturedly with each other, about how mad I actually was, what were the most dangerous countries I would face, or whether I would make it.

Everybody had an opinion on countries they had never been to; like the earnest shoe seller, who leant over my bike and said very seriously, "Monsieur, don't go to Angola! We may be thieves, but they are *killers*," stressing and lengthening the word 'killers'. Just like the Foreign Office website, if I took their advice to heart, I would never have left my front door. Having said that, I was so pleased that I was now involved with the group and it was all thanks to Albert. I hate feeling cut off from people whose country I am in, and this was a big bonus, the lively discussion really making the trip bearable and actually, fun. The thing that really struck me were the enthusiastic questions people asked about the trip and the bike; people who because of their deformities could never go on a motorbike, let alone relate to what I was doing. They were excellent people.

When the discussion finally calmed down a little, I turned to Albert, and asked, "So where are you going?" Albert explained to me that he was returning to his home in the north of Congo. He was brought up in Mboko, a small village on the banks of the Sangha River, a tributary of the mighty Congo River. But it was an incident that occurred when he was six that eventually led to him being in Kinshasa. Albert told me that he was on the roof of his father's hut, fixing a leak with some thatch, "in big, big rain" when he slipped and fell. Sadly, he fell extremely awkwardly onto the hard dirt yard, landing with his left arm under his body. "It was broken in many, many places, Mr. Spencer," he stated solemnly. "My family try their best to fix it, but it was no good." Over the next two years, he stayed in his village, helping out his family as much as he could. Over this period his arm withered up completely, and the muscles wasted away, rendering his left arm unusable.

When he was eight, a friend of his father, a Mr. Kayembe, another disabled man from the village, had come to their homestead with a proposition for Albert's father. He had explained that Albert could go with him to Brazzaville, and make some good money, taking toiletry products over on a ferry to Kinshasa, to sell. He said that disabled people can travel on the ferry for free, so it would be ideal for Albert. "Enough money to live good, and plenty, plenty to send to family," the man had boasted. Albert did not want to go at all, and was devastated as he loved his village and his life, and was scared to go to the city. He told me that, before this, he had left his village only once, to drop his aunt at the border town with Cameroon, Ouesso. Unfortunately, his father agreed with Mr. Kayembe that it was a good idea, and that was that. Within two days, Albert found himself on a boat with a complete stranger for the three-week trip down the Congo River to Brazzaville.

Predictably maybe, when they arrived in Kinshasa, Mr. Kayembe made Albert work for twelve hours a day for food, and a small room shared with five others. After two years he finally plucked up the courage to leave, and ran away to the centre of Kinshasa. He then slept in the bus station or on the streets of Kinshasa for the next six years, scraping together a living, shining people's shoes, and selling plastic bags of water and scented tissues. Surprisingly, he said that it was one of the best periods of his life, as he had "many, many friends on the street, many boys like me."

I asked him, "Why did you not go back to your village?"

Immediately he answered, "I had failed in my job, I had failed my father, I had sent no money." But recently Albert had heard from a member of his village, who he bumped into in the capital, that his father had died from "very strong sickness". Albert was finally returning to his village, at the age of sixteen, to fulfil what he felt was his obligation, to replace his father as the head of the family. Albert had undoubtedly had a tough time, but he had an infectious positivity that I hoped would see him through.

I enjoyed talking to him immensely, and learnt a lot about his childhood and his life in the village, which he obviously cherished, but I must admit that I eventually found myself hopping from foot to foot, finding it hard to concentrate on what he was saying. I was getting increasingly desperate to urinate, which was impossible on this sardine can of a ferry, as you can imagine. On top of that, black acrid fumes filled the whole deck of the ferry and my eyes were stinging and streaming tears. Nobody else seemed to be affected, I must be soft. After what seemed like an interminable period of hopping, bending double and wincing, by which time my bladder felt like a basketball, we docked in Brazzaville. I waited patiently (well, tried to), with Albert for another forty five minutes, while the crowds in front of us sloshed their way through a foot of water, and headed up the concrete slipway, pushing and shoving, to be the first in the queue at Customs.

As I arrived at the port side, an official just grabbed my passport, and pushed me forward, pointing at a grey building in the distance. I could tell that Albert and I were going to lose each other in the mayhem, so I quickly scribbled down my email and phone number that he had requested. I said, "Goodbye and good luck Albert."

Albert replied, "I send friend request on Facebook!"

That took me by surprise, as I must confess Facebook wasn't at the forefront of my mind at that moment. I laughed, and said, "Yes, that would be great!" patting him warmly on the back as I headed off. What a pleasure. I hope Albert can fill what he obviously feels are the big shoes of his father. I could tell by our conversation that he truly loved his father, and was sad that he had not seen him before he died.

I pushed my bike through the melee, unintentionally hitting carts and people with my handlebars, apologising each time, until I made it through to an overflowing toilet behind the Immigration buildings. After relieving myself, for what seemed like ten minutes, impersonating a fire hydrant, I headed out again into the unforgiving sunlight. I will never ever see my passport alive again, I thought, as I looked back at the sea of mangled humanity, swarming and surging towards me, and the official swallowed up in the whole nightmare, nowhere to be seen. I saw a relaxed-looking policeman sitting by the side of the road under a battered Coca-Cola umbrella, eating a plate of juja, and approached him about what to do. I was drowning with sweat inside my helmet, so had to remove it. He pointed me to a tatty, dusty, brick and mud building further down the road and said something like, "Douane Rapide".

To my astonishment, when I arrived there, the official who had taken my passport was sitting at a desk, looking very calm, with a fan behind him and Nat-Geo Channel blaring out of a small TV on his desk. He must have an underground tunnel from the port straight to this office; there is no other sensible explanation as to how he made it through the crowds. He stamped my passport, threw it on the counter, swivelled round on his chair to the TV, put his boots up on the desk, and that was it. I was out! I pulled around a corner and a sign over the road said, "Bienvenue à Brazzaville – You've made it alive," or something along those lines. It couldn't exactly say "You've made it in one piece," because that would be untrue of ninety percent of the people who got off that ferry.

Brazzaville was a complete contrast to Kinshasa. The city felt much smaller, more organised and much cleaner than its counterpart across the river. I made my way to a 'Hotel' called Hippocampe. It turned out to be only five minutes from the port down a steep, sun-cracked asphalt road, the cracks filled with long coarse grass. I arrived outside the hotel which consisted of an open terrace, with white pillars, blue wooden trellises, a stone floor and a solid roof. Red paper lanterns hung around the entrance and about twenty tables were smartly laid for dinner. It looked very plush and way out of my budget.

I needn't have worried though, because it turned out that the owner, Olivier, was an ex-traveller, and all travellers stayed for free. My favourite price! Olivier was a slim French guy of about thirty five, with small round glasses. He was immaculately dressed, spoke very softly and was polite to a tee. Olivier had spent two years cycling around the world, and had now settled in Brazzaville to run a restaurant and hotel, with his Vietnamese wife. He showed me to the 'campsite,' which turned out to be a conference room with comfortable chairs, a snooker table and working ceiling fans. I couldn't believe my luck after Kinshasa. Olivier warned me that there was a pond outside the room, which was a breeding ground for mosquitoes. He recommended putting the tent up, because the squadron of mosquitos apparently re-enacted the Blitz in the Conference room each night. He then pointed out the cold water shower at the other end of the building, and then apologised that he had to get back to, "things that I have to organise, the same each day."

I didn't get the chance to know Olivier very well, as he was rushed off his feet the whole time I was there. I did get some insight into him, however, through his strange library collection in the Conference room. His books included 'LSD – Spirituality and the Creative Process' by Oscar Jaruger, 'Strength and Conditioning Secrets of the World's Greatest Fighters – and How You Can Use Them' by John Saylor and 'The Hitchhiker's Guide to the Galaxy' by Douglas Adams. Hmm! I'm not sure if I wanted to get to know a karate expert on acid! No, I jest, he was a great guy, and judging from his tender relationship with his wife, another one of his titles might have helped him in life; "How to Find True Love" by Tracy Derby!

As the complete boat/customs saga over the Congo River

took five hours to complete a forty-minute trip, it was now too late to leave Brazzaville, but I felt that I had to do something constructive to keep up the momentum of the trip after such a protracted delay in Kinshasa. After unpacking the bike I decided to go to the Cameroon Embassy and try and get my visa. The Embassy sat on a steep hill overlooking the city, and consisted of a high wall, enclosing a white-washed building, with the green, red and yellow Cameroon flag fluttering outside. A friendly guard was posted at the entrance next to a metal turnstile, which he waved me through after briefly checking my passport. I pushed open the glass door and entered the building.

It was a spacious room, divided into two by an ornately carved wooden partition, depicting a busy African market on one half, and an animal filled jungle scene on the other. On one side of the partition was a single desk, with a lady sitting behind it, who was busy drying a towel and some socks. She was holding them up, and waving them around in front of the fan she had perched next to her. Watching her from the wall was the Cameroonian President, Paul Biya, and next to him was a glass cabinet with a display of various Cameroonian hats and masks. I approached the desk, staying silent, not wanting to disturb her laundry session. But she immediately stopped with her chores, looked up, smiled and asked me how she could help. She said that I needed to speak to the head of the Visa Section, who she immediately called up on the phone.

A few minutes later, in came, sorry, in stormed, the larger than life, spectacularly friendly, John James Nsangou. After an X-Factor-inspired entrance, he introduced himself and proceeded to talk to me for four hours, in which time he managed to squeeze in ninety percent of the words in the English dictionary (mostly nine letters or more, triple words score, etc.). I had very little reason to complain, as I had little to do, and he was highly entertaining. Mr. Nsangou had a wide friendly face, was suffering from a shaving rash and severely pockmarked skin, but his eyes were bright and lively and he had one of those highly contagious laughs. Luckily, he was a great fan of his own humour so each comment was punctuated with a huge guffaw, which got me going every time. He was one of those highly educated men who prides himself on his command of English, and has been waiting all his life to pounce on passing English motorcyclists so he can baffle them with his diction and vocabulary. Excellent guy.

The long and the short of it was that getting the visa would be "Very hard work Mr. Spencer, very hard work. But I think that I can do this job, but it will be very hard work." He promised to have the visa by the next morning so I returned to Hippocampe, happy that I had achieved something.

Mr. Nsangou phoned me at midnight, with a slight slur to his voice, and said he was still at the office (yeah right!) but "had managed to complete the complex and difficult task." I thanked him for his dedication and said I would see him in the morning, explaining that I had actually been asleep when he called. I registered a hint of disappointment in his voice, but didn't want to query it, because I was pretty sure he was waiting for an invite to the Hippocampe. After a couple of seconds of awkward silence he stated that there was no need to come to the Embassy, as he would drop off my passport at the campsite in the morning.

True to his word, Mr. Nsangou (which means marijuana in Siswati incidentally) turned up at 6.45am with his round grinning face sticking out of an extremely dapper suit. He was clutching my passport proudly and gave me a firm, friendly handshake stating, "I am pleased to announce that I have completed the task in hand, there were no undue hiccups, Mr. Spencer." I thanked him in the appropriate gushing manner, and ushered him to a chair and offered him a coffee or tea. "I am not going to the office today, I only have business meetings so I will take a beer graciously, Mr. Spencer."

Fair enough, graciously or otherwise. It turned out to be otherwise as he downed the litre bottle as though it were a matric students' drinking competition. I offered him another and his affirmative response was out of his mouth in a nanosecond. I left Mr. Nsangou to his beverages, and went off to pack up the bike.

I felt pretty tired, as the previous night at Hippocampe was as Olivier had predicted. Malaria was on its way. The room had glass louvres, which were jammed permanently open, and the mosquitos feasted on me, queuing all night, until I started to resemble a pile of raw mince. It was completely my fault, as I was too lazy to put up the tent, and instead, lay my sleeping bag on top of one of the Conference tables and slept there. Well, tried to. Just typical of my luck, malaria on my birthday. However, having just left Kinshasa, and not being able to sleep a wink, I had time to reflect on the two people I had been staying with for the last sixteen days in Kinshasa, and who, because so much happened, I have not mentioned yet.

Glenn and Antoinette could not have been more different from each other. Glenn was from the south in the US, was fifty eight years old, of large stature, wide girth, with a pasty complexion, but a sunny disposition. He had a tea-coloured birthmark covering half of his forehead, was a dedicated baseball fan and had a hairline that had receded behind his ears. He had an extremely gentle, almost effeminate manner, and when I spoke to him on the phone, I made the wrong assumption that he was gay. He worked for Save the Children in the city and was married to a native Congolese, Anto. Anto was as tiny as a mouse, well under five foot, and extremely thin and dark-skinned with her grey hair scraped back in a ponytail. Sometimes she would braid it in to five or six plaits, which would stick vertically in the air, making her resemble a satellite station. They were both wonderful people and showed me great hospitality, but I must admit had some strange idiosyncrasies.

Both possibly had an addiction to legal prescription medication. Every evening they would sit down and count out various different coloured pills from numerous bottles, with skull and crossbones on the labels (not really), and proceeded to swallow them for the next five minutes until they were up to their eyeballs.

Antoinette also had a fixation with trying to feed me copious amounts of food which was very touching but difficult to deal with. I ended up rolling into bed each night with more wind than a tornado – just to keep her happy. A typical meal would be four pork chops, eight potatoes, vegetables, a large buttered baguette each and this was only after being force-fed (with looks!) olives, cheese, pitta bread, tinned sardines and Guinness. Eventually half crying, half pleading, half exploding, I had to face defeat and tell her that I wasn't used to these amounts of food. My little speech must have worked, because when it came to arranging a packed lunch for my trip across the Congo River to Brazzaville, I only got the meagre fare of thirteen cans of sardines, eight boiled eggs, two baguettes, a carton of apple juice and a partridge (no, not the last one!).

I quickly realised that I had to choose my words carefully when discussing food. When I first arrived at their fourth floor apartment in the city centre, I mentioned in passing that I was fond of canned sardines and chilli. The very next day fourteen cans of 'Sardines à 'l'huile pimentée' were perched (get the double-fish joke!) on the kitchen shelf along with an eye-watering concoction of chilli (bird's eye), garlic and onions boiling on the stove in a pot so vast that cannibals could have easily squeezed three people into it, with space for vegetables.

This was another hidden condiment I found nestled in my suspiciously heavy back-pack when it was finally time for me to depart, an industrial size jar of chilli sauce. Anyone would have thought that I was circumnavigating Africa for God's sake! I knew that if I stayed with Glenn and Anto much longer I would firstly forget how to speak (every time I opened my mouth, she would put food in it), and secondly, that I would end up weighing the equivalent of a small whale. However, they were the perfect hosts, and I must say that I have never met a couple who get on so well with each other. They proudly told me that they were celebrating their 25th wedding anniversary next month. They still kiss each other and still hold hands in the street but not in a mushy self-conscious 'look how much we still love each other' way. Good luck to them both! I said my goodbyes and headed to the ferry, distributing the kilogrammes of food Antoinette had tried to bury me and the bike under, to the local Cheges.

I know I have laid it on a bit thick with my negativity about DRC and how depressing it was, but I was only reporting what I saw. I can truly say, hand on my heart, that it is the only country in Africa where I felt true hostility and, in some cases, outright hatred. This really struck home when I was confronted by a huge grin of pearly white teeth from a waiter in Brazzaville. I realised that no one in the streets of Kinshasa had actually smiled at me during the sixteen days I had been there. What an incredibly positive effect a huge smile had on me. Conversely, it really sunk in how constant aggressive and suspicious looks can make you feel so low. Don't get me wrong, I was not feeling sorry for myself, but I think we all need some positive acknowledgement of our common humanity. But I had had a lot of that, from a lot of people, on this incredible journey and I was more than spoiled. It was now time to continue into the heart of the Gabon jungle.

Chapter Ten
2000 Beers

'I met a lot of people travelling, I even encountered myself.'
James Baldwin

'If you want to be original, be yourself.' Gabon border guard

As a child I was always fascinated with geography, and knew all the countries in Africa (and most around the world) and their capitals, by the time I was thirteen. When my brother Simon and I were children, we frequently took long car trips with our parents, from Swaziland to South Africa to get our monthly shop from the large discount hypermarkets that had started to spring up in South Africa at that time. I used to love these trips, as my dad had a Ford Granada Coupe, which was bright red, with black, plastic, fast fins on the back window. To me, at that age, it was the ultimate, cool racing car.

We would set up the back of the car like a campsite with loads of cushions, strips of biltong (dried and salted meat made from beef, ostrich, kudu or any other red meat), and soft drinks. We also had a pair of black binoculars and I felt very important looking out for animals as the African landscape rushed by. We would keep ourselves busy by testing each other on general knowledge: capitals of the world and rivers and mountains were my forte. Eventually I would nod off from the motion of the car and wake up in a new place raring to go. The whole family seemed to share my enthusiasm for travelling, facts and geography, and I learnt a great deal about this world we live in from these journeys. But everything I learnt in my childhood, especially about Africa, only increased my fascination with the people and cultures contained within these countries. I did undertake some rudimentary research on the countries I was going to visit on this trip, but only half-heartedly, for two reasons. Firstly, I knew there was no substitute for going – and I was the luckiest person on earth, I was going to thirty four countries (!!), and secondly, I somehow wanted to cross each border with no preconceptions of what it would be like. Consequently, there were certain countries that I only had the most basic knowledge about, and Gabon was one of those.

Libreville, the capital of Gabon, has a population of roughly six hundred thousand. In 1846 L'Elizia, a Brazilian ship carrying slaves for sale, was captured by the French Navy near Loanga. The slaves were freed and founded Libreville ('free town' in French). Along with Abidjan in the Ivory Coast, Libreville is one of the few African cities where French is becoming a true native language. The city is home to shipbuilding, brewing and saw mills. This is all I knew about the city I was heading to next, oh, and that it is the most expensive city in Africa. I also knew that to get through to it, I would undoubtedly be passing through a dense tropical forest because it makes up 85% of the country. It was with these sparse facts in my head that I entered Gabon.

I knew immediately that the roads in Gabon were dangerous for motorcycles even before I heard of the accident. I would go so far as to say, I knew what was coming – and I am not that kind of mystical person at all, so don't take this lightly – I really did have a premonition. The roads were not dangerous *because* they were like many in Africa; potholed, muddy, rutted, stony, and full of children, animals and lunatic drivers, trying to traverse collapsed bridges, swollen rivers or forest paths that are supposed to be roads. No, it was the opposite. The roads were perfect. They were so beautiful that they could not help but lift the spirits, and were also capable of removing any riding sense that even the most seasoned of riders would have embedded in their heads. Common sense could disappear in such an environment. It was a biker's dream ride, and by the same vein, his Achilles heel. On each side of the road was pristine jungle, so dense, so green and so stunning, it formed a solid, lush, impenetrable wall that seemed to force the focus of all my concentration onto the road, like a real life computer game, but so much more mesmerising. The surface was perfect, brand new asphalt with not a single blemish. The route through this dense jungle consisted of long sweeping bends, which rose and fell depending on the contours of the jungle terrain that the road snaked through.

I'm the first to admit that I have never been a speed freak, and even in my younger days I used to get hassled for driving like a grandfather. Nothing had changed since then. But on this particular section, I felt myself getting carried away with this stunning adrenaline-filled race track, fuelled by the fact that I had not passed a single vehicle that I had to negotiate. Without realising it, my speedometer slowly crept up, and it was only two incidents that brought me back to my riding senses. It would only be the first one that I would treasure.

Thundering around a bend, I spotted a black shape in the middle of the road, about a hundred metres ahead of me. I pulled on the front brakes and changed down through the gears as quickly as I possibly could and, as soon as I had slowed down sufficiently, I pulled in the clutch to freewheel and deaden the noise of the bike. To my absolute amazement, it was a chimpanzee, sitting in the middle of the road, presumably enjoying the heat radiating off the tar. It was a fleeting encounter, as he was immediately up and gone, vanishing into the safety of the thick undergrowth. Our meeting was so brief, but it was enough to bring me back to reality. I pulled up on the side of the road, determined to take a minute to think. I was angry with myself for driving at what I considered a dangerous speed. I had just seen a chimpanzee in the wild, for God's sake. What am I doing rushing through this breathtaking Garden of

Eden, like Valentino Rossi? Slow down, enjoy the moment. I wish I had never been cursed with the mentality of restlessness, always looking for the next stimulation, the next superb view and next encounter with man or beast, so much so that I miss the pleasure of the present. I was doing it again. I would probably never come here again, and I had the absolute privilege of experiencing it completely alone. I must always keep in mind that yesterday is history, tomorrow is a mystery. Today is a gift. That's why it's called the present.

I pulled off my helmet and sat down on the side of the road to slow my mind down and soak in where I was. The first thing that hit me was not the silence, but the cacophony of noise emanating from the walls of the jungle. There was an orchestra of birds, interspersed with hundreds of other unidentifiable sounds; roars, grunts, whistles and constant snapping and rustling noises as the jungle wildlife got on with their busy day.

I knew from a chance encounter with a biologist in Swakopmund, Namibia that the 753rd bird species had just been found in Gabon (the Olive Backed Forest Robin). As well as this little fellow, he informed me that there was an abundance of Yellow Whiskered Greenbuls (greenish brown birds with yellow beards, that I had seen frequently along the road), as well as Egrets, Crowned Eagles and African Grey Parrots. Add to this the forty two medium and large mammals, including elephants, lowland gorillas, forest buffalos, sitatungas (large antelopes), leopards, arboreal monkeys as well as cats like civets and genets it was obvious that I was sitting in a truly primeval jungle. This is an environment that sustains thousands of species, including Homo sapiens, and here I was letting it fly by, while I hid inside my head, my thoughts, and my helmet. The best thing I did was to stop at the side of the road and give myself this reality slap. From the noises surrounding me I could swear that those seven hundred and ninety five recorded species were all there, just beyond my sight in the undergrowth, chatting between themselves, wondering what I was, what I was doing, and possibly whether I tasted good. It was beautiful and although thunderous it was somehow peaceful because it was pure nature, and not manmade. It had the desired effect of bringing me back to the here and now. With this new frame of mind, I took off again at a more leisurely rate, smiling at the vision of the chimp sitting in the middle of the road.

As I made my way further north the road began to change. The bends became sharper and I started to see the occasional village, consisting of a couple of thatched mud huts in small clearings. Outside most of these homesteads, hung on hooks, or held up by children, were displayed the profits of their hunting. As I got closer to Libreville, this sight became more and more common, and I saw, in one day, maybe a hundred dead animals, including crocodiles, pangolins and spotted civet cats, strung up on trees or held on the end of poles, like fishing rods.

Bush meat boy

I know the locals are only doing what they have done for thousands of years, but I couldn't help wondering how long the jungle could sustain this hunting. I would have preferred to see these animals alive. If you consider that I saw 100 dead animals in one day, which is seven hundred dead animals a week on this stretch of road only. Consider the death toll countrywide.

I had already had a glimpse of the massive scale of the slaughter of jungle animals when I visited an illegal bush market on the outskirts of Kinshasa. Yves, the Reuters reporter who I met in Kinshasa, was doing a story on the escalating bush meat market, and invited me to come along. I readily agreed, and we made our way out of Kinshasa to the slum areas in the south of the city. The market was an incredible spectacle. The first thing that struck me was the explosion of colour. All the women working in the makeshift market were wearing beautiful, brightly coloured dresses and headscarves. They were sitting behind twisted wooden stalls of ripe, succulent, tropical fruit, piled up in pyramids of colour, sitting on sheets of newspaper.

In total contrast to this explosion of colour, were the bush market stalls. They were dank, dark, stinking piles of darkly coloured meat covered in flies. At the back of the stalls were shirtless, sweating men in white plastic aprons, which were splattered with blood. Most were wielding machetes and hatchets, chopping up football-size pieces of buffalo meat, and wrapping them up in brown waxed paper for the customers crowding the stall front. The others were brandishing large brooms, sweeping up the blood that was dripping onto the floors, pushing it into a corner, where it congealed into a jelly-like, crimson puddle. Monkeys were on display, split open and splayed out on the counters for people to inspect.

There were also stalls that specialised in 'muti' – traditional medicines that were often made out of animal, and in some places in Africa, human parts. There were huge clothsacks full to the brim with dried monkey heads, monkey hands and an array of potions. Next to this was a stall selling many different types of antelope meat, warthog and elephant. I would be lying if I said I enjoyed this, but I tried not to make judgments. I found it very sad, but at the same time it's part of life. Let's hope that the animals do become protected, before it is too late. I suspect that this will not be the case, and that like many

Market monkey heads

habitats in the world, it will eventually be destroyed by the most voracious predator of all: us.

My worries seemed to become more justified as I travelled further north. Firstly, I came across a huge road-building project and it was no surprise that it was the Chinese who were undertaking this. For the economy and the drivers of the country these perfect two-laned highways make obvious economic sense, but at the same time they have the effect of opening up huge swathes of forest that before had remained inaccessible, and therefore were naturally protected.

The reason for this project also became quickly obvious. Within a short space of time I was suddenly being forced off the road by huge logging trucks, the drivers of which obviously had no respect for my life, or the trees. They were absolute maniacs and instead of slowing down when they saw me, they would accelerate, causing a huge dust cloud to rise up off the road surface, engulfing me and the bike and making it impossible to see. I was worse off than a blind pig in a snowstorm. The wind from these huge lorries buffeted me in all directions, and it only took a few of these encounters and some serious bike wobbling to realise that I would have to pull right off the road and stop to let them pass, if I ever wanted to see another African sunrise.

I didn't really warm to these drivers, not only because of their road manners, but also because in my mind their trucks represented huge, jungle-eating machines. The fact that vast oil reserves have also been found in Gabon seems to suggest that the destruction of the jungle will only increase exponentially. See, negative thoughts again, my emotions were a rollercoaster of wonder and despair, but that was bound to be the case. This was Africa after all. It was so wonderful being alone on the bike, but if you are the type who is not happy with your own company, and your own thoughts, a trip like this could become torture. Your mind can go into freefall and you need to constantly reign in your thoughts and concentrate on the task at hand. I have, on occasion, ridden for more than half an hour, and then suddenly realised that I have not noticed the road at all, because I have been so wrapped up in my own thoughts. I'm sure many people reading this have had a similar experience, arriving at their destination, and not really knowing how they got there. It was a miracle I had not come off.

I continued on towards the coastal capital, Libreville, having covered over four hundred kilometres, when I came over the brow of a hill and once again spotted some shapes in the road ahead of me. No mistaking this one though, it was an Army roadblock. There was a group of four soldiers all in green camouflage outfits, army boots and red berets, with machine guns slung casually over their shoulders. Parked on the edge of the road was an army Land Rover, with another soldier sprawled out on the front seat, fast asleep.

I knew from experience that African officials could be exceedingly awkward, and I had a routine I always went through when I encountered them, which seemed to help. I tensed up nonetheless (not that I have any problem with officious officials), so I slowed the bike up a fair distance from the roadblock, to give myself some breathing space.

Right, here we go, follow the routine; pull up slowly, turn

off the engine, get off the bike, take off the helmet and approach the official, with arm outstretched and a seriously over-exaggerated grin on your face. Through experience, I have found a combination of friendliness and respect can often disarm officials and, if not, at least I always started in the right vein. Before I faced this Gabonese army road block let me just say something about manners. Manners are everything in African society.

It is a very vital and important part of African life and business that you follow certain rules of politeness and etiquette. Whether you are meeting someone socially or officially, there is often a complex ritual of greeting that verbally can extend from, "How are you? How is your health?" all the way down the family tree to, "How are your cousins, uncles, aunts etc.?" This is often combined with a lot of handshaking, hand slapping in the air, numerous kisses, or touching shoulders, depending upon which country you are in. It's impossible to know the differing rituals as soon as you cross the border, and mistakes will be made, but the universal behaviour of respect and friendliness is the best start. One of the biggest errors made by first-time visitors to Africa is to try and rush officials into activity. Western concepts of time-wasting and urgency are not appreciated. Outwardly displaying the emotions of frustration and impatience are unacceptable in Africa, and are the quickest way to meet a brick wall.

If you rush into an office and demand a visa it is possible, in fact probable, that you will be kept waiting not minutes but hours and even possibly days. In many African countries, a very important judge of how important an official is, is how long they can keep you waiting. This makes it very clear that they are extremely busy and might just be able to squeeze you in at some point in their hectic schedule. This is a fact of life in Africa and can be either hilarious or extremely frustrating depending upon how you approach it. I fall into the former group and find it highly entertaining. Let me give you an example, which occurred before I had even left the UK.

I went to pick up an African visa from an Embassy in London – I can't remember at this moment which one, but it doesn't matter, it could be any. I arrived in Trafalgar Square with fifteen minutes to spare before my appointment. Luckily, the Embassy was only ten minutes away, and easy to find, and I made my way through the double glass doors, mentally prepared from previous experience for a lot of people and a bit of chaos.

Surprisingly, there was no-one in there. Nevertheless, I was still told by the uniformed guard, standing just inside the entrance, to "take a ticket" and sit down until my name was called. I ripped number sixty four from the ticket machine and sat down in the row of connected, plastic chairs which seemed to be specially designed to be as uncomfortable as possible. The back of the chair was too straight, the bottom section too short, and it was so hard and slippery that I found myself bracing my shoes on the carpet just to stay on it.

Opposite me in the officials' glass booth sat a traditionally built, African woman in a colourful print dress, with the type of bored expression that people in those kind of positions seem to practice. Also visible was a microphone speaker, the one where it seems like the commentator is holding his nose and has a tennis ball in his mouth, and you can't hear a word that is said.

I sat there for half an hour watching the official pick her nose, check her fingernails every five seconds, and tap her pen on the desk top, until I decided to take the situation into my own hands.

I walked up and said, "Good morning Madam, my name is Spencer Conway and I had an appointment to pick up a visa, about half an hour ago."

She looked up at me slowly, begrudgingly and, in slow motion, said, "Ate teel yo nunba ees cold," or something along those lines.

Quite understandably, I said, "Pardon?"

She said more loudly, stretching out all the words, "Wait till your number is called."

I started, "But I am the only person in... "

She cut me off, repeated her request and literally glared me back to my seat, showing me the direction with her eyes. Frustrated, I turned round and went back and sat on my chair. No sooner had I sat down, when she called out officiously, looking around the room as she shouted, "Number sixty four, number sixty four." I stayed put. She hesitated for a few seconds to see if anybody was coming up, and then said, "Spencer Conway, Spencer Conway." Excellent theatre.

So, after that diversion, back to the etiquette of my present situation, and the Gabonese Army road block. Luckily, there was no need to panic as these were extremely friendly guys and after checking my paperwork I was allowed to move on. As I was pulling off slowly, the friendliest of the group put his hand on my shoulder, to slow me down. He leant into my helmet, so that I could hear him clearly, and said, "Mr. James... " (I was often called this, as it is the middle name that appears in my passport and I suppose more recognisable than Spencer, maybe because of James Bond)... "Please drive with great care, two Europeans are dead on this road last week, one on a moto like you."

As I said earlier, I *knew* what he was going to say before he said it. It transpired that a young English couple had rolled their car on a sharp bend and the driver had died instantly. The soldier also told me I would see the car in a "short while", on route. The details of the other accident only came to light when I met a Canadian in Libreville who filled me in on the horrific details. Apparently two Germans and a 22-year-old Canadian were attempting a ride from Cape Town to Senegal where the two Germans guys had procured medical jobs in Dakar. The Canadian was to continue onwards to Morocco to meet up with his girlfriend. Apparently he was the hyperactive livewire of the group, fast talking and fast riding and they quickly got into a riding routine where he would rush ahead and then wait for the other two to arrive at various points. Apparently, he was also keen on playing 'thrash metal' on his iPod as he rode, which is obviously not conducive to mellow riding. As they were making their way through this area, between the main towns of Lambarene and Libreville, the young Canadian took a sharp bend on a mountain pass too wide, as he was evidently travelling too fast. A logging truck was coming the other way and although they both tried to take some evasive action, it was too little, too late. The biker managed to avoid a head-on and scraped along the side of the oncoming vehicle but was unable to maintain control and hit the massive rear end bumper of the truck, splitting his helmet in half like an eggshell. He was killed instantly. God only knows what hell the German riders must have faced when they came round the corner, but it is nothing compared to what a family in Canada will have gone through after expecting to meet their son again, full of the stories of Africa after his trip of a lifetime. Unfortunately, I know it sounds callous to say, but motorbikes are very dangerous no matter how you gloss it, and if you ride like there's no tomorrow, there won't be.

With these sobering thoughts in my head I continued on my way and did indeed come across the wrecked shell of a burnt-out car sitting on its roof at the side of the road. As I rode, I felt my mood deepening and for some reason I started to lose my physical strength and timing. Within a short space of time I realised that I needed to stop for the night as I had been shaken more by the Army officer's news than I realised. I inevitably thought about how my parents, girlfriend and two girls would react if it was me that didn't make it back. I started to think about all the close shaves and crashes I had had in the last months, and how much further I had to go. Everyone crashes. Some get back on. Some don't. Some can't.

I felt pleased that I was in the first group, but I couldn't shake this dejected feeling. I couldn't believe how quickly these thoughts drained my physical energy reserves and all I wanted to do was stop. It is incredible how sensitive one's riding skills become depending on your frame of mind. It is a fine balance between brain and body. If you are depressed, down, or even slightly tired, your riding immediately suffers and you start making small, but important errors. In a car you can afford to make the odd swerve but on a motorbike a small error can have grave consequences. The Canadian guy had made a fatal mistake because of an opposite emotion to mine; euphoria had got the better of him. I have no doubt that he was having the time of his life, with fellow bikers, in a beautiful country, on a perfect road and listening to his favourite music. It was because of this mind frame, and his love of speed, that he had paid the ultimate price. These thoughts brought it home to me that riding a motorcycle is so much more than just transport. I knew I had to stop soon. I felt weak.

I immediately slowed down to scan the jungle canopy for a suitable place to bed down for the night. The biggest problem I faced was getting the bike into the jungle and hidden from view. Although I felt safe in Gabon, and in ninety percent of the places I had travelled, I always liked to disappear into anonymity in the evenings so that that I could get an undisturbed rest, ready for the next day's challenges.

I rode on for another twenty minutes, getting more and more frustrated that I could not find a break in the jungle when, out of the corner of my eye, I spotted a small path on the left-hand side. I turned the bike round to investigate. I normally avoid any sort of path when camping, as they tend to indicate the presence of people passing through, but on this occasion I was tired, down, and it was also beginning to get dark. The path turned out to be no path at all. It looked as though someone had just recently trampled their way through, but it was definitely not a regular thoroughfare. This was not surprising as I had not seen any settlements for hundreds of kilometres. I wondered who had made their way into this jungle and why, as I pushed the bike off the road and out of sight. I managed to wheel it along this rudimentary track and into the undergrowth, where I covered it with large ferns and moss that I cut with my bush knife. I then continued deeper into the jungle to find a suitable place to pitch my minute tent, following the slightly trampled undergrowth, until I was almost fifty metres from the main road. Although I was fully prepared to come across various jungle animals, not in my wildest dreams did I expect to come across what I did.

I pushed my way through the undergrowth and made my way out into a small clearing. In front of me, there must have been at least two thousand bottles of the Gabon beer, Regab, stacked up in red plastic crates. What the devil!? I couldn't believe it. I sat down and contemplated whether God had possibly dropped them there for a fatigued, tired and, above all, thirsty biker, to raise his spirits (almost literally). Realising this was not the kind of tacky miracle *He* would waste his time performing, and that two bottles would have sufficed anyway, I busied myself making a sandwich, extracting an extremely squashed roll and a can of sardines from my rucksack, while I worked out what to do.

I toyed with the idea of cracking open just a single Regab to have with my dinner but decided against it. This turned out to be a wise decision. As I was finishing off my fish delight, drifting through the forest came the sound of voices. As I hastily packed up my rucksack and stood up, my heart beating, a local man came into view, pushing aside a large banana palm frond with his hand. He was about thirty, ebony black, wearing a torn black vest, khaki shorts and sandals and was built like a bus, but what I noticed first was the absolute look of shock and surprise on his face. He had obviously not noticed the bike camouflaged in the undergrowth, fifty metres back down the path, and I could tell by his expression that he had definitely not predicted that a white guy dressed all in black, smeared in sweat and mud, would be waiting for him at the end of this path. His eyes widened visibly and he stopped dead in his tracks as the others came into view behind him. I thought now would be the best time to break the ice, so in my best schoolboy French I stepped forward, with my hand outstretched, and greeted them all, trying to explain what I was doing there, as I shook each of their hands in turn.

To my relief, 'steroid man' was extremely friendly and also spoke English. He told me his name was Samson (very applicable), and after clearing up the reason I was there, he explained the mystery of the beers. I must say he was the most honest, straightforward thief I have ever met. In a very matter of fact tone Samson explained to me that they had stolen the beers from a depot in Lambarene, the town I had started from, and that they had stashed them here until they could find a buyer. It transpired that they had now found one in the form of a bush bar owner in a nearby village and were here to load up their truck. I offered to help them and they readily agreed.

It turned out through our conversation, while struggling and stumbling to get the truck through the undergrowth, that they were full-time thieves. They spent their time roaming between Lambarene, Port Gentil on the west coast, and Libreville, relieving people of anything that was not screwed down. I realised that I was now an accomplice to one of their crimes but I wasn't going to get all moral at this stage. To be completely honest, I was just pleased that they were so friendly, and now, I secretly had my eye on a couple of those beers! I was not to be disappointed and after the half hour it took us to load up the truck, they thanked me and we all cracked open a beer.

It turned out that 'Samson, the muscular' had been to university in Russia and had studied Politics and Economics with the promise that on his return he would be given a highbrow job in the Government. After four years of study that he absolutely hated – "I missed Gabon daily" – he eventually returned to find that not only did his job offer not exist anymore, as there had been a shift in power, but also that his brother had gone missing under suspicious circumstances.

His brother was an outspoken critic of the way the government was run and rumour had it that they were involved in his disappearance. Samson stated that he felt unsafe in the main cities and moved to Moanda in the far south of the country where he drifted into criminal activities. As we spoke, he seemed to sadden significantly and eventually, sighing and standing up, announced that they had to be getting on their way. Before leaving he thanked me, wished me luck on the rest of my journey and said, "Remember, Gabon is the world and the world is Gabon." I think the beer was going to his head but I was pleased that he felt I was important enough to impart philosophical advice too, whatever it meant.

Samson stumbled down the path and returned with four more bottles of Regab, handing them to me and saying, "Good luck Mr. Spencer, I wish you safe journey." I wished them luck too, and returned to the clearing to sort out my sleeping arrangements. Unfortunately, I was now left with no option but to drink the remaining beers because, as I am sure you will appreciate, it is very dangerous to ride a motorbike with glass bottles in your luggage. Strangely enough, after my liquid dinner I slept very well that night, lying on top of my tent and marvelling at the brief, but wonderful encounters you have with people living a completely different life to you.

I woke up at sunrise in my jungle paradise with a slight headache, but reinvigorated for my day ahead. I checked over the Tenere for five minutes while soaking up the first rays of the sun and the atmosphere of the jungle. Then I was off. Another day, another learning experience...

Before I leave Gabon, and its vibrant life, I add that I learnt that the country was first 'discovered' by Pierre de Brazza and that a European conference awarded it to France in 1885. In 1910 it became part of French Equatorial Africa when the colonies of Gabon, Congo, Chad and Ubangi-Shari were formed. Don't know what happened to Ubangi-Shari but no doubt it is possible to Google it for information. Gabon actually became independent in 1960 at the time when many other African colonies also did so.

What language do people speak in Gabon? I got by using French, no problem then, but a third of the population speak Fang as a mother tongue. Great to listen to but had me lost. Actually French is the medium of instruction in schools and France still has an influence in the country. Regrettably, I wasn't able to learn much more of this beautiful country

Cameroon

Cameroon was a strange visit. I was thrown into two different worlds. The British High Commissioner had heard about my trip and had kindly invited me to stay with his family. They were incredibly accommodating and welcoming but it was strange to enter a guarded, gated community with manicured lawns and evident wealth. The district, Bastos, which I was staying in was in the north of Yaounde, the capital, and was very tranquil because of its exclusivity. The most lavish residential properties, top restaurants, various embassies and the presidential palace were all located here. The rest of Yaounde was shut out. I preferred the 'outside' and spent two days wandering the city.

The downtown 'African' setting was more my scene, hectic and unpredictable. There were crowded fish stalls selling grilled Tilapia and superb goat and beef kebabs with onion. The French influence was clear to see and there were smart boulangeries selling baguettes, pain-au-chocolat and various other cakes and desserts. Yaounde was a riot of colour set amongst manic streets. Thousands of bright yellow taxis with blue stripes, minivans and highly decorated scooters careered around the place. Street vendors clogged the pavements, each with a colourful umbrella to protect them from the sun. The rainbow theme was continued with the traditional clothing. Women wore long flowing dresses called Kabba or a wrap-style long swathe of fabric called Pagnes, with batik or tie dye patterns. Men wandered around in 'Boubou avec Pantaloons'; an undershirt flowing over shirt, loose pants and matching hat. Everyone looked superb. In the central square, Place Ahmoudou Ahejo, my favourite sight by far was the shoe sellers. They all walked around with a single shoe balanced on their heads. This could be a pink suede shoe, a baby's bootie, a leather or rubber sandal or a high heel, teetering precariously. It was an odd sight, seeing a sea of umbrellas with a variety of bobbing footwear weaving around them. Not once did I see anyone falter or drop a shoe, despite the manic activity everywhere. Their selling method was absurdly laidback compared to other countries in Africa. They simply stood in front of you for five seconds, with the shoe on their head. If you didn't show any interest they simply moved on, yawning, to the next potential customer. It's a wonder that they sold anything. Some of them probably forgot completely that they had a shoe on their head. They would go home, eat dinner, have a bath and go to their local with the shoe still sitting there.

The shoe sellers competed with the food, fabric and clothes sellers. Most of the stuff was severely sub-standard. One guy was selling T-shirts that were so large they were almost touching the road despite his efforts to hold them aloft. He did have a superb Cameroon football jersey which he persuaded me to try on. One sleeve was so tight I could hardly get it on whereas the other would have welcomed Arnold Schwarzenegger's bicep. He did not see any problem with this and offered a small discount when I pointed it out. I declined the offer; I wasn't keen on restricting the blood flow to my left arm just for 'a souvenir's sake'. Hats off to them – or on!

My interview on the Cameroon TV chat show 'Good Morning' was the highlight of the visit and still makes me laugh every time I think about it. It was complete chaos, highly unprofessional and superb entertainment. Firstly, the presenter,

Patrick Patrick, forgot that he was live and missed his cue. (I never found out if that was both his first and last name or if he was being introduced twice.) When he finally realised he was live he mumbled an introduction and I was called onto the stage where my back blocked out the camera. Unfortunately, they had also forgotten to provide me with a microphone so a sound engineer had to crawl on stage and mike me up. (If you look at my website he can be spotted crawling next to my bike on the left hand side of the screen.) The volume was too low so I cannot be heard, which is probably a good thing. Patrick Patrick also decided to mount my bike but failed dismally in his traditional robes. He then had the bright idea of wearing my motorcycle helmet instead. This led to us both sounding like mumbling idiots. When he wasn't messing up Patrick Patrick was looking at his script or at his director who was just out of camera shot. He was so useless, but so enthusiastic, that it didn't matter a jot. I left the interview with a grin on my face that stayed with me into Nigeria.

The newspapers were just as professional. The day I left Yaounde the national newspaper, with the slogan 'Nothing hidden under the Sun' was celebrating its 50th anniversary. The front page article was an interview with the British High Commissioner, accompanied by a large photo of him. Unfortunately, the photo was of some random person from Malaysia. The reporter who had spent an hour with the Commissioner returned to his office to complete the article. He Googled the Commissioner's name to obtain a photo. Evidently, there is a Bharat Joshi in Malaysia also.

Great place, but time to get moving. I still had to travel from Yaounde through the second largest city, Douala, and on to the Nigerian border. I was not destined to travel this section alone. On the afternoon I was leaving I was approached by the only other white face in Yaounde (apart from the British High Commissioner and his family). A tall, slim, curly-brown-haired backpacker introduced himself and we had a chat over a beer.

For the sake of this book let's call him Paul from the US of A. Within minutes of meeting him I was regaled with Paul's life story. Apparently he had spent three years alone in the mountains of British Columbia growing huge amounts of marijuana. He told me he saw not a single other person and had guarded his product day and night with the help of a sub-machine gun. He had almost gone insane from lack of social interaction and lack of sleep. The outcome of this endeavour was that he amassed four million dollars having sold his weed exclusively to the Hells Angels. He had then embarked on three years of travelling – so far. His aim was to visit every country in the world, and he had apparently ticked off more than 150. As money was no object he generally flew from place to place. I had no idea how much to believe but one bit I did not believe - that he had nearly gone insane. I think he did go insane. He was extremely agitated and spoke constantly, even if there was nothing to say. He was the most un-mellow person I had ever met, in the guise of a mellow hippie. He didn't fool me, and being the idiot that I am, when he mentioned that he was heading towards Douala, I decided to offer him a lift on the motorbike. It was a fantastic decision. We had a top class couple of days. I had a mad American nattering in my ear for the whole journey. He was like a woodpecker at my helmet. I loved it. Added to this was that we were both privileged to be travelling through such a beautiful country.

The trip turned out to be a real eye opener to me. Touristically (I hate that word), Cameroon is so attractive that it is perplexing that it is so little known or visited. The north west of the country turned out to be beautiful, with volcanic peaks covered in bamboo forest rising to over 2,000 metres and picturesque waterfalls and villages scattering the landscape. Most impressive of all were the massive number of lakes created by volcanic activity and tectonic shifts. We travelled through virgin forests, home to abundant wildlife including lowland gorillas and so-called pygmies.

It was a region with the lowest density of services and the lowest quality roads and was one of the most challenging areas to travel through. Especially with a weirdo on the back of the bike. We stopped in Bamende, the capital of the North West Province, and also the heart of the English-speaking opposition movement to the French-speaking dominance of the country. The landscape changed from terraced fields in the mountainous areas to strangely English-like meadows where the Fulani grazed their herds. I was surprised to find that people recognised me in the streets. Patrick Patrick was more famous than I realised. Fame may have eluded me elsewhere, but not in North West Cameroon – for five minutes at least. What did Andy Warhol say in 1968? "In the future everyone will be famous for 15 minutes... if they are in Cameroon." Or something like that.

We stopped at the Ideal Hotel which was anything but. There was almost no space for me in the room as it was taken up by the whole Cameroon population of mosquitoes. I didn't sleep for more than fourteen seconds at a time but at least it gave me the opportunity of witnessing the nightlife sounds of Bamende; people shouting, dogs barking, gunshots, etc.

I woke up the next morning (not strictly true, as I hadn't ever fallen asleep), after receiving enough mosquito bites to fell a fully grown bull elephant. After rousing prolific-loon Paul, we headed off towards Nigeria. It was a dangerous route. The police were intent upon killing as many motorcycle adventurers as possible. They had set up the world's most dangerous roadblocks.

The countryside was undoubtedly beautiful but the police were evil. Let me explain. The road blocks consisted of two or three speed bumps on a corner, followed by a rope or chain across the road. The police had a little hut on the side of the road that they slept in, and only woke when they had decapitated a tourist. They never managed to do it to me so I woke them every time to rub it in.

The police were not the only peril on the journey to Lake Awing. Paul was the worst pillion passenger imaginable. He hung on to me like a baby orangutan and on every corner I leant into he did his upmost to pull us the other way, sending me into a dangerous swerve. He also head-butted me every time there was a change of speed. I had to stop the bike and try and teach him to relax. I would have had as much chance with Pol Pot. To add to the instability of the bike plus Paul, a plague of bugs decided to infest this part of Cameroon. Inevitably, they were all heading in the opposite direction to us, maybe to Yaounde.

It also started pouring with rain so I was unable to wear my goggles. Now, one or two bugs hitting you in the face at 100 kilometres per hour can be suffered. Ten or twelve of them swimming around in my eyeballs is not conducive to safe riding. It hurt like hell when they hit me directly in the eye, like a miniature Mike Tyson with a needle in his glove. I had to stop and ride out the storm.

When it cleared the riding was superb. We slid around blood red, mud roads through fragrant Eucalyptus forests. The rolling hills looked down on glimmering crater lakes nestled in the emerald green valleys. It is a beautiful country. We stopped at Lake Awing for a bite to eat. I found a sunken Pirogue (traditional carved wooden canoe), and decided to bail it out, using one of my petrol cans. It took about twenty minutes to make it seaworthy and about twenty minutes to persuade Paul to join me on the lake. I wanted to try and film a diary cam as the clear blue water and magnificent steep, jungle banks made for a stunning backdrop. We weren't very successful: Paul was more unstable in a Pirogue than he was on a motorbike. His eyes were huge with fear and he lurched back and forth for no apparent reason. He was like a drunk on a roller coaster. I could see us upending and losing the camera and maybe Paul too. Perhaps he couldn't swim. I never asked. I cut the rowing trip short and we headed back to shore, wobbling like a blancmange in the wind.

Once on dry land we sat down for some, you guessed, sardine sandwiches and a bottle of Kadji Beer Blonde, a light ale of remarkable quality. Beer in Africa normally ranges from appalling to undrinkable so it was a pleasant surprise. The lakes were such jewels and so unexpected. I was unaware that they existed, let alone that they were famous for their beauty. I subsequently found out that they are famous for a much more dubious reason. One of the stunning lakes, Lake Nyos, experienced a huge natural tragedy and is now the site of a deserted village. It holds the unenviable world record as the lake with the most number of deaths attributed to it, drowning excluded. On 21st August 1986, in the throat of an old volcano in the Oku volcanic field under the lake, there was a mysterious natural gas eruption. A massive cloud of suffocating carbon dioxide and other gases were expelled by the lake with such velocity that vegetation and trees were levelled. The cloud travelled north-west towards Su-bum, the only substantial settlement in the area. An estimated 2,000 people and hundreds of thousands of animals were killed. Lake Nyos is one of only three lakes in the world known to be saturated with carbon dioxide. The others are Lake Monoun, also in Cameroon, and Lake Kivu on the Rwanda/DRC border. Scientists disagree on the source of the tragedy. Because the lake lies in the crater of a volcano, some believe the gas was volcanic in origin. Other scientists argue that the decomposition of organic material at the base caused a natural gas build-up.

When we headed into Mamfe, the town where I split from Paul, we found out more details of the crater catastrophe from an exceedingly friendly Inspector of Police. His name was Ndinwa Chiki Edmond, Police number 77830719 S.B. WUM. Don't ask me why I know his number. Over a meal of fried chicken, Njeme (green spinach with onions and red chilli), Fufu (carpet glue, I think), and tomato and onion sauce he told us more. The reason he knew so much about it was because he was there. He told us that his people, the survivors, were rehoused and forcibly relocated into an infertile area. They were put in grim, concrete two-room houses with no amenities at all.

"Our sense of being displaced and forgotten is very high," he said earnestly as he ordered another Castel beer. (Dishwater, with a hint of garlic.) He also told us that the estimate of 2,000 dead was absurd. "It is many much more, like 7,000. Many have died slowly, slowly from breathing problems." Whatever the exact details it was a massive event, unreported by the world's media. It is tough for African tragedies to make the news; there are so many of them, natural and manmade.

After eating, I said my goodbyes to Ndinwa Chiki Edward and saw Paul off in a taxi. "I'm heading to London for a mega party, Spence. I need a break." Africa is dazzling but draining; my words, not his. I understood and anyway I was quite happy to head on alone.

In a sombre mood I headed off to the Nigerian border, but not without one more incident. Cameroon continued to stun me with its abundance of flora and fauna, right up to the border. It was lush beyond words with bubbling rivers and spectacular waterfalls everywhere.

After a few hours' riding I stopped at a roadside hut and sampled palm wine and kola nuts with a student called Rene. The wine was grim and the kola nuts bitter as hell, but I put on my grin-and-bear-it face. No need to offend such a welcoming guy. I pushed on but after ten minutes the bike started jumping around like a kangaroo. I suspected water in the fuel or dirt in the air filter. I pulled up on the side of the road under some massive palm trees and set to work. It was the filter. As I was about to head off two young guys came out from the middle of nowhere. They were about fourteen or fifteen. One, wearing a Jimi Hendrix T-shirt, looked like Will Smith, ears and all. Except he was so short he had to look up to look down. The other was taller and as muscular as a praying mantis. He was sporting a 'Nani' Manchester United football jersey. Midget Will Smith pulled out a tiny pen knife and said, as menacingly as a dwarf can, "Give us money," as he waved the knife back and forth through the air.

I just said, "Fuck off, you're not having any of my money, not in a million years!"

He looked taken aback but pulled himself together. "Give me money now."

I laughed and said, "Come and get it then," as I swung my helmet back and forth by my side. They both looked totally perplexed. This was not going the way they had envisaged. They started arguing between themselves in French, which they didn't realise I spoke. A rough translation; they were shitting themselves. They both backed up and disappeared into the forest. The bloody youth of today: no respect, I say! On to Nigeria before anyone else wanted to use me as a pin cushion. Cameroon, beautiful – yes: muggers, hopeless – yes.

Chapter Eleven
Charly Boy Oputa Grand Commander of the People's Army

'Four wheels move the body, two wheels move the soul.'
Laconia Harley-Davidson

'You must act as if it is impossible to fail.' Ashanti proverb

Within two hours of entering Nigeria one man and his entourage were to change the nature of my trip beyond recognition. My eight months of roughing it in two dollar accommodation, or camping it on the cheap, were to come to a spectacular halt. Eating an endless cycle of sardines or corned beef (which I still do) in the sweltering sun was to be replaced by five star meals in air conditioned luxury. Well, for a week at least! I was about to witness the beautiful insanity that is Nigeria thanks to 'Charles Charly Boy, Grand Commander of the People's Army, Jewel of the Nation, His Royal Punkness, Area Father Oputa!'

There is no denying that Nigeria and Nigerians have managed to attract a massive amount of criticism in Europe and worldwide. They have gained a reputation for being involved in all sorts of shady deals ranging from drug dealing, murder and prostitution, to the forging of everything on earth, from sunglasses to designer clothes, from money to passports.

This stereotyping was evident and strong in the surrounding African countries. When I stated that I was going to cross the whole of Nigeria, the severity of comments ranged from, "the drivers are crazy, the road is too dangerous," to "my God, you don't want to go there; they will rob you," to "they will kidnap and kill you, they kill all foreigners," and finally, no more optimistically, "Nigeria is the most dangerous country in the world, they are all criminals that side!" I am not going to enter into a discussion of the truth of these claims but I am pretty sure that they do not kill all foreigners, maybe just a few! I didn't intend to be one of the killed and, from experience, if I had listened to all the warnings about different countries in Africa, I wouldn't have left my front door.

So, it was with an open mind and a soaring heart that I crossed the border from Cameroon into Nigeria. What a transition it was. The immediate impression was that once again I would have to update my 'Worst Drivers in the World Award' and present this dubious accolade to the Nigerians, wrestling the award away from the previous country I had been in, and the one before, and the one before... The whole of Nigeria, all 923,768 square kilometres, is a race track! Unfortunately, the cars do not meet Formula One safety standards with the inevitable consequences. As in all of Africa, there were burned-out shells of cars, taxis and buses littering the side of the road. But in Nigeria this was exponential, with accidents seemingly on every corner. The accidents also seemed more violent, with the mangled and unrecognisable skeletons of vehicles paying testimony to the speeds that must have been involved in the crashes. I have been known to exaggerate slightly but during my week in Nigeria I was almost knocked off the bike over one hundred times, and I was almost killed on about twenty, heart-stopping, mouth-gulping, jelly-legging occasions.

I quickly learned that as pedestrians Nigerians are impeccably polite, but put them behind the wheel of a car and they turn into demented lunatics. I soon became used to the wide-eyed maniacal glare of various drivers as they leant over the steering wheel, nose to the windscreen, pushing their vehicles to warp speed. (Well, as fast as their bangers would go.) The main road to Abuja was fairly good but peppered with potholes, and the landscape was unspectacular, mainly flat and semi-arid scrubland. I travelled at a steady 120 kilometres an hour. This was interspersed with bouts of wild weaving, braking and dodging as I was nearly knocked into the gullies bordering the road, by the rest of Nigeria, who were all entrants in the 'Castrol Rally to Abuja'. The massive lorries were the worst. I was swatted like a fly by the powerful winds they generated. It was like riding in a cyclone for fifteen seconds every time one whooshed past at breakneck (my neck!) speed. So it was with relief and not a little surprise that I entered the outskirts of Abuja with all limbs intact but a few nerves shredded.

Abuja was the strangest African city I had driven into. Normally you are confronted with bustling mayhem, a stimulating and wonderful assault on all the senses, as teeming masses noisily get on with their African day. But Abuja was like a ghost city. The eeriness of the scene was accentuated by Aso Rock, a 400-metre monolith that rises out of the flat terrain and looms silently over the city. I coasted quietly and slowly past the Presidential Complex, the National Assembly, the Supreme Court and much of the city that extended to the south of the rock. I stopped to photograph the Nigerian National Mosque, a grand, gold, anodised, domed prayer hall with four towering minarets at its corners. The organised and clean boulevards were empty, apart from the occasional plush car coasting past. The pavements that bordered the gleaming modern tower blocks were devoid of hawkers and litter. Trees were planted at intervals along the pavement and flowers splashed out of pot stands on street corners. A couple wandered hand in hand down the street and the sound of laughter emanated from a roadside café, but generally the streets were silent. Too silent, too clean and too organised. I felt almost like I was in a European city. It was odd, but only because I was ignorant of two facts.

The first and obvious fact I should have realised was that it was Sunday. I had been travelling so long that I only infrequently kept track of the days of the week. This partially explained why it was so quiet. The second fact that I was ignorant of was that Abuja was a new purpose-built city, built in the 1980s and only became the capital in 1991. It was a city planned to be geographically neutral, and to relieve some of the pressure from the old capital, Lagos, which had become clogged and unmanageable, with its sprawling population of twelve million. This explained why Abuja was so clean, new and organised. Even the roads were set out in a highly organised grid system! After the chaotic capitals of the last sixteen African countries I had recently visited, I was mesmerised by the tranquillity of the place and rode around savouring the contrast. As I surveyed the streets I would have guessed the population of the city as a few thousand but it turned out to be over two million. I would quickly find out that this shining metropolis was a sleeping giant, but only on Sundays.

I turned off the main boulevard at random, on to a sand-covered tarmac road. On my right was a skeleton structure of a small market, made of wood and corrugated iron. It was empty except for a young boy selling pirate DVDs to the rare passing car. (I don't think there is any other sort of DVD but pirate in Africa.) On my left twenty metres further down the road was a small yellow sign with 'Hotel' written on it. The letters were fashioned out of black duct tape. There was a crude hand-painted picture of a Guinness bottle, and a duct tape arrow pointing to where the Hotel and Guinness bottle could be found. Unfortunately, one of the nails had fallen out so the sign had swung on its side. It indicated that the Hotel and the bottle of Guinness were to be found in the heavens. Seated below the sign, on plastic chairs, were a group of eight immaculately dressed men. Judging from the empty bottles on their table they were evidently in the process of doubling Guinness Extra's daily profit. I pulled up near to the group, avoiding a large crack and pothole in the road which was gushing with water, crisp packets and coke cans. I kicked the stand down, removed my helmet and dismounted. As soon as it was obvious that I was approaching the group, all eight men stood up in unison. The man nearest to me turned, walked forward and extended his hand in greeting. He was clothed in traditional gear: a bright gold-coloured Buba with black triangular patterns emblazoned on the front (a loose shirt that reaches midway down the thigh), a pair of gold Sokoto (loose trousers) and a gold Fila (traditional round cap). He finished his elegant and suave look with a pair of red suede shoes. I guessed him to be about forty, his face unlined, but with a smattering of grey on his perfectly shaped sideburns.

With a thousand-megawatt smile of Cheshire cat proportions and beyond, he said, "Welcome to Nigeria, welcome to Abuja. My name is Phrank Shaibu."

I replied, "Thank you very much, my name is Spencer Conway," shaking his outstretched hand warmly. (I had just shaken the hand of someone who, like Ashraf Mohammed in Egypt, would remain in my heart forever.)

"I am looking for somewhere cheap to stay for a few days," I continued. He politely ignored my question. I was to learn quickly that you don't under any circumstances skip the greeting rituals vital to Nigerian etiquette.

Phrank put his arm around my shoulder and said, "Come and meet my friends, Spencer Conway. You must be sweltering in that protective motorbike jacket. Come and imbibe in some Guinness Extra and be leisureful for a time. It will do you the world of good, of that I am sure."

There was no way I could refuse such a polite and persuasive invitation. Little did I know that Phrank Shaibu had hundreds of eloquent speeches and stories hidden up his sleeve. He was the master of the quick retort, the master of wit and repartee, the smoothest of the smooth, the purveyor of Jane Austin vocabulary; with a Nigerian twist of course. Listening to Phrank speak was a privilege. It was, without a doubt, pure poetry, regardless of the fact that it was poetry in three languages and many dialects and eras. Phrank could be a posh English gentleman from the 18th century or he could be a Nigerian shoe polisher. Push him further and he could be an

English lecturer at a top US university. He could be many things but what was most important to me was that he could be relied on in every circumstance, every situation. Phrank was a pure James Bond of Africa. Just a bit chubbier.

Phrank introduced me to Felix Achile, his righthand man. Felix would turn out to be a quiet but solidly dependable man who was proud of his family, culture and country.

Next to him was the stocky Sam Dave Ocoha who was introduced as "Sam Dave, the Head of the Rotary Club Nigeria". He was the most casual and Western-dressed of the group. He was sporting a white shirt, blue corduroy jacket and denim jeans. Perched on top of his large round head was a blue baseball cap with the rotary club logo emblazoned on the front. It was five sizes too small but somehow managed to stay put. After being introduced to the rest of the group we all congregated around the bike. Phrank called over a young girl of about twelve and ordered nine bottles of Guinness. The group started to point at all the country stickers and flags that adorned most of the bike, raising their eyebrows and letting out long low whistles of exclamation.

"You have travelled too far, too, too far," said one.

"All the way from England to Cape Town and back actually, 45,000 kilometres," I replied. This fact set the whole group off into a frenzy of animation and comment, repeating my words, whilst whistling, laughing, clapping their hands and clicking their fingers.

"From England to Cape Town and back!" exclaimed a distinguished-looking, elderly gentleman with thick black rimmed glasses and a Fedora. He slapped his palm on his thigh for emphasis.

"All the way on that moto?" questioned another.

"Yes," I replied.

"Alone?" asked another, his eyes widening in anticipation of my answer.

"Completely alone," I nodded. This set them all off again,

high fiving, whistling and raising eyebrows to each other. Phrank took my hand (strange for me, but great) and led me to the table. We all sat down and the questioning continued.

"You are too, too strong, Spencer Conway. Where are your wife and children?" enquired Felix in his serious baritone voice. (I loved the way, because of my age, it was just assumed that I was married and had children.)

"Where do you stay?"

"What do you eat?"

"Why are you doing this?"

"What about wild animals?"

"What about bandits?"

"Are you not scared of the dark?" I lost track of how many times I was asked this particular question in Africa. I answered as best as I could until we were interrupted by the girl with the Guinness. She proceeded to open all nine bottles and place one in front of each of us. She then proceeded to balance a beer mat on the top of each bottle. "To prevent the flies from enjoying your Guinness," Phrank offered in explanation. "You must be very hungry, Spencer Conway. Let us have the pleasure of rumbling up some food and condiments for you to feast upon." Despite my protestations, Phrank was not taking no for an answer and sent the girl to the kitchen.

After about fifteen minutes she returned with the worst meal I would ever eat in Africa. (Let me point out that I am not in the slightest bit squeamish; I made the mistake of eating a live worm in front of my two young daughters and after that I had to eat one, or more, every time their friends came round or I would be nagged relentlessly.) I had just sat down with eight of the nicest men I had met and now they were all going to sit and watch me eat. The meal that was placed in front of me looked like a piece of jellied meat that had been sneezed on by a multitude of people suffering from the bubonic plague. It turned out to be a raw cow's cheek marinated lovingly in Ogbono soup, bitter leaf spinach in palm oil. I don't want to cast aspersions on Nigerian cuisine because everything I had after this particular offering was delicious. But this was worse than it looked. I suspect the girl had been under pressure to come up with something quickly and had not even bothered to cook it. Before I started eating I asked for a bowl of water to wash my hands. This impressed them all and Felix quickly berated the poor waitress for her foolish oversight in not bringing the distinguished guest a bowl. The meal was stone cold, the cow's cheek tasted like a lump of sinewy jelly and the Ogbono soup was so slimy it stuck to my fingers and left a long trail to my mouth, not unlike a horrific green, putrid tasting bubble gum. The only thing that stopped me retching was the Fufu that I scooped the glutinous mass up with. Fufu is made by boiling starchy vegetables like Cassava, yams or plantains and then pounding them into a dough-like consistency and it was tasty enough to save my blushes.

Although they were in no way openly staring, I could tell that the gentlemen at the table were covertly assessing how I dealt with the meal. Luckily, I was armed with a little bit of knowledge. I knew not to ask for cutlery as this food is eaten with your hands. I also knew that you only ate with your right hand; reserving the left for activities in the ablution department. Also, being from Swaziland, I was familiar with Fufu which is called Pap in southern Africa and Ugali, Sadza or Posho in eastern Africa. This, I deftly dealt with, rolling a small ball into the fingers of my right hand and then scooping up the accompanying 'soup'. There were nods of approval all round and when I had finished I swear they nearly broke into applause. I smiled and said, "That was excellent, thanks," when what I really wanted to say was, "Give me Ethiopian sour pancakes any day. Long live Injera!"

"You are a true African!" exclaimed Felix.

"No, you are a true Nigerian," said Phrank. They all laughed and nodded in agreement.

"Nine more Guinness!" Rotary Sam Dave said, turning to

the waitress and pointing at the empty bottles.

Phrank turned to me and said, "Spencer Conway, you are a crazy man and I believe that it is important that on your visit to Nigeria you have the esteemed privilege of meeting another crazy man, who also happens to be a motorbike enthusiast, like your good self. His name is Charly Boy."

"Who is this Charly Boy then, Phrank?" I asked. They all started at once. "Charly Boy is a very famous Nigerian." "He is a rap singer and also has his own television programme." "Charly Boy helps the poor of Nigeria!" "Charly Boy is very controversial!" "Nigerian people love him very much."

Phrank put up his hand and they all stopped talking. "If you wish Spencer, I will call him now and arrange for a prompt rendezvous, possibly this afternoon, or even tomorrow when you are fully rested and recharged."

A little overwhelmed with the speed of activity I just spluttered, "Yes, yes, that would be great." Phrank sprang into action making numerous animated phone calls interrupted by loud suggestions from the assembled group. Felix disappeared for ten minutes and returned with a pair of neon lime green flip-flops. "I bought these for you Spencer; you cannot walk around hot Nigeria in those big leather boots." He presented them to me with both arms outstretched. I was touched, thanked him profusely and immediately changed into my effeminate footwear. It was a good look when combined with my all black bike gear and general hard man image. After ten minutes of activity Phrank turned off his phone with a flourish and said, "We will meet Charly Boy tomorrow morning at ten and then we will have a press conference and then a TV interview."

I was flabbergasted and just said, "Fantastic, amazing, yeah great, thanks Phrank."

"It is my pleasure to help you, Spencer Conway. Welcome to Nigeria."

I felt very welcome. It was impossible not to. Most Africans are very animated and tactile in their relations and Nigerians took it to the extreme. All discussions involve a great deal of hilarity, smiling, back slapping, knee slapping and various complex handshakes. It is not uncommon for men to walk down the road hand in hand. One of Phrank's nicest traits was taking hold of my hand when he really wanted me to listen, or leading me, by the forearm, away from the group when he wanted to talk quietly or give me some advice, which was always pertinent and useful. On this occasion he took my hand and said, "Come Spencer, I have arranged for you to stay here tonight, no fee. I will show you the room."

We wandered into the hotel which only had four rooms set in a quadrangle. The room I was shown was the cleanest I had stayed in for seven months. "Phrank, that is fantastic, but please let me pay."

"It has already been arranged, there is no negotiation on this particular point, Spencer," he stated, grinning widely, his plump cheeks wrinkling up his face.

"I don't know what to say, except thank you so much for everything."

"It is my pleasure. I suggest you relax and take a shower and we will meet outside here at nine tomorrow. Does that meet with your approval?" I shook his hand warmly, "I look forward to it, see you at nine."

'Nigeria time' is a well-known concept. If someone says 'see you at 9', it really means 'nine is the earliest I will arrive but it could be two hours later'. I somehow knew that Phrank was not going to be late and I was proved correct when he swung in, all bright and breezy, accompanied by Baritone Felix and Sam Dave Rotary Club Chairman for Lokoja. Phrank Shaibu Head of Communications for Media in Nigeria, once again looked suave and sophisticated in his immaculate traditional gear which on this occasion was jungle green colours, finished off with a pair of brown leather shoes in which I could see the reflection of my face. Not a crease could be seen. They all greeted me warmly and then we headed off in Phrank's car. It took us about forty minutes weaving through the fully-awake city during which time we had animated discussions on various topics. It was such a pleasure to chat with people who had a magical command of the English language, especially after struggling to communicate with my schoolboy French in Cameroon. I cannot remember the context of the comment but Phrank came up with the statement, 'Racism is just a pigment of your imagination.' I thought it was great and stored it away in my memory bank. We headed into an obviously wealthy suburb, and turned onto a road called Charly Boy Avenue. And so it was I was thrown into the world of 'Charles Charly Boy Chukwuemeka, Grand Commander of the People's Army, His Royal Punkness, The Area Father, Oputa'.

We arrived outside a large set of black wrought iron gates with a small guard tower on the left and a large sign, 'The Punk Palace,' on the right. A uniformed guard came out to meet us and after checking our credentials opened up the gates.

Charly Boy's mansion looked exactly like The White House, right down to the massive white pillars framing the entrance, but with some significant adaptations. There were only two outer pillars instead of four because suspended between them was a black human skull, the size of a Mini car, fashioned out of stainless steel.

We pulled up on the driveway in front of the house. I looked out of the window on my right, across an immaculate lawn, in the centre of which was suspended on a pole twenty five foot in the air, a Harley-Davidson motorbike, silhouetted sharply against the clear blue sky. We exited the car and headed up to the front door. Jutting out of the wall, on the righthand side of the massive wooden doors, was the front end of a Harley Davidson, giving the impression it had smashed its way through at high speed. (I would soon find out that the rear half of the bike was on the other side of the wall, jutting into Charly Boy's sitting room.) As we approached the door, it was opened by a tall, good-looking man of about thirty, with waist-length ebony dreadlocks, a wispy beard and moustache and the largest smile humanly possible.

"Welcome to The Palace, I am Mike, Charly Boy's advisor," he said, heartily shaking all our hands in turn. He pointed back out the house, over the lawn to a large thatched gazebo and stated, "We'll wait over there, Charly Boy will come shortly." Once inside the gazebo, which turned out to be a mini bar, Mike offered us drinks from a gold-coloured fridge and told us to make ourselves comfortable. Although it was only ten in the morning I was sweltering in my jacket, so removed it and hung it on the back of a gold-sprayed wicker chair, before sitting down. We only had to wait two minutes before Charly Boy came swaggering across the lawn towards us, grinning and waving his hands in the air. He shook all our hands and when he came to me he said, "Welcome to Nigeria."

As he spoke I noticed that he had his tongue pierced, one of many piercings that were visible. I found out later, that in addition to his androgynous style, his piercings and tattoos were frowned upon by conservative Nigerians, who viewed this form of modification as Satanic and Occultist. Charly Boy's appearance was different to say the least.

I judged him to be about forty five. This proved to be wildly wrong as he was in fact sixty one. It was obvious from his taut muscles and energetic demeanour that he kept himself in shape. He was dressed in green combat trousers and a green camouflage vest. Draped around his neck was a gold-edged, diamond-studded cross about five inches long. As well as the tongue stud he had a lip, nose and eyebrow ring and his arms were adorned with various tattoos. Every finger on both hands was decorated in large silver Gothic rings. He had a black bandana wrapped around his head, and a number of thin dreadlocks cascading down his back. Strapped to his right bicep was a digital distance counter, the type used by keen runners.

Although he was not late he apologised, saying, "I was just finishing my workout, sorry Spencer Conway." (How do they all know my name?) The conversation flowed easily and Charly Boy was laid back and full of questions about my "crazy man travels".

Throughout our chat he dabbed the sweat off his forehead with a crisp, white handkerchief. His mannerisms were extremely effeminate, I must admit, and I knew from Phrank it had caused him to suffer from some troublesome rumours in a country where homosexuality is illegal. But contrary to popular belief he was not gay and has actually been married to an African-American singer Diane for over thirty years. Charly Boy and I hit it off immediately and over the next five days we embarked on a whirlwind cycle of TV, radio and newspaper interviews, photo shoots and bike rallies. Under the watchful eye of Phrank, who became my unofficial 'Nigerian etiquette advisor,' I learnt a great deal about the Nigerian phenomenon that is Charly Boy and the phenomenon that is Nigeria.

Charly Boy was the second son of a former well known and respected Supreme Court judge. He was raised as a Catholic in a strict family. Although he describes his parents as friends who always encouraged their children to speak out and question things, he has also spoken of their extremely conservative nature. He had set out to become a priest but left the seminary school after a year. In his late teens he went to the States where he was expected to study Law but graduated with a degree in Communications. What he achieved upon his return and up to the time I met him can be summed up in the words of a presenter on Radio Nigeria that I heard the day I left the country:

"Charly Boy is a Nigerian singer and songwriter, television presenter, publisher, producer and one of Nigeria's most controversial entertainers. He is best known for his maverick lifestyle, biker style, political views and strength of character in the face of criticism. But most of all Charly Boy is known as an advocate of the masses as he has steadfastly fought for the rights of the average Nigerian. He has on several occasions been tortured by the Nigerian police and the military for standing up to his country's government. As Head of the Okada Riders (small motorbikes), an organisation that has been frowned upon by the government (they have been regarded as a menace and unsafe transportation), he has fought for the rights of Okada users, most of whom are poor individuals. They make their meagre living as taxi drivers. Charly Boy's efforts have earned him the status as a cult hero among the poor and have earned him the name 'Area Fada' (Father).

"Charly Boy also fought for the rights of military pensioners during the Abaca-led military dispensation by marching to Defence Headquarters in Abuja and demanding payments. He has also fronted campaigns for Nigerian widows. During the fuel subsidy protest he was arrested for civil disobedience. Charly Boy continues to be a thorn in many people's sides, but is undoubtedly loved by the masses."

The report ended with the slightly incongruous comment: "Let us not forget that Charly Boy is one of the richest people in Nigeria and possibly in Africa". As if to point out that the final comment was not a criticism, the commentator added, "But let us *also* not forget that Charly Boy has imported more than two thousand Okada motorbikes to help our young people."

So there we have it. The Charly Boy I knew in those five days was a gentleman of note, but undoubtedly a well-oiled media machine/circus. His entourage consisted of Mike The Dread, various sunglassed-up minders, random unidentified photographers and cameramen, his secretary, his beautifully elegant wife Diane and the Wasp. I called him The Wasp for strikingly obvious reasons. The Wasp was evidently Charly Boy's 'main man bodyguard'. He rode a massive yellow and black road bike. He was decked out in black leather bike gear with yellow lightning strikes emblazoned on the front. A black bandana and wraparound black sunglasses with yellow lenses finished off his look. The Wasp was at least six foot six, had dark, flawless skin, perfect teeth and strikingly chiselled cheekbones. His hands were the size of shovels and his handshake predictably vice-like. I would like to say that I warmed to him and that he is on my Christmas card list but I would be stretching the truth. I do not even know The Wasp's name. He did not utter a single word the whole time I was there. The odd nod of acknowledgement was all I got from behind his mirror glasses. I loved it. It was like being in a movie.

Charly Boy put me up in a five-star hotel and dragged me into the Nigerian equivalent of The Oprah Winfrey Show for an interview. He chloroformed and kidnapped me for a Village People-style photoshoot involving Chinese construction workers, two Caterpillar diggers and an angry site manager.

Everywhere Charly Boy went, people lined the streets and shouted, "Charly Boy, Charly Boy, Area Fada, next president of Nigeria!" On a number of occasions he jumped out of his car or stopped his motorbike to run along the road waving his white handkerchief to the crowds. (How the hell did he keep it so clean?) During one sortie he even resorted to throwing money to the crowds, but a riot almost ensued and it was decided that this was too rock and roll, or maybe too tacky for words? I was swept up in the road show but always had the wonderful Phrank Shaibu, Head of Media and Communications, to guide me.

"Spencer, Charly Boy is organising a bike rally from Lagos to see you out of Nigeria. Felix and I have decided we will escort you down to Lagos to facilitate a smooth journey."

"Phrank, it is five hundred and fifty kilometres to Lagos, you can't possibly follow me down!" I exclaimed.

"It is decided, Spencer Conway Adventure Motorcyclist, there will be no swerving from the plan. We are already packed and greased to go," he said, smoothing down his grey-flecked sideburns. "The road will be smoother and the journey more serene with our knowledge and guidance." Baritone Felix piped in: "It is our pleasure to escort you to the border, although it is evident that we do not wish you to leave."

So it came to pass, as they say, that I found myself hurtling towards Lagos. I use the word hurtling because unfortunately Felix fell victim to the Formula One disease that is rife in Nigeria. We covered the five hundred and fifty kilometres in six hours on potholed, car crash-strewn, cow wandering and goat grazing roads. If you asked me anything about the landscape I could not give you a single detail as all my concentration was focussed on saving the only life God had given me. It was hair-raising and on a number of close shaves I wanted to confront Felix about his Kamikaze driving, but I never did.

As we came into the outskirts of Lagos, shanty town settlements sprang up sporadically on the edge of muddy, litter-strewn hillsides. On my left a massive landfill sight stretched on for kilometres, the litter spewing out onto the road. Massive yellow trucks squashed the refuse into the tarmac creating the impression of a patchwork road made of plastic bottles, bags, cardboard boxes and flattened tins. Scurrying around on the mountain of refuse at the side of the road were thousands of children. In one hand they all gripped a wicked-looking metal hook with which they scoured through the stinking, putrid rubbish. Recyclable items such as rubber and plastic were skewered with the hook and swung into a Hessian sack they had slung over one shoulder. As more yellow dump trucks came into the site the crowd swarmed around it, risking life and limb to be the first to search the next rotting offload. A shanty town of cardboard and corrugated iron hung dangerously on the muddy hillside adjacent to the landfill site. This was obviously where these children were born, brought up, worked and died. As we progressed into the city the shanty town became one never-ending entity, sprawled along both sides of the road as far as the eye could see. It was spectacular in its scale. As we entered the central area of Lagos the shanty towns gave way to blackened high-rise buildings, tatty soot-covered shops and cafes. The pavements were covered in a spectacular array of umbrellas; white, blue, neon green, striped, spotted and branded. The streets were heaving with thousands of yellow taxis and mini vans, Okada scooters and handheld carts.

The Okadas regularly weaved past me, transporting two, three, even four people, plus luggage. The gaps between the traffic were filled with hawkers; women in brilliantly coloured traditional gear, selling bananas and nuts, stored in a tin bowl balanced on their heads. There were children with frozen lollies and cell phone cards, and men with an array of sandals and shoes, pinned to strips of cardboard. It looked like all of the twenty one million people that make up Lagos were out and about. The whole colourful, yet dust and dirt-covered scene was surging and heaving with life and I loved it, but it did not make for easy riding. After much weaving, dodging and gulping I made it intact to the city centre, scarcely disguising my jelly demeanour from Phrank Shaibu and Felix Achile when I got off the bike.

"A little bit different to Abuja, hey gents," I said, understated.

"Lagos is a very exciting city; you will enjoy it greatly for the next two days. Charly Boy has booked you into the Water Park Hotel," Phrank said, pointing to a smart high-rise building set back from the main road. Me in a smart hotel, would you believe it. I can't say I complained too bitterly after the previous seven months' accommodation.

"You can enter and give your name at the reception, everything is organised. We are going to Victoria Island to fulfil a previous obligation. Have a good night and we will see you in the morning," said Baritone Felix. I thanked them and headed into the foyer. I was feeling great. I didn't know it then but I would be leaving Lagos in two days' time with calls for my arrest being voiced on Radio Nigeria.

The hotel was wonderfully clean and I must confess I did not feel overly guilty escaping the poverty outside. After all, I was a guest and I knew it would be very rude to spurn Nigerian hospitality. Well, that was my excuse anyway. Charly Boy had the penthouse suite at the top of the hotel and after I had showered, Mike the Dread knocked and invited me up to Charly Boy's. We had a fantastic evening and when I demonstrated my extensive knowledge of obscure reggae bands, my acceptance in the group was complete. The next day we undertook Radio and TV interviews at the Nigerian Institute of Journalism and various other locations around the city. Throughout our meanderings we were joined by hundreds of Okada riders, their bikes spluttering and spewing smoke in their attempts to keep up. There were the constant chants of "Area Fada," "Charly Boy," and "Next President!" Charly Boy waved his white handkerchief theatrically out of the car window. It was blatantly obvious that the Lagos 'street public' loved the 'Charly Boy Show'. I was enjoying my fifteen minutes of fame greatly but the next day was to be the absolute pinnacle of mayhem.

Charly Boy had arranged for a bike rally to see me out of Lagos on my way to Benin. But nothing could have prepared me for the scene outside the hotel when I woke up. There were at least thirty journalists waiting outside with foot-long camera lenses swinging on their chests. There were crowds of people swarming the entrance to the hotel. In the distance, at the junction to the main road I could see hundreds of Okada riders waiting patiently for the arrival of Charly Boy. I met him in the foyer and they swung into a well-rehearsed formation, before we entered the mayhem. The Wasp took his position next to Charly Boy. Mike the Dread and another fearsome-looking bouncer with traditional scarification on his cheeks took their positions ahead of Charly Boy. Their objective was to keep the crowds back and prevent them from squashing their hero.

I positioned myself behind the group along with four or five of Charly Boy's media team. We plunged into the chaos and made it to the main road unscathed. I could not believe my eyes. I looked down the arrow-straight, two-way thoroughfare and all I could see were not hundreds, but thousands of Okada motorbikes stretching into the distance. It was a spectacular sight of dust, exhaust smoke and colour. Everyone of the riders was wearing plastic construction hard hats in every available colour on earth. The hard hats would be as useful as goldfish in a pillow case in protecting the riders in a crash but it was a hilarious and multi-coloured visual experience I shall never forget.

Charly Boy jumped onto a block of concrete on the central reservation and raised his bejewelled fist in the air. Engines were turned off, voices were lowered and the thousand strong bike rally hung on his every word.

"Thank you everybody for coming down today. We are here to support a fellow rider who will have the honour of becoming the first person to ride around Africa on a motorbike. He is also raising money for our precious African children. Let us welcome motorbike hero (I liked that bit) Spencer Conway to Nigerian warmth," he shouted, sweeping his hand towards me. The crowd screamed, waved and hooted.

"Let us ride with Spencer Conway out of Lagos and show the power of the Okada riders!" he bellowed out above the noise. He then transferred to Nigerian patois, or Pidgin English. I understood little but the effect on the crowd was unmistakable. They roared in approval to every statement, hooted and clapped at every pause, until Charly Boy had managed to whip up a carnival atmosphere in five minutes flat. Completing his speech he jumped off his concrete pedestal and started jogging down the road. This was the signal for the rally to start.

The Wasp and I hurried to our bikes and with much bodyguard jostling we made it to the front of the bikers and behind Charly Boy. He set his distance counter to zero (an incongruous touch I felt), whipped his white handkerchief out of his trouser pocket and began waving it to the crowds.

The TV crews were on motorbikes at the head of the rally. The passenger cameramen were balanced precariously, facing the wrong way, to catch the action unfolding behind them. A pick-up truck with a camera mounted on the back hooted its

Lagos rally with Charly Boy in the lead

way to the front. Radio interviewers in smart shiny suits were jogging next to Charly Boy, attempting to undertake a breathless interview.

We made our way under overpasses, people screaming Charly Boy's name from above us. People ran out in the road to shake hands with or just touch him. As we weaved our way around the city, more and more bikes joined the rally and our progress became slower and slower until after only twenty minutes we came to a shuddering halt at a huge roundabout. Cars were coming in from six different directions: it was total gridlock. Charly Boy ran into the centre of the roundabout, waving his arm in circles above his head, screaming to the crowds. This in no way helped with the gridlock and I suspect that he was enjoying bringing the centre of Lagos to a complete standstill. The snaking horde of bikers stopped but kept their engines running. The air became thick with fumes, which engulfed the whole scene. Crowds pushed into the centre and then Charly Boy, floating in and out of view behind the fumes, once again made another tacky but showbiz decision. He started handing out fifty Naira notes which he pulled out in wads from his stuffed pockets. This caused absolute chaos and for the first time I thought, 'I might get caught in the middle of a riot here.' Somehow Mike the Dread, The Wasp, two incredulous traffic policemen and various bodyguards managed to keep the crowd under control. No matter how much I was enjoying this it was evident that no traffic was going anywhere and I was definitely not going to Benin today. I called over to Phrank above the sound of the engines, as Charly Boy gave me the thumbs up through the smoke. The Wasp smiled at me. (No, I made that last bit up.)

"Phrank, this is amazing but there is no way I will make it out of here today."

"Do not fret Spencer, we have many plans up our sleeves. There are alternative routes we can access, to make good your escape," he said, smiling and slapping me on the back.

"This is incredible, how did Charly Boy organise this so quickly?"

"He is the Area Fada," Phrank answered.

"I will never forget this experience and really it is all down to you."

"Your happiness is my happiness," was his simple answer.

"Well, I really don't want to leave, Phrank. You and Felix had better come to England one day, so I can repay your generosity."

"This will indeed happen and we will take the fullest advantage of your hospitality, do not fret."

"Good," I answered, laughing.

I was interrupted by the blast of some powerful speakers, emanating from a black pickup truck. The words 'Ninja biker' pounded my ears.

"Charly Boy's most famous song," Phrank shouted above the bass. I shook my head in wonderment. What an organised but at the same time chaotic team! Fantastic! The next two hours were superb but, true to his word, Phrank had a plan.

"I feel now is the appropriate time for us to depart. I feel we must say goodbye and make our way to the outskirts." I agreed. Despite having a great time I knew this was the Charly Boy Show and I was beginning to yearn for the silence of the open road. I don't want to sound ungrateful, but fame and celebrity is not me. I love to be alone. Sensory overload has never been high on my list. Peace and tranquillity, the space to think, always have been. I had thoroughly enjoyed my days of super stardom (by proxy) but it was now time to be me and focus on my goal: to circumnavigate this mind-blowing continent. Bring on the next experience.

Amongst the chaos I managed to thank and say goodbye to all the characters who had made my experience so rich. Before I knew it I was on the outskirts of Lagos, alone. I drove for an hour, my mind swimming. I felt like I needed to stop and take some deep breaths. I pulled up outside a grotty little roadside stall, flopped down on a plastic chair and ordered a bottle of water and a piece of fried chicken. A radio was blaring and to my absolute shock I suddenly heard my name, clear as day. And then it was repeated again. And again. I quickly called the waitress over. "Sorry, please tell me what they are talking about on the radio."

She stood still, listening. After a short while she said, "There are many traffic problems in Lagos. They are wanting to arrest Charly Boy and some European who is riding with the Okadas." She put my bottle of water down, unscrewed the cap and poured a small amount into the cloudy plastic glass. "Do you know Charly Boy?" she asked.

"No, never heard of him," I replied, a bit too adamantly. "Thank you," I said, turning to my drink. She hesitated as if to say something but then thought better and wandered back into her cooking hut. How bloody brilliant, what an experience. I felt not a drop of worry or fear, just a feeling of incredulity (plus a big smile), that I was a fugitive from Nigerian justice. One for the grandchildren.

I sat there thinking about the last five days. It was Phrank Shaibu that shone through in all my thoughts. He had guided me seamlessly through the myriad of Nigerian customs, giving me a massive appreciation of the manners of the past. Gone were the sulky teenagers of England, with manners for no one. Nigeria respects age. Unfailingly, every elder of Nigeria would be stood for, greeted and the first to be seated. They would be the first to eat. They would be deferred to in an argument, despite disagreement. Everyone would be greeted with questions about their family's health and wellbeing. Women would be accepted into the group with the same introductions. Phrank made me aware that you do not offer a handshake to Muslim or married women. With extreme tact, Phrank led me through the maze of manners that I feel are so lacking in Western society nowadays.

The only way Nigerians let themselves down is when they are behind the wheel of a vehicle. Their every intention was to try and kill me. On my way out of the city I became afflicted with road rage and Tourettes. Luckily most of my screaming and cursing was confined to within my helmet, so I really just ended up shouting at myself and not offending any of my would -be-killers in the slightest. My wild hand gesticulations as I careered wildly past the oncoming missile vehicles were just met with baffled expressions and quizzical looks. It was as if they were saying, "Look how that crazy white man drives," seconds after nearly forcing me off the road over a hundred foot cliff. Ok, there was no hundred foot cliff in this area of Nigeria, but I am sure you get the point.

Despite my surreal and deeply entertaining time spent with Phrank Media Manager Minister and Special Advisor to Public Communications and Strategy Shaibu, Felix Side kick Achile, Sam Dave Rotary Club Lokoja Chairman Okocha, Charly Boy Area Fada Oputa, Dreadlocks Mike and The Wasp I was elated to be out in the bush again and left to my own devices. After a half hour ride I was out of the city and I set up camp. I was relieved to be back amongst my other friends; snakes, spiders, lizards and the various other things with wings that always surround my campsites. In many journals I have read of Westerners travelling through Africa, a common thread runs through all: complaints. Moaning, extended paragraphs about the heat, the mosquitos, the food and the people seem to slip into their writing at regular intervals. As I sat there on my groundsheet, spread over a rocky uneven piece of Nigeria, I felt so lucky. For some reason I seem to be utterly indifferent to personal comfort, have been blessed with an impregnable digestive tract and seem capable of eating everything or nothing. I had loved ninety nine percent of the 'local' people I had met in the previous nineteen countries (ones that shoot at me are obviously in the one percent category). Most of all I had conquered one hundred percent of the challenges I had faced. I am not blowing my own trumpet; I am just stating what I had learnt on this journey, about myself and my body. My complete lack of fear in any situation had also pleased me. Maybe certain people are more suited to Africa than others. As I sat there I even welcomed the familiar sound of mosquitoes buzzing around me as the arches on my feet itched crazily from their attacks. Excellent. Benin and Togo, here I come.

Despite various mating crickets, mozzies and some largish creature snorting outside my tent during the depths of the night, I slept well. I was awoken by the sound of an axe splitting wood and popped my head out the tent. A grizzled old man as wiry as a wire grinned at me toothlessly. He had on a pair of ripped shorts, and sandals fashioned from car tyres adorned his dusty, gnarled feet. A dead animal skin, with a long tail of some sort, was wrapped around his head, giving the impression of a wizened Nigerian Davy Crockett. He seemed completely unfazed that a motorbike, a tent and a white man had sprung up on his land overnight. I looked around and realised his homestead was only thirty metres away from where I had sat the night before. I must have really been wrapped up in myself congratulatory thoughts. Idiot. Anyway, no harm done. I introduced myself and he turned out to be Happy. Well that's what his name sounded like. I thanked him for the campsite and after I had packed up my things I helped him carry the split logs up to his hut, handing him a yellow can of Blue Ocean Africa Best Taste Sardines and a red can of Nigeria Titus Sardines as I left. Not a lot of variety. He seemed pleased and I was pleased to make Happy, happy.

Guardian of the tree

The border crossing into Benin was easily reached along the Lagos Badagry Way and before I knew it I was cruising along the tarred Atlantic coastal road. On my left was a beautiful palm fringed white sandy beach which stretched for almost the entire width of the country. I drove through the capital Cotonou without much of a look and it was only when I was approaching the town of Ouidah in south western Benin that things started to get interesting, well, shocking is a more appropriate word. Three words were to define my brief visit to Benin; Ignorance, Slavery and Voodoo.

The ignorance came from me. Although I was fully aware of the history of slavery along the west coast of Africa, I had no idea that the city I was about to stumble into was so historic and of such massive significance to all of West Africa. It seemed such an unassuming, pretty, but almost nondescript city. This impression started to change as I turned from the city centre down a sandy, four-kilometre track to the beach. It was a beautiful road, bordered by verdant green marshes and lagoons. Fishermen were casting their nets in an arcing spiral over the surface of the vibrant turquoise water. Others were punting their way on perfectly carved wooden pirogues out to their houses – beautiful thatched longhouses set on stilts in the water. Strange round fishing boats, fashioned together with branches, bobbed on the shoreline and large white herons floated by on the breeze. A woman in a bright traditional dress sauntered down the road, waving to me, a large reed bag balanced solidly on her head. Ten foot high statues started appearing at the side of the road. A monkey in the stance of a man, a mermaid of some sort and a circle of life snake, amongst others. The atmosphere was beautiful but somehow strange.

I rode very slowly, taking it all in, but the tranquillity was shattered when I suddenly came under a serious and sustained attack. Something stung me, or bit me, and then another and another, burning into my back. I swerved to a halt, dropped the bike and ran down the road like Basil Fawlty. I ripped off my jacket and vest which flew, windmill-like through the air, such was my vigour. I started slapping my entire upper body wildly, manically, whilst leaping around the road, banshee style. (Section that man at once, Nurse!) Unbeknownst to me, during the night, and not for the first time, Schwarzenegger Red Ants (genus: Arnoldius Maximus) had steroided their way into my motocross boots which were strapped behind me. They had obviously become bored with the journey and had decided to relocate up my back for some sadistic fun.

After pulling myself together and pulling the armies of Arnies off my reddened skin I regained my composure and carried on down the track. Luckily, no one had witnessed my camp, shrieking dismount. Credibility intact, I say.

The road opened up into a beautiful, lemon-coloured beach, the sea swirling with greens and blues. There was a very light wind blowing through the palm trees. Wispy clouds moved lazily along the otherwise clear blue skyline. Far out to sea the silhouette of two traditional wooden fishing pirogues added to the picture postcard scene. It was exquisitely beautiful but the history of this area was far from beautiful, as I was about to discover. Standing at the head of the beach, dominating these stunning surroundings both by its size and symbolism was a monument called The Door of No Return. I parked up the bike and walked across the powder soft sand to the monument. I spent the next half an hour stunned and shamed by my ignorance of the area but pleased to be now getting educated.

The Door of No Return is a large ochre and white archway set on a white circular base facing the sea. Around the base are various murals and Voodoo symbols. The arch itself is covered in murals depicting shackled slaves. On either side of the arch are Voodoo statues welcoming the souls of dead slaves back to their homeland. The 'history' that this monument is commemorating is staggering to me and the facts speak for themselves. During the seventeenth, eighteenth and nineteenth century Ouidah became known for its central role in the slave trade. The Portuguese, English, Dutch and French all constructed forts in the city to protect their interests in slavery. The tranquil four and a half kilometre track I had just ridden from Ouidah was the same route that more than a million slaves walked, the 'Route des Esclaves'. Before they walked the route, however, the slaves were chained to cots, in a building with little ventilation to simulate the conditions on ships. The weak and sick were tossed into massive graves, sometimes still alive. The beach that I was now standing on was the same one that these million (yes, it's worth repeating, considering that this is just one tiny beach on the massive West African coast) innocent Africans from the Kingdom of Dahomey were branded for ownership and forced onto longboats. From the longboats they were loaded onto large slaving vessels where they were crammed in like sardines for the horrific journey to the New World. Many, let's be honest, most, would not survive the trip and none would return to Benin. Barbaric.

The lovely houses on stilts that I admired on the Route des Esclaves were also a legacy of the slave trade. Villages were built on stilts, to protect civilians from the water-fearing Kings of Dahomey, who were raiding the country for slaves. Thirty thousand people still live in this way, perched atop the water in the village of Ganvie. I cannot deny that my ignorance, countered quickly by revelation, did not have an effect on me. As far as I was concerned this was a beautiful ride through a quaint town, down to an idyllic beach, where I would remove my boots and rest my weary legs, nothing more, nothing less. After the hectic chaos of the Nigeria/Charly Boy scene, maybe I wasn't looking deeply enough. Maybe I wanted a 'no brainer easy' destination. But Benin could never be that.

I realised quickly that the other vital ingredient of Ouidah, and Benin life, was the Voodoo religion or Vodun as it is officially called. That explained the strange statues along the route as well as the symbolic murals on the Door of No Return. Voodoo is completely normal in Benin. People across West Africa, especially Togo, Ghana and Nigeria hold similar beliefs but in Benin it is recognised as an official language. Voodoo is more than a belief system; it is a complete way of life including culture, philosophy, language, art, dance, music and medicine. The Voodoo spiritual world consists of Mahou, the Supreme Being and about one hundred divinities, or Voodoos who represent different phenomena such as war, illness, healing, the earth, lightning, justice and water, to name just a few. Hence the baffling array of murals and statues around Benin. Voodoo priests ask these gods to intervene on behalf of ordinary people but local adherents stress that they have nothing to do with sorcery or black magic. People here do not stick pins into dolls to cause misfortune to their enemies, as you can see in some Western films. These images may have arisen from the icons of a particular God which a priest may have had in his shrine. It suited Westerners to discredit Voodoo with comments about wicked spells, black magic, violence and sacrifice. European colonialism tried to suppress Voodoo. However because Voodoo deities are born to each clan, tribe and nation, and their clergy are central to maintaining the moral, social and political order and ancestral foundations of its village, these efforts have not been successful. Voodoo was even 'exported' by slaves to Brazil and Haiti and is as strong as ever in Benin. How absurd that Europeans were trying to paint Africans as violent savages whilst they enthusiastically engaged in the traffic and slaughter of people who had done them no wrong.

Another jigsaw piece fitted into place when I realised the significance and importance of Voodoo 'fetishes'. Throughout the West Coast countries, I had to try to come to terms with and accept the slaughter of the wildlife. Bush meat markets were everywhere and in Congo and Gabon I came to expect a slaughtered animal on display on every corner. I had to rationalise it. It was tradition and had been going on for thousands of years, but I did not manage to persuade myself. In Benin however the slaughtered animals were of a different kind; dried out. I realised that they were not for food but for Voodoo. All creation is considered divine and therefore contains the power of the divine. This is how medicines such as herbal remedies are understood and explains the ubiquitous use of mundane objects in ritual. Voodoo talismans, called fetishes, are objects such as statues or dried animal parts that are sold for their healing and spiritually rejuvenating properties.

In historical and religious terms everything in Benin now made sense to me and I realised why there was such a strange and different atmosphere to anywhere I had been before. It was the terrible weight of history in an unlikely setting – Eden. Somehow, if a place is ugly one expects ugly events to have occurred there and the opposite is also true. The beauty of Benin was not the 'right' film set for such atrocity and was all the more shocking because of this fact. I will never forget those four and a half kilometres of Benin.

I headed out of Ouidah and stopped at yet another faultlessly beautiful beach about five kilometres from the Togo border. I set up camp, built and lit a fire and settled down to my meal of sardines, bread and alcohol. I had managed to collar a bottle of Flag Lager, which was horrible and a bottle of La Beninoise, a pale lager that was delicious. As I sat by the fire letting the day's revelations sink in, a crab decided that he was a good friend of mine. He kept wandering (well, scurrying sideways) up to the camp fire only to be repelled by the heat. I eventually decided that his fixation with the fire was his downfall. I picked up a coconut and threw it at him. It was a perfect shot and I cracked him dead. On the fire he went, and my canned sardine meal was upgraded to Fresh Crab Beninoise. Lemon would have been good but can't really complain.

The next day would become the first occasion in my life where I would be in three countries in one day. It was mainly down to a coconut-climbing, machete-wielding geriatric.

I cruised through Benin/Togo customs and after a short ride stopped at another dazzling beach and lagoon to watch fishermen throwing out their early morning nets. As I stood in a coconut plantation a local man of about 200 literally ran up a coconut tree and started hacking off coconuts with a machete. I was stunned by his athleticism and by instinct grabbed my video camera and started filming. As soon as he saw me he rocketed down the tree and approached me like the wild man of Borneo. I made a hasty retreat, shouting that I had been in Togo for half an hour and couldn't he make an effort to be more welcoming. Actually I said, "Bugger off you moody old fart," which I felt was a very square and mild response. I knew I was wrong on this occasion as many Africans are extremely sensitive about being filmed and see it as some sort of exploitation. I suggest it is them exploiting the situation, because if you agree to pay them (which I never did) then their moral high stance rapidly disappears. I was in Togo for such a short time that I only have three interesting observations. Firstly, the armed forces are FAT – Forces Armees Togolaises. Secondly, the locals do not like you filming them climbing coconut trees. They will chase you with machetes, whether they are infirm or not. Thirdly, Togo has a fifty six kilometre long beach with a coastal road running next to it and, after my machete scare, before I knew it I was in Ghana. Sorry Togo.

Ghana was an easy deal; good roads, reasonable drivers and the official road rage language was English. I rode a mammoth distance of five hundred and forty seven kilometres in seven hours, twenty three minutes from the Togo/Ghana border to Busue beach in south west Ghana. I arrived at Alaska Beach resort late in the evening and extremely shattered. It was still light enough to see immediately that using the word 'resort' for this place was stretching it to the extreme. More like, this was a last 'resort'. The accommodation was shabby, leaking huts with broken windows and even more broken beds. The facilities were broken and the chap running it also seemed a broken man. The light in my room consisted of a bulb taped to a broomstick and connected by terminals to a car battery. The dusty hut was a menagerie of spiders, mosquitoes, cockroaches (my favourite, especially fried in butter). Actually, bear this in mind, if you don't brush your teeth when you go to bed, cockroaches nibble at the side of your mouth when you are sleeping. This fact puts them at the bottom of my Christmas card list.

I slept very badly, which in English means I didn't sleep at all, mainly because of the surly insects fighting for my affections. I woke to find that the staff were as surly as the insects and they chained up monkeys for tourists' pleasure. This alone put me off the place. It was inevitable that I would get stuck here and that is exactly what happened. The next morning I woke up in my hut sweating like a lunatic and feeling remarkably weak. My joints felt like they had been bent back and forth in the wrong direction and my eyeballs felt bruised as if they had been punched repeatedly during the night. I had contracted malaria.

Malaria is one mean bastard, not to be underestimated. It is caused by falciparum which is a mosquito-borne disease. The bite of the female Anopheles mosquito causes 219 million cases per year worldwide with a death toll of 1.2 million, mostly among African children. I knew that the signs and symptoms begin 8-25 days following infection. So I must have contracted this blasted disease in Congo, Gabon or Cameroon. It could have been any of those countries, as I was bitten raw in all of them and ended up resembling a lump of uncooked mincemeat. Very rapidly I exhibited the classic symptoms – paroxysm, which is a cyclical occurrence of sudden coldness followed by rigor and then fever and sweating. I knew that I needed to go to hospital but quickly lost the logical part of my brain and instead writhed in my hut for four sweaty, hellish days.

When people who have had malaria tell you that they did not care if they had died, believe them. Your mind also plays tricks on you. The 'resort' owner's wife was an unfeasibly skinny Ghanaian woman wrapped in a skin-tight sarong. She had tried to dye her hair blonde but it had ended up a dirty tobacco yellow. In my addled state she resembled a giant used cotton bud. Every time she came into my hut to feed me water and mop my brow I giggled like a lunatic. I appreciated the concern but really wasn't sure where I was and who this cotton bud was. I knew that if I had cerebral malaria there was a good chance that I would die. Individuals with cerebral malaria frequently exhibit neurological symptoms including abnormal posturing, conjugate gaze palsy (failure of the eyes to turn in the same direction), seizures, coma and usually death. Pretty serious then. Thank God, or Jah, or whoever, but on the morning of the fifth day I started to regain my sanity and lucidity and slowly climbed out of the abyss that is malaria.

I was still too weak to escape the motley crew that had gathered at Alaska Beach. The cotton bud who had nursed me turned out to be a right royal pain. Her favourite pastime was to creep up behind the male guests and poke them in the ribs with her index fingers, or punch their spine with her knuckles. She also had a habit of slapping men across the back of the head and screaming, "Hello my darling, what's up?" It was obviously some strange form of flirting that you are supposed to evolve out of when you turn eleven. It was extremely annoying and in my fragile state even worse. I had to watch my back at all times.

There was also a middle-aged, lank-haired French surfer called Kofi. He adopted the name himself and refused to answer by any other. He insisted that he was from Ghana and spoke in a pseudo Ghanaian accent and had mastered local mannerisms, when he was sober enough to do so. When drunk he forgot his strong Ghanaian DNA and he became more French than Napoleon eating garlic snails. He had taken a shine to me (not in the Biblical sense) and hung around like an annoying mosquito. He even looked like one – skinny, brown, with the thinnest, longest nose ever conceived. He religiously covered his Concord-inspired nose with sun block factor 1000, which was fluorescent white and gave the impression he was wearing a sail on his face. Kofi droned on about all aspects of surfing; the right weather conditions, the best shape waves, the top equipment, the most beneficial surfing exercises, diets etc, etc. It transpired that during the year he had been festering at Alaska Beach, he had never been within twenty metres of the sea, let alone surfed on its flat-as-glass surface. He was a friendly enough chap but could not respect personal space. It was obvious that I was suffering and just wanted peace and quiet, but he just buzzed around my head blithering on like an idiot. The only time he stopped talking was when he broke into a hacking cough that doubled him over, blowing sand off the beach and nearly knocking palm trees down. 'Hacking' was too gentle a word to describe his cough. He hopped and jolted around between fits. I was convinced that he was going to cough so violently that he would turn inside out. Thankfully, like many, many ex-patriots he had a serious love affair with alcohol. By about three in the afternoon he would generally be laying comatose on the beach surrounded by empty bottles of Star lager. Silence! Bliss! Split personality Kofi was the last thing I needed to relieve my splitting malaria headache.

In my delirium the only other people I vaguely remember were a couple of Germans travelling in a DAF truck. Irene was also suffering from malaria, writhing around in terrible pain. Her boyfriend Stefan just ignored her and sat glued to his lap top looking very much like a sunburned Boris Becker. He scowled at her every now and then and showed zero sympathy. When I hobbled over to see how she was coping, Irene whispered, "I am fine, thank you very much. But I cannot talk to you, Stefan will be angry."

I tried to get more out of her but it was blatantly obvious that she was in a panic and didn't want me there. I returned to my own woes. Stefan did speak to me at some point. Unless I was hallucinating he seemed to quiz me on the availability of S+M partners in West African clubs, whilst his girlfriend lay there dying. I think that's what we discussed.

After another three days of laying in the shade of a coconut tree, having surreal conversations with the world's marginalised, I finally felt strong enough to slowly pack up the bike and head along the Ghanaian shoreline road. Although I felt as weak as a kitten it was nice to be making progress again and the good sealed road was kind on my battered joints.

In two laboriously slow days I made the 650 kilometres to the border with Ivory Coast. Customs was a nightmare with serious jostling, red tape and harassment. It didn't help that I felt about 25% as strong as I normally did. But after an hour of hassle I was finally in the Ivory Coast. But not for long! The border guard, Morris, who finally guided me through the lengthy rigmarole seemed a decent, if strange looking fellow.

He didn't have the classic West African bone structure – strong with chiselled cheek bones. He had a very flat, shockingly wide face, like a plate with features. We chatted amicably about my trip and what road conditions I could expect ahead. As we finally stepped on to Ivorian soil Morris said in a soft voice, "Monsieur Spencer, tell me why you are doing this, and alone!"

I then made one of the bigger mistakes of my trip. For some reason, I suspect because my guard had dropped, I blurted out, "I am hoping to write a book on my journey." It was as if a switch had been turned on in his brain and he changed from the chatty, soft-spoken Morris into a psychopathic border guard. "So you are a journalist!" he screamed.

Instantly recognising my mistake, I replied urgently, "No, not at all. I am a teacher and just want to write about my experiences."

He ignored me and continued, "You are a journalist and you want to come in our country and spy on our people."

Oh no, now I had been upgraded to a spy. He shouted across to the other border guards and they rushed over, chattering animatedly in French. It was rapid fire colloquial French but the gist was; "You are a spy and now you will die." No, it wasn't that extreme but I knew I was in poo canyon without a paddle. Morris continued proceedings. "Where is your journalist permit? Who do you work for? Why you tell us you are professeur? Why you no speak true?"

I tried interrupting him, "I am a teacher, I don't work for any... " but he continued, "You want to speak bad of our people, speak bad of the black man and make us to be stupid."

Oh no, now I am a racist spy. The tension was calmed slightly by the arrival of a coal-black customs officer who was evidently more senior than Morris. I was physically manhandled back into the sweaty, tin customs hut. After at least an hour of animated discussion it was decided that I would be fined $80 and returned immediately to the Ghanaians. I was over the moon with relief and was out of there like a shot. No torture or imprisonment for me tonight! Little did I care that it was a good five hundred kilometres round trip back to Accra. From there I could head directly north into Burkina Faso and thereby circumvent Ivory Coast.

Unfortunately, during my enthusiasm for escape I ran into the only speed gun camera in Africa and was fined £150 by Takoradi Court. This was only because I refused to pay a second bribe in one day. Enough is enough. I made it to Accra and 'booked' into a brothel. Without going into detail let me just list the bonuses and drawbacks of staying in a brothel.

Bonuses: Very cheap.

Drawbacks:

1. Communal toilets are generally brimming.

2. There is a constant flow of prostitutes who all have the same modus operandi; they approach you in short leopard print skirts and absurdly badly-applied make up and fluorescent lipstick. At night, it's like being accosted by a variety of neon lips floating towards you through the air at differing heights. When the lips arrive, you are bound to be prodded, your hair stroked, and your biceps felt, as you hear, "Oh you are so strong, buy me a drink." They generally burst into song at this point; usually Mariah Carey or Celine Deon, whilst wiggling their bums and boobs in your face. Then in slurred words, the chat up line: "Buy me a drink, I love you." It is all very romantic and touching but I managed to kill the vibe by stating in a deadpan voice, "You buy me a drink." If this doesn't work, you have to fight for freedom. Some of those ladies are large.

3. Noise; banging doors, banging windows, banging people, buckets being filled and emptied, food being fried and eaten, washing being done, arguments being had, dogs barking and scratching, feet shuffling down corridors, cars hooting, doors opening and slamming shut, doors locking, flip flops flapping, music blaring, people bartering, drinks clanging. Everything but blissful silence. Right, I have pointed out the pros and cons. The choice is yours.

Evidently I slept like a baby and the next morning staggered to the bike bleary-eyed but excited to hit the road to Ouagadougou, the capital of Burkina Faso (a country that many people don't even realise is a country). Ouagadougou: do you get anything more exotic-sounding. Ougadougou was a complete let-down. It was a dusty uninspired city with two jewels, a beautiful Mosque and a fantastic reggae singer who I met on the side of the road. On my only night there I noticed a curious competition going on. The Mosque would start up its chanting followed by the Catholic Preachers/Evangelists. It would get louder and louder until there was just a cacophony of sound penetrating all the streets. Everyone just carried on as if there was no Battle of the Bands going on. I wandered the streets and ordered some disgusting fish and rice. The fish was burnt to a crisp and the rice was soggy and gooey. Maybe it was supposed to be risotto. It was crap.

As I ate I spotted a bit of African graffiti. It said: 'Direction in Life – Are you looking for it? Did you ever find it? Don't bother – We are all going to die!' – Manfred the Mouse – The Man with the Mouth'.

A little bit negative, I must say. And why was Manfred scrawling in English in a French-speaking country? I never found out.

My only other highlight was buying a T-shirt on the side of the road which said, 'Have you been to Ougadougou too?' The T-shirt was great but the man who sold it to me was greater. His name was Rocky Emmanuel Pata Pata but it could have been a made-up name, or his stage name. His music was beautiful. I will never forget it. I went to his house which was a mud and corrugated shack. In the one room he had a bed, a drum and a guitar. We sat down and he played me the most beautiful reggae song that he had written himself. I asked him if I could film it and the transformation was incredible. Rocky Emmanuel put his heart and soul into the song. It was hauntingly beautiful and was one of the three minute snippets of my life that I will never forget. I left with my heart soaring from the music, but decidedly underwhelmed by the country in general.

Senegal was as shocking as Burkina Faso was an anti-climax. The Savannah of Guinea quickly collapsed into a drought-stricken landscape. It was dusty, dry and empty of vegetation except for the gargantuum baobab trees that dotted the forlorn landscape. It was more as I had imagined Ethiopia to look. I don't know why I was surprised how barren it was; after all, Senegal is a stone's throw from the Sahara Desert. I just didn't expect the scale. There were dead animals everywhere, littering the hillsides and the verges of the road. Dead cows, donkeys, horses, sheep and goats had literally stopped in their tracks and given up. I drove past a horse that was lying prone but still seemed to be breathing. I doubled back. It was immediately evident that I had been wrong. Its face had collapsed and was just parched skin on bleached bones. The breathing movements that I thought I had detected were in fact hundreds and thousands of maggots writhing around in the remains of the stomach. I was quite relieved actually. What would I have done if it had been alive? Given it mouth to mouth, or a can of sardines? I didn't even have a gun to put it out of its misery. I just said, "Why the long face, I'm the one who has to get out of here." No I didn't. It was actually quite horrific. The remaining living herds were painfully thin and scrabbled around in the dust for wisps of green. It was a futile attempt and eventually their nutritional intake would drop below the energy expended in searching for it. They were doomed.

The small villages that I drove through looked equally arid but the people were in slightly better shape than their animals. I continued on towards the capital, Dakar, feeling pretty down. It was a very bleak landscape. Dakar was another iconic landmark for me simply because it was the finishing line for the famous Paris Dakar Motorcycle Rally for many years. I had followed it for most of my life until it was moved to South America (due to security problems along the African route). Somehow the Rally seemed irrelevant once I was amongst this death and desolation. God also had a comedown set for me. The last hundred kilometres into Dakar were plagued by problems. I had four flat tyres, the chain broke and the bike just gave up completely on four or five occasions. I managed to muddle through but didn't miss the irony of limping into an iconic Rally destination at a snail's pace. The outskirts of Dakar are sprawling and I felt like I would never get to the centre. It was one of those mirages; the closer you get the further it gets. Once I did get into the centre I wished I hadn't. I was an absolute beacon to every single conman, hawker and hustler in the city. I was accosted constantly. I do not blame them one tiny bit, but that doesn't mean I have to pretend to enjoy it. It was hell. In fact I wasn't accosted, I was assaulted, verbally and physically. I stayed only one night but can produce a long list of my social interactions.

The first were the three guys who attached onto me like limpets. They insisted that they had the best hotel deal in town and when I said I could sort myself out they literally pushed and carried me to various dodgy establishments. I had to turn psychotic to get rid of them.

Second were the crack cocaine and hashish dealers. I had to act similarly with them.

Third were the hawkers who would put T-shirts on you while you were walking. If you weren't careful you could find yourself in a completely new set of clothes by the time you got to the end of the road. An accomplice would run in front with a mirror, saying, "It looks good no, it look good, you buy, very cheap, I like you." If you started running they would just run too, keeping up their salesman spiel. I acted similarly with them too.

Fourth were the pure con-men. A middle-aged man in a suit came up to me and was my best friend. "Remember me, my friend. Good to see you again. Is everything OK? Can I help you?" I am good with faces and knew for sure I had never clapped eyes on this fellow. "Sorry, you have the wrong person. I have never met you."

"No, no, it is me. I see you at airport." Now I knew for sure. I had never been near the airport but it was a gamble that probably paid off for him nine times out of ten.

"I came here on a motorbike, please leave me alone." This had absolutely no effect and it took me a good ten minutes to lose this particular character.

Then there are the ones who walk around with empty bottles of medicine and say they are sick and need help. They might cough dramatically to show you how sick they are. They might show you a festering boil. This is a much more difficult moral dilemma as some of them have obvious serious problems, like no legs. They are not con men just desperate and destitute.

Fifth, but not least, are the out-and-out thieves. They don't bother with conning, they just get to it. A rucksack is the biggest tourist beacon on earth (apart from the person connected to the rucksack of course), so it is important to keep it on your front, in full view. You will still get pickpocketed somehow. Add to this mix paying for parking, paying for looking and paying for breathing and Dakar is a nightmare. They are poor, I am not. I understand. But I was so glad to get out of there and head into the outskirts and on to Mauritania.

Chapter Twelve
Red, Yellow and White Sandstorm

'Ears that do not listen to advice accompany the head when it is chopped off.' African proverb

'The continent is too large to describe. It is a veritable ocean, a separate planet, a varied, immensely rich cosmos. Only with the greatest simplification, for the sake of convenience, can we say 'Africa'. In reality, except as a geographical appellation, Africa does not exist.' Ryszard Kapuscinzki

Right, here we go: Mauritania. A country with a reputation in the same league as, say, Nigeria or Angola. But I knew from experience that you can't judge a country by its reputation. Nigeria and Angola were two of the highlights of my trip. Nevertheless, some of the undeniable statistics about Mauritania were too sobering to ignore. So here we go.

Slavery still exists in Mauritania. Yes, slavery still exists in Mauritania. Though legally abolished in 1981 it did not become a crime to own slaves until 2007. Discrimination against black populations is open, mainly against Fula and Soninke, who are seen as contesting the political, economic and social dominance of the lighter-skinned Arab Moors. It has been estimated that 10% of the population are still slaves and that 20% of the population live on less than $1.25 per day. To add to this cheery scene, female genital mutilation, child labour and human trafficking are common. Furthermore, extremist activity and violence has increased radically since 2007 when two French picnickers were killed and numerous tourists kidnapped. The famous Paris Dakar motorbike race was cancelled in response to the deaths of the two French nationals. The activity of Al Qaeda of the Islamic Maghred has only increased exponentially since and foreign office websites strongly recommend avoiding travel in all of Mauritania. Still, as I say, if you listened to all the negative worldwide news, you would never travel anywhere. Nevertheless; all of this in a country that is 80% desert and where it's very difficult to survive. Bloody hell!

The landscape of a country rarely mirrors the turmoil of the people who live in it and my introduction to Mauritania was no exception. If one had to describe the country in one word, it would be 'sand', but this would be a serious insult to Mauritania. The desert was staggeringly beautiful and majestically serene.

Entering Diamma (Keur Massene), the southern border with Senegal, I was confronted with picture postcard sand dunes of a vivid red, swirling around me in huge ice cream cone shapes. The fine red sand particles, whipped up by the wind, floated diagonally across the road creating an optical illusion of the snaking road actually moving back and forth across the desert. Fifty kilometres in, the sand changed to a more traditional tropical island yellow (picture a Seychelles or St Lucia beach). The large sand dunes gave way to expansive fields of yellow/ white sand cones about five foot high that stretched out on my left all the way to the coastal cliffs.

Gradually, as I travelled further north the sand became whiter and whiter until it looked exactly like snow. My vision began to play tricks with me but I loved every challenging minute of it. Over a distance of 300 kilometres I saw five camels and exactly zero humans. This just added to the intensity of the nothingness, and the atmosphere of aloneness in this mega space was electrifying. I was revelling in the constantly changing sandscape until I was forced back to reality by a swirling wind that was picking up from the east. My bike began to jolt heavily westwards and it became more and more difficult to control. The sand began to burn my cheeks and fill my boots and within fifteen minutes it became impossible to ride. I pulled over, weaving as I pulled up.

I hunkered down beside the bike to protect myself against what was now evidently a massive sandstorm, but to no avail. The bike threatened to fall on me and sand was attacking my whole body. I felt like a sandblasted wall. I had little option but to unpack my tent from the rucksack and use it as a sleeping bag. This proved extremely difficult as the tent ballooned into a massive sail and threatened to carry me off with it across the vast desert expanse – never to be seen again. I finally tamed the flapping tent and tied myself into it. Time to ride out the storm, as they say. This proved to be a two-hour ordeal and when I finally mounted the bike I was red raw from the sand, my eyes, cheeks and ears stinging from the blasting. I physically rode out of the storm, and the feeling of relief as the wind dropped and the bike stopped bucking this way and that filled me with elation. Come on, the Sahara!

After forty minutes of tough riding I paused to take in fluids. Whether I was mentally groggy from the conditions or just an idiot, I put the stand down and jumped off the bike. The foot stand promptly sunk in the deep sand and the bike toppled over. The handlebars landed with a thud, directly on the *only* rock in this part of the Mauritanian desert and the clutch lever snapped in half. Fantastic luck. I looked up to the vast blue sky and screamed at the top of my voice, "Oh dear!" (or something similar). No need to panic: only 150 kilometres to Nouakchott in first gear. Using my superb mechanical skills I strapped the clutch housing to the handlebars with two bungee cords. I then cut a small piece of siphoning hose and pushed it on to the end of the snapped clutch lever. Hey presto, brief hiccup, and I was off, changing gear with ease and singing 'Misty Morning' by Bob Marley at full volume. Only the odd camel to annoy with my radically out-of-tune voice. (Strangled cat and all that.)

Within an hour and a half I started seeing signs of civilisation; the odd road sign half hidden under sand, broken sections of camel enclosures being reclaimed by the desert, plastic bags and eventually an Arab Moor in a flowing blue

Boubou (robe) and black cheche (a length of fabric wrapped around his entire head, revealing only his coal black eyes). He was riding a camel at a blistering pace next to the road and we gave each other an enthusiastic wave as I rode past. Within ten minutes I was cruising through the outskirts of the sand-swept city and into the centre. Nouakchott was a bloody weird place. The whole city was built on a completely flat plain, and I mean flat. The outskirts were basically shanty-town shacks, huddled close together. Most were losing the battle to fight off the salmon-coloured sand dunes that advanced from the east and invaded their doorways. Nouakchott derives from the Berber, Nawaksut, which means 'flat as hell'. No it doesn't, it means 'place of winds'. I should say!

Looking at the sprawling mass of urban expanse around me it was difficult to believe that the population of this city was 200 in 1958. The area was chosen as the capital in 2000 due to its central location and now boasts a population of two million. The exact population is difficult to know because there is a large sector of nomadic people who sweep in, set up and then move on.

The dilapidated dwellings, salt and cement works, and streets empty of people gave way to a more vibrant, lively feel as I entered the centre. Everything was on offer and the central market was abuzz with traders selling camel wool rugs, carpets, embroidery, earrings, bracelets and camel saddles. Tea and food stalls were on every corner. Women in black and multi-coloured robes sold mangos and bananas, delicately balanced in fruit towers, on the top of upturned cardboard boxes. Blue and white cooler boxes lined the streets, full of lukewarm water to fend off the dehydrating effects of the swirling desert winds and vicious temperatures. Scattered amongst the market sellers and on the street corners were deformed, homeless people, begging for money. They congregated near the three ATM machines in the central plaza and shouted at me in Arabic as I drove past.

Moors on camels with vibrant red saddles watched me

unblinkingly as I turned in to the main street. The camels followed my progress by turning their heads lackadaisically, whilst chewing on something or other much more enthusiastically.

A spectacular cream-coloured Mosque, which I later found out was donated by Saudi Arabia, stood majestically against the blue horizon and on my left a wind-battered edifice resembling a hotel cast me in its shadow. I pulled up outside the entrance. A flight of five steps led up to a sliding glass door that was cracked from top to bottom. A man in a traditional Boubou robe and sheepskin sandals was squatting on the top step. As soon as I stopped, he sprang to his feet and ran into the building. Within seconds, four men rushed out and literally went into kidnap mode. One of them, clutching a strap of some kind, threaded it through the back wheel of my bike and passed it to another on the other side. They lifted the back wheel while the third took the handlebars and guided the bike up the steps. Within seconds they had disappeared into the foyer. It was all done in a spectacularly organised fashion. The fourth man grabbed me forcefully by the arm and pulled me up the stairs, beckoning wildly with his free hand for me to follow.

"OK guys, calm down. I promise I will stay in your illustrious hotel tonight and forgo the luxuries of other competing establishments," I said. I didn't say that, but before I could, he hushed me up and continued pulling me through the large open foyer and into a smaller room behind the reception desk. In his rush he pulled over the reception desk which consisted of two chairs with a piece of plywood balanced precariously on top of them. He slammed the door behind him with such force that it just bounced open again. He turned to me and said, "American is not safe here".

"I realise that now, I have just been kidnapped." I didn't say that either because he continued in a forceful staccato tone: "No American, it is not good. Many men, Al Qaeda, are coming in hotel, in city, to ask where tourists, when they go, where they go. You must not leave here, this place. It is bad, it is not good."

Now, I am not denying that I was pretty worried but I also wondered whether this was a typical, well-rehearsed ploy to get customers, literally, into the hotel. But then I thought, that's ridiculous, there are no tourists. When I looked into his concerned face and beseeching eyes I realised that either he was an Oscar-deserving actor or he was telling the truth. I decided he was telling the truth and after everything had calmed down, Abut explained to me what was going on, with the other three gesticulating and murmuring in agreement in the background. Trusting him was one of the best decisions of my trip.

Abut turned out to be the only one in the group who spoke English, thanks to a five-year stint in London as a youngster. He enthusiastically and patiently translated everything he asked me and my replies. It was evident that he was the 'main man' in the group and they hung on his every word, clapping and nodding. Abut was a short man with a very slight frame. He looked rather odd though as his large paunch stood out incongruously from his otherwise stick insect frame. He looked like he had swallowed a basketball.

He beckoned us all through to another room, the floor adorned with a large, ruby red, woven rug. Green tea with sugar and mint leaves was served and what a pleasure it was. Abut poured the tea from a great height into impossibly small mugs without spilling a drop. He swung his arm towards and away from the cup in a manic arc, creating foam in the cup – a process called ragwa. We were each served three different cups of tea which started out bitter but by the third was smooth and sweet.

During our 'tea party' Abut explained that Al Qaeda activity had increased in the area and many hotel owners had warned him that suspicious groups of men had been questioning them about the whereabouts and plans of foreigners presumably with the intention of setting up kidnappings. He said that the effect was being felt from the radical extremists in Algeria and Mali who were spreading their activities further south. Then, two weeks ago Abut had three men question him about his customers. "So I know it is the truth," he said quietly. "Anyway, now is time for to rest and later we eat."

"But how much are the rooms?" I queried. "It's 40 US," he replied bluntly. I knew that Mauritania was expensive so thought that was extremely reasonable and accepted.

The room turned out to be simple but clean and I flopped on the bed. I must have fallen asleep and was quickly dreaming of being kidnapped and dragged across the desert by 'armed to the teeth' Al Qaeda operatives, when a knock on the door woke me from my peaceful slumber.

It was moustachioed Abut and not a group of terrorists, which pleased me no end. "You come and eat now," he said, once again grabbing my arm and pulling me into the corridor. This seemed to be his modus operandi in persuading motorcycle adventurers to follow his orders. I yanked the door to, as I was pulled sharpishly away from it, and stumbled down the stairs to the foyer, still connected to Abut's arm. He sat me down in a cavernous dining room which looked as though it could accommodate two thousand seated customers, at the least. There were rows and rows of well-laid tables as far as the eye could see. A bit like the desert. OK, I exaggerate, but it was large. It looked like the O2 Arena. It wasn't difficult to find a table as on this particular morning as I was the only customer. Judging from the long silent corridors, it also seemed as if I was the only resident of the hotel, full stop. It was a bit like 'The Shining', set in Mauritania, except Abut was a lot more friendly and stable than Jack Nicholson, but he did have the eyebrows.

Abut sat down opposite me, and almost immediately, another stick-thin basketball swallower (must be Abut's brother) approached with a steaming hot plate of food. Abut gestured me to eat and sat with raised eyebrows, waiting for my reaction. It was delicious and I said so. Abut looked delighted and clapped his hands. He explained that it was camel meat cooked in peanut sauce. Apparently the peanuts are ground down into oil and then combined with tomato paste and jachtini (ground okra), fried with strips of camel meat and served on a bed of rice. "My brother is too much the best Cooker in City."

I had to agree, although his reputation didn't seem to have spread far and wide, judging from the lack of queues through the door. More green tea followed as I explained to Abut that I needed to get some cash from somewhere to pay him and to refuel. He stroked his jet black moustache thoughtfully and said, "It is better you go to auto bank when is dark, maybe three in morning. Petrol open at four and then you go. I walk with you, it is much not far." So that was the plan, after a few more hours' sleep.

When he woke me up and we headed out into the street, all furtively (well, he was), under the 'cover of darkness', I had to have a little giggle. Abut was acting exceedingly suspicious, whispering to me, looking around constantly whilst hugging the walls and doorways as we went. Now anyone who has been in the open desert in the middle of the night will know that it is not far from daylight. However, Abut seemed convinced that we were incognito and melting into the darkness effortlessly, so I kept quiet and tried to keep a straight face.

I knew I was potentially in a very dangerous situation but watching Abut ahead of me I felt like I was in some Z-rate movie. We made it safely to the cash machine but it refused to eject any money. We tried another one on the opposite side of the square but with the same result. Now I was stuffed. I was stuck in Mauritania, with Al Qaeda on my tail (maybe), owed Abut for the hotel (definitely), and had no way of buying petrol to get the hell out of Dodge (for sure).

I smothered the rising panic in my throat and said to him, "Let's go back to the hotel and I will call my bank. I am sure it is not a problem."

He agreed (shiftily looking around), and we hurried back, once again under the cover of daylight. I called NatWest Bank, located in a village in rural England and probably issued one of the most surreal requests the operator had ever heard.

"Hello, yes, my name is Spencer Conway and I have a bit of an emergency. I am in Mauritania in the Sahara desert and I am hiding from Al Qaeda. Unfortunately, I cannot buy petrol to escape as my NatWest cash card is not working." After a stunned silence, the lady on the other end asked me to repeat what I had just said. After a while and many questions she seemed to conclude that I wasn't a hoaxer, or completely off my trolley, and sprang into action. After taking all my details, there was a lengthy spell of elevator music, as she put me on hold. I eventually ascertained that my card had been cancelled due to suspicious transactions spanning many African countries.

I explained to her that I was circumnavigating Africa and that it was indeed me making those transactions. As I was in imminent danger of kidnap could NatWest possibly reinstate my card? She said she would do her best to have it functioning within a couple of hours. Thank God for the 24-hour hotline and mobile phones. Little did I know that this would be the very last phone signal I would ever get in West Africa. It was fortuitous, however, as this last call did the trick and after paying and thanking the lovely Abut I headed north into the desert of Western Sahara.

The slight fear I had felt, dissipated quickly, as the beauty of the Sahara once again flooded my senses. I rode 477 kilometres in seven hours and eighteen minutes without spotting a single person and definitely no terrorists. It was tiring riding as I was continually buffeted by winds that constantly changed direction. On my left, the rocky Hamada stone plateau dropped away to steep cliffs battered by sandy winds and the blue ocean waves. On my right was the vast empty desert stretching endlessly into the horizon. A sea of water and a sea of sand kept me company for over seven hours, not a second of it boring. Most people assume that a desert, by definition, has to be hot and sandy. In fact a desert is defined as an area that struggles to sustain life.

The Arctic and Antarctic are the two largest deserts but the Sahara, at 9,400,000 square kilometres is a respectable third. I travelled through a vast, arid plain, broken by occasional ridges and cliff-like outcroppings. On occasion, this gave way to the more visually stunning ergs; large areas covered with sand dunes which swept across the arrow-straight sealed road, threatening to erase it from the landscape. These were superb fun to ride through as long as you kept your nerve and your throttle tightly back. The solitude and otherworldly landscape was a tonic to my soul.

It was not until I reached the Mauritania-Morocco border that I once again came into contact with people. This was my thirtieth border crossing to date, and one of the strangest indeed. The customs office consisted of a large cream and green tent pegged into the desert sand, swaying and swirling in the harsh winds, fighting to maintain its foothold in this shifting environment. Everything manmade in the desert – the clothes, the buildings – the tents, are all designed to fight off the never-ending sand assault. I pulled back the flap and there in the relative tranquillity of its interior lay three men sprawled out on carpets in a corner of the tent. Two were under covers and the third was pouring tea from his prone position swathed in a black robe and headdress.

He beckoned me over and without getting up, gestured with his hand, "Passport".

I unzipped my rucksack and handed it down to him. He paged through it, pausing to look at my photograph. He reached out to his left to retrieve a small ink well and stamp. Unfortunately, it was slightly out of reach and he struggled with his fingertips to reach it. I momentarily considered picking it up for him but before I could he rolled over on the carpet until he was within reaching distance.

After stamping my passport he asked, "Money change?"

I pulled out $20 and held it out to him. He turned and kicked the second man who was completely hidden from view under his blanket. He groaned, stuck his head and arm out, took the money and disappeared under his blanket. After a few moments of mumbling and rummaging he popped out again with a few tatty notes. I had no idea how much money he had given me and what currency it was but was too tired to argue.

The passport stamper gestured that I could go and I ventured into the howling winds once again. I headed away from the border but after a hundred metres or so I realised that I had not an inkling of which direction to go in. There was no discernible road whatsoever, just indistinguishable desert. I returned to the customs tent where a lone truck driver was just mounting his vehicle. I went up to him and said, "Sorry, which way?" pointing quizzically from where I had just come.

He seemed to understand and motioned for me to follow him. I jumped on the bike and fell in behind the slow-moving truck, the dust and sand immediately coating my goggles and the inside of my mouth. I wiped my goggles every thirty seconds to try and maintain my visibility but it was a losing battle. I had no choice but to fall back and follow his dust cloud from a distance. To this day I have no idea how he found his way to the Moroccan side. All the landscape looked identical to me but he took seemingly random right turns near a small rock here, random left turns over a dune there, and sweeping unnecessary arcs on flat plateau sections. After twenty minutes I began to suspect he was having me on and was going to drive around the desert forever, until I died. Just as I was losing patience with this practical desert joker, not to mention hope, I saw a brick building in the distance. Simultaneously the truck driver gave a long burst on his horn.

Thank God, the Moroccan border.

Chapter Thirteen
The Norwegian and the Bee-Sting Victim

'The further one goes the less one knows.' Lao Tzu

How strange people are. The Moroccan customs officer wasted no time in filling me in on the disgusting habits of the people of Mauritania; how backward, useless, lazy, untrustworthy, ungodly they were – and they couldn't spell! He continued: "You have see the road, the food, the life. Yes, the Life! Now Morocco, today, you see good life, nice people, one hundred percent good food. All is good, not like before, in Maroc. One hundred percent good time for. You see, you choose, good do this, yes?"

I definitely got his gist and he was extremely friendly but the more he spoke the more random his combination of English words became. Eventually he was saying things like, "Dyson, good Manchester, big brother, like London, fish and chips, Rambo, no, yes, you accept, thank you, yes, Ronaldo, happy, happy."

I must confess that he was right. Everything was more organised in Morocco. For a start, they had recognisable roads, customs officers that were not lying down, hidden under blankets and the banks actually had money, without terrorists loitering outside, but somehow I felt sad. The trappings of organisation were filtering in. I wasn't ready for it. I had become enmeshed and ingrained in the chaos of Africa and, no matter how strange it sounds after nine and a half months, I wasn't ready for an organised world. I found it predictable, almost boring. The roads were good, the road signs prominent, and the shops organised and clean. It was too much. But what hit me the most was the fact that this country was fully jacked up for tourists. After DRC, Congo, Angola, Gabon, etc. it was as if I was heading out of the continent I loved and closer to the continent I respected, but did not love, Europe. I had almost come full circle. From the safe, to the raw, to the safe. I hated safe. My heart sank. I felt as though my journey was wrapping up to an anti-climax. I rode in a blur, not taking in the landscape until I drove into Rabat on the west coast. I felt like I was wrapping the trip up and my problems were over. I was wrong.

In the central market square I spotted a youth hostel and despite being 30 years out of my youth I approached it with the hope of a cheap night. Cheap it was indeed, but I lay all night listening to annoying hippies singing the praises of marijuana whilst putting the world's problems to rights. I had heard it all before, probably said it all before myself, when I was seventeen. But from my now 'mature' perspective it was inane and childish and I couldn't wait for morning to come.

The spectacular morning sun did rise over hippieville but not before I met Per the Norwegian at the darkened breakfast table. I am sometimes a spectacularly bad judge of character and I took to Per immediately. He was tall, blonde, with striking sea-blue eyes and a wicked laugh. His enthusiasm for life and his sense of humour were contagious and we spent the next three days meeting up at various agreed points on our way to Spain. I suggested that he come over on the ferry to Tarifa in Spain and spend a day kite surfing with me in one of the windiest coastal resorts in the world. Per was super keen but had to wait in Tangiers for a bank transfer from his mother in Norway. We went to a roadside café to indulge in Moroccan meatballs and couscous. During the meal Per phoned his mother to check the progress on his bank transfer. His mother assured him that it had all gone through and that the money would be with him within two days. Hearing this news I offered to lend him 150

Euros and he could pay me when we got to a bank in Spain. Per was extremely grateful and we headed off on the ferry to Tarifa. We found a campsite less than one hundred metres from the beach and after setting up headed into town for some lunch. Per popped off to the cash machine just around the corner from the café and I never saw him again.

I had been 51,000 kilometres around Africa and then I got robbed by a dodgy Norwegian in Spain. I was gutted and felt naïve and embarrassed. I sat there for twenty minutes, not really wanting to believe it, and then made a half-hearted swoop around the centre of the town. But I knew he was gone. There was no way his mother had been on the end of that phone. You made a fool of me, Per, and if you are reading this I hope you suffer one day for what I suspect is not a one-off, but an immoral lifestyle choice; the opportunist conman who preys on decent adventure motorcyclists. Bastard Norse!

Having my streetwise ego battered as well as my wallet I sank into a mood of extreme glumness. I am a serious expert at glumness and can wallow in it for days. Luckily for others I decided to do this trip solo. I could be a nightmare on many occasions and hyper-enthusiastic and cheery on others. Maybe I have got ADHD. My mood did not improve as I headed up the Spanish coast. The Costa del Sol in all its wonder flew past me. The truly traditional Spanish lifestyle was evident everywhere I looked, pubs called The Red Lion and The George, fish and chip shops called Gary's Fish Bar and The Codfather.

I stopped to camp in northern Costa and the theme continued when I headed into the town centre. The high street consisted of tacky curio shops selling rude T-shirts (which shrank to the size of a handkerchief after the first wash), temporary-tattoo parlours, hair braid and nail painting salons, and general holiday paraphernalia; blow-up dinghies, blow-up dinosaurs, blow-up dolls, etc. Peppered between these garish shops were the ubiquitous bars offering drink deals that had a great chance of killing you. 'Drink one Supercharger in one minute and get the next 300 drinks for free,' or 'Drink this bowl of Spirits as big as your head and win a free ticket to Slime World.' Or 'Sample our nine strongest cocktails without ejecting them and win a 'Top Plasterer' cap'. The promotions were everywhere and by mid-evening were obviously having their effect. Nine-year-olds were lying in the gutter paralytic, crying their eyes out whilst being consoled by sun-burned pink, eight-year-old boys with lopsided caps. The more mature eleven-year-olds were having swearing and vomiting competitions between playing chicken with the traffic. It was all very pleasant and the ideal holiday, not, so I skulked back to my mini tent where I gladly zipped out the scene, but unfortunately not the noise. I slept not at all, what with the death throes of a camper nearby, and the ensuing ambulance and paramedics, fighting their way through a crowd who were keen on swearing them to death also.

I was elated to get away the next morning and hide my ears under my helmet and escape the lunacy that is the Englishman abroad. The open road and the freedom of thought that goes with it led me to ride for two nine and a half hour days with only a short camp break. I ate up the 1,538 kilometres from Tangier to Toulouse without noticing such places as Malaga, Murcia, Alicante, Valencia and Barcelona. I was on a mission to get back and no magnificent city was going to stop me. It was in this vein, in a semi-stupor, that I suddenly realised I was in France and had missed most of what Spain had to offer; Gaudi, bullfighting, Tapas bars, a miniature England in the sun, etc.

Now there will be those of you who are saying, "How can he travel the length of a country without noticing it, I have always wanted to go to Spain, the spoilt brat!" My only answer is that this was the nature of my journey. I had to travel vast distances and I never promised a travelogue of thirty five countries. Some places were so awe-inspiring that you had no choice but to stop and marvel. Others were difficult and arduous to get through and demanded to be noticed. Others were a soft touch and my motorbike distance-riding brain took over; cover the miles, do this trip, nail it! The only thing that was impossible to ignore in Spain were the number of cars that flashed me as I rode past, waving huge blocks of hashish out of the window. They were so enthusiastic to sell their wares, that I was almost knocked clean off the bike on numerous occasions, by large blocks of illegal smokables. But they were barking up the wrong plant with me and I steadfastly ignored their shouted sales pitches, conducted as they drove alongside me. It was a bit like being in The Fast and the Furious.

It was with some relief that my trance-riding subsided when I arrived in Toulouse and after stocking up on baguettes, cheese and red wine I found a wonderfully secluded campsite on the outskirts of the city. It was a superb evening and I had an excellent conversation with myself. I sat by a river bank, there were no arguments or interruptions and I completely agreed with everything I said. Very peaceful – the only way sometimes, I suggest. Other people can be so annoying with their opinions, especially if they are different to mine. I went to sleep under the stars contemplating the fact that I only had 963 kilometres to Calais. From there, it was but a short trip over the Channel to England and my final destination, the metropolis that is the village of Biddenden (population five, or thereabouts) and the starting point of my epic circumnavigation. My job was nearly done, nothing could go wrong on this last section. It would be plain sailing. Ha! Ha!

Never count your *poulets* before they hatch, as they say in France.

At sunrise I headed off towards Limoges and after a good four hours of riding was making steady progress. My stomach was beginning to rumble when I spotted a portable roadside café set up in a dirt clearing on the side of the road. It is generally my rule to avoid roadside cafés in England, or anywhere for that matter. From my experience, there is a reasonable chance of contracting various food bugs and spending the evening violently ejecting one's stomach contents from various orifices. On this occasion I deemed it a risk worth taking. After all, my stomach was now as hard as nails having dealt with the various culinary delights Africa served up over the last nine months. I parked the bike under a large tree and weaved my way through the rusty metal chairs and tables and up to the food counter. The surly, lank-haired, acne-ridden teenager who was serving did little to allay my hygiene fears in any way. Against my better judgement I ordered a hot dog. He poked unenthusiastically at the pinkest frankfurter I had ever seen and rolled it around in some grease and unidentified black lumps. He plonked the flaccid offering into a floppy roll and handed it to me. I asked for a dollop of mustard, he scowled at me, leant down below the counter and passed me a filthy plastic bottle with dried lumps of yellowy-brown mustard encrusted around the lid. I squeezed the bottle and it ejected a stream of water, followed by a pea sized piece of mustard, onto my already soggy roll. I thanked him for this five-star fare and sat down at a nearby table.

An exceedingly obese couple were perched in the open side door of a sky blue Kombi van opposite me. They were earnestly involved in an eating competition. Both had chipmunk-sized cheeks and were chewing at an alarmingly high speed. Both were smeared in a multitude of different sauces and the male driver seemed blissfully unaware that he had a slither of onion dangling from his bulbous nose. I assume he was unaware, otherwise I suspect he would have retrieved it and gobbled it down. As they ate they eyed me in a manner which I can only describe as disdainful. It could only have been due to the inferior size of my sausage. I ignored their looks and took a bite of my hot dog. It was a cold dog. A squirt of grease and cold water hit me on the cheek and the majority of the frankfurter shot out of the roll and landed forlornly in the dust. It wasn't finished yet. The frankfurter then rolled around in the dirt for a few seconds coating itself fully in dirt and tiny stones, winked at me, and then came to rest next to my boot (maybe that bit didn't quite happen). I looked up and both the Weight Watcher avoiders looked at me and then at my sausage. The husband said to me telepathically, with a knowing nod, 'It is your own fault. Firstly, you should have ordered the double extra jumbo-jumbo sausage and secondly, you should be more careful to protect your precious food. The correct technique is to stuff the food in your mouth as quickly as possible, preferably in one piece, and then chew as quickly and aggressively as you can before any escapes.'

I decided to cut my losses. This was not a memorable food stop. I nodded to the obesities as I went past, avoiding a large bin swarming with bees. I mounted the bike and pulled off. Immediately, I felt a burning pain in my foot, careered to a halt, jumped off the bike and ripped off my boot, hopping along as I did. I fell onto the grass, shook my boot, and no, not one, but two stricken, bees fell out. Now this does not seem like much of a story until I tell you that a bee sting kills me within an hour. Within ten minutes I tend to look like Pavarotti, my tongue swells up, I go into anaphylactic shock, my airway becomes restricted and I die. Nothing to worry about then. I had to think quickly. I had an epi-pen (adrenaline) self-injector in the bottom of my rucksack but didn't fancy injecting myself at the side of the road. I strapped my boot to the back of the bike with a bungee cord and rocketed off to find the nearest *pension*. My foot was already on fire and was twice the size it had been ten minutes ago. It felt like the skin was going to split.

Luckily, within twenty minutes I spotted a shabby blue hotel sign on the front of a peeling white building, with rickety rotting blue shutters. Nice in its heyday, maybe eighty years ago. However, bee-sting victims can't be choosers and I parked up, and hopped into the reception. The walls were painted bright red and the semi-circular tongue-in-groove counter was furnished with a yellowed calendar and some dusty plastic flowers. It looked like the entrance to a brothel and probably was. Behind the counter stood a shocked-looking, camp-as-

Liberaci, middle-aged Frenchman. I explained my predicament in my best French, combined with sign language and miming. I acted out the dive bombing bees with all the sound effects, whilst at the same time pointing at my elephantine foot. I mimed plunging an injection into my thigh and swept my finger across my neck to denote death.

Just as he was about to call the police to eject this hopping foreign madman, I said, "Pardon moi Monsieur, je ne parle pas bien Francais. Je cherche un chambre pour la nuit. C'est un probleme ici (pointing to my foot) avec le buzz-buzz."

I slipped back into miming sounds but he seemed to get my gist and answered, "C'est 60 Euros pour un nuit."

I scrabbled around in my bag and handed him the money. "Donne moi la chamber, silver plate," I begged. He showed me to a tiny room and I gratefully closed the door on him and fell onto the bed. I put my grossly swollen foot up on both pillows and nearly passed out from the change in blood flow. I had no option, I had to inject. I rifled around in my bag, pulled out the epi-pen and the HD camera and prepared to film my self-medication. I sat up on the bed and nearly passed out again as the blood rushed back into my constantly expanding foot. My foot was as heavy as a brick and every toe felt like it had a lit cigarette inside it. I removed the casing on the hypodermic needle, said a few words to camera and then filmed my thigh as I plunged the needle into it. 'Plunged' may be a slightly misleading term. A half-hearted little jab is a better description. It did nothing. I psyched myself up and tried again, this time howling in pain as the needle pierced my thigh muscle. I managed to inject a micro gram of the liquid before pulling the needle out. I screamed as a small chunk of skin came out with it and a fountain of blood followed. It was bloody painful.

I grabbed a bit of toilet paper and held it against my throbbing thigh. This is not right. I held up the injection against the silhouette of the window, to inspect it. The end of the needle was bent over itself, forming a vicious little hook; hence the little chunk of thigh and the big chunk of pain. The needle must have been damaged on my travels. I could also see that only about a quarter of the fluid had been injected, but there was no way I was going to go through that again. Disheartened, with a swollen thigh and ultra-swollen foot, I lay down to face my fate. I make it all the way around Africa and then I am nailed by a Norwegian in Spain and stung by two Frenchmen in France. Typical luck. I eventually nodded off into a fitful night's sleep. Luckily, I woke up alive which was a good start to the day, but my foot was grotesquely large and turning a lovely Chelsea Flower Show, winning shade of purple. How could two tiny bees cause such carnage and why were there two of them? Although I am not familiar with their methods of copulation I assume they were having sex when they flew into the hole in my boot and were angry with the coitus interruptus. So not necessarily Frenchmen bees, it could have been a mixed sex attack.

Chapter Fourteen
Not Home, Just Visiting

'The only man I envy is the man who has not yet been to Africa – for he has much to look forward to.' Richard Mullin

'Twenty years from now you will be more disappointed by the things you didn't do than by the ones you did do.' Mark Twain

'I haven't been everywhere but it's on my list.' Susan Sontag

I still had the dubious pleasure of making the final 663 kilometres with a club foot. No point in panicking, better to adapt my clothing to cope with the present situation. It was in this positive frame of mind that I dressed myself in preparation for the final hurdle (not literally, because that would be stupid on a motorbike). I have always been acutely aware of the need for protective clothing. I see no point in years of surgery and skin grafts just for the thrill of riding in shorts and a vest in the hot weather. I pulled on my black, padded Cordura (not-quite Kenyan-bullet-proof, but close) trousers and jacket, my black, hard core helmet and need-a-mortgage-priced black gloves and my hard-as-nails bike boots… well, one bike boot.

I had as much chance of putting a whale in a Mini as I did putting on my left boot. I had no choice. It was going to have to be the fluorescent, neon green flip flop with the pink flower design that the superb Felix bought me in Nigeria. I slowly and painfully pulled a black sock over my absurdly shaped foot, cut a little slit in the sock between my big toe and the next and daintily put on my flip flop. I looked down. What a vision. I was bound to get some looks, but so what. 'Onwards and upwards,' as they say. What does that mean? Was it coined by astronauts or mountaineers?

I thanked the shell-shocked camp receptionist for his close

care and attention (not too close thankfully, as I am not that way inclined – not that there is anything wrong with it obviously), and headed off towards the city of Tours, Le Mans and then the Channel Tunnel. The bike was throbbing, as was my thigh and foot, and I have to confess, my head. I omitted to mention that before I injected myself I did indulge in a bit of French courage (translation: Courvoisier brandy).

Despite the communal, human-machine throbbing, I made the Channel Tunnel in 10 hours 23 minutes. My foot was now so large the flip flop was beginning to split and my weight had probably doubled. Nevertheless I was proud to have driven near on 700 kilometres changing gear with a bare foot in what was now becoming the only cold section of the trip. My frozen, swollen foot was being welcomed back to English weather already. As I pulled into the train terminal it began bucketing with rain. I was glad to get out of the elements but not before a little girl decided to open her father's car door just as I was heading past. I was knocked off the bike, bounced down the road and landed on my club foot.

I said, "What do you think you are doing?" or similar words, but before my imminent arrest for road rage, the father jumped out, helped me with the bike and apologised profusely. I think he could see that I was a man on the edge and I calmed down. This was getting more and more absurd. I would not be at all surprised if the Tunnel collapsed over our train and once I had dragged myself and my club foot out of the wreckage, found that England had been annihilated by a war I had no idea was going on. With trepidation in my heart and poison in my foot I managed to manoeuvre the bike into the train.

The fluorescent tube strip lighting running the length of the train only accentuated the garish colour of my flip flop and I could see the owner of the car parked in front of me checking out the stickers on my bike and my weird foot attire. Behind me were the classic German biker couple, heading for a two-week, organised trip, Ja! They had religiously clean BMW 650s, matching outfits, down to matching sunglasses and water bottles. Except hers were pink and his black. I stood there, with my chain hanging off, dripping grease, most of the bike tied up with wire and bungee cords, mud and Saharan sand everywhere, the number plate flapping off, a bullet hole in my swing arm, bald tyres, clutch hanging off – and that was only the half of it! But it was not only the bike that had changed. My physical appearance had changed completely. I had lost forty five pounds since I had left these shores and looked ten years younger (although I say it myself). My skin was chestnut brown and I was fitter than I had been for twenty years. But that was just my exterior shell, what people saw. Internally, I felt different, I felt proud, and I felt privileged. But I also felt unexpectedly depressed.

Within the next forty eight hours my incredible journey would be over. A wave of melancholy washed over me. I tried to brush aside the feelings of deflation as the train arrived in Folkestone on the south coast of England. I had always felt alien in England and when I drove out into the grey, dreary streets the feeling of not belonging was magnified tenfold. England was always going to feel small, enclosed, organised and claustrophobic after what I had been through, but it was the intensity of my feelings that surprised me. I felt like crying, felt like my heart was being crushed. Leaving Africa felt like bereavement. Part of me felt guilty for these feelings; after all, I was soon to be reunited with my girlfriend Cathy, my daughters Jesamine and Feaya, and my parents. That reunion would have to be slightly delayed as I had already been forewarned that the village, the BBC and newspapers were only expecting me in two days' time. I also knew that a huge street party had been arranged. I had no choice but to hole up for a couple of days.

A few hundred metres from the train station was a traditional pub with a B&B sign outside. I felt lethargic and demotivated and couldn't be bothered to look for anywhere else to stay. This place would be as good as any. I wandered into the pub and was confronted by a row of locals all supping on pints, but I couldn't motivate myself to indulge in small talk. I ordered a pint of Stella Artois and went and sat in a darkened corner, absentmindedly dragging the beer coaster back and forth across the table. I felt devastated: the energy and verve for life that had lifted me to the highest heights over the last nine and a half months had drained away instantaneously. I felt like I was back to square one. The sun had set on my adventure.

Geographically, that was true. I had to pull myself together for my family. I took out my mobile, which of course had reception. Everything works in England. How annoying. I called Cathy and made a concerted effort to sound cheery. "Hi, it's me; I'm in The George pub in Folkestone." (I toyed with the idea of saying, "Honey, I'm home," the famous quote from 'The Shining', but it wasn't appropriate as I never called her honey and it wasn't my home.)

She sounded great on the phone. I had always loved her South African accent. "I'm coming down right now, don't go anywhere," she replied. Where was I going to go, to circumnavigate Africa? Cathy was down within an hour, walked into the pub, looked at me as though she wanted to slap me in the face and said, "Don't ever do that again." Then she gave me a massive hug. It was great. The next day we focused on the homecoming which did me a lot of good. I was desperately trying to be positive about leaving the continent I should never have left. I had to put on a show for everyone who supported me. We headed up the motorway and spent the next night in a polytunnel, in a farmer's field, only five miles from Biddenden, the village I had left 278 days earlier.

At ten the following morning, after my very last night camping, I made my very last diary cam, my bottom lip quivering. I had zero elation in my heart about what I had done. It's impossible to explain but I felt as though I had not been around Africa at all. It felt like I had been away for only a few days. At the same time, I knew that the village would be exactly the same but I was totally and utterly different. It would be impossible to explain my experiences to anyone and I felt very lonely. How absurd that I could travel alone for so long and never feel lonely and then when I returned to 'civilisation', I felt more isolated than ever.

I remember very little about the homecoming except that I was met by more than fifty bikers. We tried to create a spectacle for the cameras by all over-revving our motorbikes and waving enthusiastically. I was in pole position and as we rode into the village and under a banner saying, 'Welcome Home Spencer', everyone lining the streets started cheering and waving. Cameramen were jostling for space in front of the bike as I pulled into the car park. I was so glad I was wearing my helmet. It hid my glum expression. Everyone had been so welcoming and helpful but all I could think of was that the sign should have said "Welcome *Back* Spencer". I was not home. I would always be a visitor in the Garden of England. It is a beautiful country, it is just not me. I was already missing the chaos, unpredictability, anarchy, danger, vitality, grandeur, beauty and vastness of the continent that is AFRICA. I had never been one for safety, security and routine and never would be. Africa was flowing in my blood, its soil embedded in my hair and its magnificence seared into my heart. But I have also always been one for reality and the present. This was the present and I was being exceedingly selfish.

I took a deep breath, banished my Africa thoughts and dismounted the bike. I removed my helmet and the crowd all broke into a round of applause. My two girls came running through and I lifted them off the ground, hugging them tightly, cameras flashing around us. My mum and dad rushed over too. They both seemed so small. It's strange that I had that thought because one of the first things my mother said to me was, "You seem to be even taller." John, my bearded, hippie, web designer friend handed me a pint and there were congratulations all round. I muddled through some interviews, saying corny and totally untrue things like, "I am just looking forward to normal things, like making a cup of tea without lighting a fire." It couldn't have been further from the truth. I never want 'normal' and would love to build a fire every night for the rest of my life.

I stumbled through a typical English garden party, organised by my mother, and accepted a speech of thanks from a Save the Children representative. I was not really there. I was in my own head space. Don't get me wrong; I love my family more than anything in the world. It was just all too sudden. It's difficult to be fighting through a sandstorm in Mauritania one minute and eating scones and jam in a quaint English country garden the next. I was emotionally all over the place. Frankly, I was glad to head home and to my bed. Sleep would relieve the thoughts whirling around in my head.

The next day I was totally shell-shocked but realised I had to snap back to the present. I had a family relying on me and despite all I had achieved nothing would come of it until I had finished the book, DVD and programmes. There was no getting away from the fact that I was unemployed. It was a proper

352

reality slap and with a heavy heart and a light wallet I headed down to my local job centre in the grey town of Ashford. I parked my beautiful, wonderful, multi-coloured bike, which had been through so much with me, and plodded up the stairs to the Employment Office. I looked back. My bike looked so incongruous in this environment. I sat in a queue of depressed, bedraggled looking people and watched the rain drops sliding slowly down the dirty glass windows. Eventually I was called to a desk where an unenthusiastic, down-trodden, middle-aged woman asked, "How can I help you?"

"I am beyond help," I said. No I didn't.

"I am looking for a job. I wondered if you had any companies that were looking for a lost soul who has just become the first person to circumnavigate Africa solo and unsupported on a motorbike," I said. No I didn't.

"I'm looking for some work. Here's my CV. I wondered if you had anything suitable on your books," I did say.

She reached for my CV, sighing as she did, as though it was an imposition to ask for a job in a Job Centre. She glanced at it briefly, shuffled a few papers on her desk and tapped a few keys on her computer. "I'm afraid that in the current economic climate there is not a great deal to offer." She looked back at the screen. After a few moments she looked up and said, "There is a position for a Japanese-Speaking Curtain Maker."

I looked at her, waiting for her to add, "Only joking, you're on Candid Camera. Got you!" But there was not a glimmer of humour in her stoic face. Now I know I may be a lot of things, but I definitely knew that I was not The Japanese-Speaking Curtain Maker they were looking for. I thanked her for her help and trudged back out to my forlorn-looking, unemployed motorbike. Two peas in a pod. Just goes to show. I started out with nothing and I've still got most of it left.

The first person to circumnavigate North and South America. Now that would be something.

Acknowledgements

I would like to acknowledge the following people for their support, help and contributions to my adventure:

Firstly, to my girlfriend Cathy and daughters Feaya and Jesamine. Thank you for putting up with my lunacy.

To John Lacey, friend and artistic web and book designer.

I have to thank the following businesses and organisations and their officers; Shaun Fenton of Diesel Films and Hoxton Moto, John Lagerway of Jofama Lindstrands, Sendra Boots, Antonio Barras, Shark Helmets, Simon Neil of Lagunas, Andy Howeth from Dexterity Motorcycles, Paddy Tyson and Overland Magazine, Jim Martin at Adventure Rider Radio, Dominic King at BBC Radio, Dallas Hageman Wild Ride Radio, Michelle Constant SABC and TED Kettler, Motorcycle Men Radio.

For inspiration and encouragement; Sam Manicom, Nick Sanders, Lois Pryce, Austin Vince and Alun Williams of Wales, who kept me in fits of laughter with his quick wit and humour.

Also many thanks to those on the road, too many to mention; to Phrank Shaibu, Felix Achile and my dear Ashraf. All my Adventure Motorcycle friends and other mad bikers.

A heartfelt feeling for Carl Routhier, who rescued me in time of danger. Thank you, Canadian!

Greetings to my brother Simon in Swaziland and his daughter Ysa who followed my journey around the continent.

To Biddenden villagers who constantly sent messages of support to keep me going.

To Save the Children and the British High Commissioner in Cameroon, Tim Foster, who helped when I had problems in that country.

To Michael Ball, who interviewed me on ITV and to Richard E. Grant, my patron.

To Anna Foster for her expertise in copy-editing and compiling the book, and Alan Copps for advice on final copy.